THE

GROWTH and DEVELOPMENT

of

SOCIAL SECURITY

in

NEW ZEALAND

(A Survey of Social Security in New Zealand from 1898 to 1949)

Published by the Social Security Department with the co-operation
of the Health Department

WELLINGTON, N.Z.
R. E. OWEN, GOVERNMENT PRINTER

1950

Price 6s.]

CONTENTS

	Page
PREFACE	
New Zealand's Location, Area, Population, and Economic Structure ..	11
INTRODUCTION	17

PART I—CASH BENEFITS

CHAPTER I—EARLY DEMAND FOR PENSIONS	21
CHAPTER II—PENSIONS LEGISLATION, 1900 to 1930—	
Old-age Pensions	24
Widows' Pensions	26
Maori War Pensions	26
Miners' Pensions	27
Epidemic Allowance	28
Blind Pensions	29
Family Allowances	29
CHAPTER III—DEPRESSION, 1930–35—	
Pensions Reductions	30
Unemployment Relief	30
Pre-depression Developments	30
Depression Measures	30
Preliminary Schemes	31
Farm and Land Settlement Schemes	31
Scheme 5	31
Hospital Board Relief	32
Clearing Rabbit-infested Lands	32
Single Men's Camps	33
Alluvial Gold Mining	33
Maori Land Development	33
Building Subsidies	33
Issue of Boots, Blankets, and Food Rations	34
Provision of Full-time Work	34
Sustenance Without Work	35
Assistance For Women	35
CHAPTER IV—RECONSTRUCTION PERIOD, 1936–39—	
Promotion of Employment	35
Number Receiving Unemployment Relief	37
Improvement in Pensions Legislation	38
Invalidity Pensions	38
Deserted Wives' Pensions	39
Old-age Pensions	39
Widows' Pensions	39
Restriction on Asiatics	39
CHAPTER V—FINANCING OF PENSIONS AND UNEMPLOYMENT RELIEF TO 1939—	
Pensions	39
Unemployment Relief	40
CHAPTER VI—ADMINISTRATION OF PENSIONS AND UNEMPLOYMENT RELIEF TO 1939—	
Pensions	41
Unemployment Relief	43
CHAPTER VII—PRELIMINARY CONSIDERATION OF THE SOCIAL SECURITY SCHEME—	
Recommendations of Select Committee	47

CONTENTS—*continued*

CHAPTER VIII—SOCIAL SECURITY, 1939 to 1949—   *Page*
Scope of the Social Security Act, 1938 48
  Benefits in Respect of Age 50
    Superannuation Benefit 50
    Age-benefit 50
      Residence 50
      Character 50
      Rates of Benefit 51
      Additional Benefits—
        Dependent Wife 51
        Dependent Children 51
        South African War Veterans 51
      Income and Property 51
      Voluntary Withdrawal From Employment to go on to
        Age-benefit 57
      Benefits for Aged 59
      Private Resources of Age-beneficiaries 60
  Widows' Benefits 61
    Widows With Children—
      Residence 61
      Character 61
      Rates 61
      Income and Property 61
    Widows Without Children—
      Residence 62
      Rates of Benefit 62
      Income and Property 62
    General—
      Application for Widows' Benefit 62
      Number of Beneficiaries 63
    Deserted Wives—
      Recovery of Maintenance 63
  Orphans' Benefits 65
  Family Benefits 66
  Invalids' Benefits 71
    Qualifying Conditions 71
    Residence 71
    Character 71
    Rates of Benefits 71
    Additional Benefits—
      For Dependent Wife 71
      For Dependent Children 71
      For the Blind 71
    Income Exception—
      Married Men and Widowers With Dependent Children .. 71
      Married Women 72
      Special Assistance for Married Women Invalids 72
      Others 72
    Medical Examination 72
    General 73
  Miners' Benefits 75
    Basic Rate 75
    Benefit for Widow 75
    Medical Examination 75
  Sickness Benefits 78
    Qualifying Conditions 79
    Rate of Benefit 79
    Income Exemption 80
    Friendly Societies 80
    Waiting Period 81
    Payment of Benefit 81
    Miscellaneous 81
  Unemployment Benefits 86
    Income and Property 87
    Rates of Benefit 87
    Dependants 87
    General 87
  Emergency Benefits 88
  War Servicemen's Dependants' Allowances 92

CONTENTS—*continued*

CHAPTER IX—RECIPROCAL BENEFITS—   *Page*
    Reciprocity with Australia 93
    Reciprocity with Great Britain and Northern Ireland 95

CHAPTER X—INTER-RELATIONSHIP BETWEEN SOCIAL SECURITY BENEFITS AND WAR PENSIONS AND OTHER ALLOWANCES—
    War Pensions 97
    Rehabilitation Allowances 99
    Demobilization Allowances 100

CHAPTER XI—ADMINISTRATION OF CASH BENEFITS—
    Administrative Organization 101
        Social Security Department 101
    Administrative Procedure—
        Application for Benefit 103
        Verification of Information 103
        Grant of Benefit 104
        Records and Index 104
        Appeals 104
        Time Taken to Grant Benefit 105
        Date of Commencement of Benefit 105
        Renewal of Benefit 105
        Reviews of Benefit 105
        Income and Property—
            Definition of Income 106
            Method of Ascertaining Income 107
            Property 107
            Deprivation of Income and Property 108
        Payment of Benefits 108
        Payment Outside New Zealand 109

CHAPTER XII—GENERAL STATISTICS—
    Number of Cash Benefits in Force, 1939 to 1949 114
    Expenditure, 1939 to 1949 116
    Means Test 121
    Relation of Cash Benefits to Cost of Living 122

PART II—HEALTH BENEFITS

CHAPTER XIII—INTRODUCTION TO PART II 126

CHAPTER XIV—MATERNITY BENEFITS—
    Cost of These Services 130
    Medical Services 130
    Hospital Services 130
    Obstetric Nursing Services 132
    St. Helens Hospitals 132
    Effect of Maternity Benefits 133

CHAPTER XV—HOSPITAL BENEFITS—
    Hospital In-patients 133
    Out-patients—
        Hospital Out-patients 135
        Artificial Aids 136
        Miscellaneous 137

CHAPTER XVI—MEDICAL BENEFITS—
    The Refund System 138
    The Direct Claim System 138
    The Token System 138

CHAPTER XVII—PHARMACEUTICAL BENEFITS 140
    Turnover 142
    Cost of Prescriptions 143

CHAPTER XVIII—SUPPLEMENTARY BENEFITS—
    X-ray Diagnostic Services 144
    Massage Services 145
    District Nursing Services 146
    Domestic Assistance 147
    Laboratory Diagnostic Services 148
    Dental Benefits 149

CHAPTER XIX—THE MEDICAL SERVICES COMMITTEE REPORT 150

CONTENTS—*continued*

PART III—FINANCE

CHAPTER XX—FINANCING OF SCHEME—   *Page*
  Source of Funds 158
  Social Security Contribution, 1939 to 1949—
    Original Rates 158
    Changes in Rates of Contributions 158
    Income Exempt From Social Security Contributions 158
  Methods of Collecting Contribution—
    Charge on Salaries and Wages 159
    Charge on Income Other Than Salary or Wages 160
    Charge on Income of Companies 161
  Equitable Adjustment 161
  Receipts of the Social Security Fund 161

SUMMARY OF CASH BENEFIT RATES 163
LIST OF HEALTH BENEFITS IN ORDER OF INTRODUCTION 164
ACKNOWLEDGMENTS 164

APPENDIX—
  Appendix I—Chronological List of Legislative Measures Relating to
    Civil Pensions, Social Security Cash Benefits, and Finance .. 165
  Appendix II—List of Legislation Affecting Health Benefits 170

INDEX 172

CHARTS—
  Chart 1—Old-age Pensions : Number Granted and in Force Each Year,
    1899 to 1939 45
  Chart 2—Age-benefits : Number Granted Each Year, 1935 to 1949 .. 54
  Chart 3—Age-benefits : Number in Force Each Year, 1935 to 1949 .. 54
  Chart 4—Proportion of Population Aged Sixty Years and Over on Age
    or Superannuation Benefit, 1940 to 1949 56
  Chart 5—Age-distribution of Age and Widows Beneficiaries Sixty Years
    of Age and Over, 30th September, 1948 59
  Chart 6—Widows' Benefits : Number Granted and in Force Each Year,
    1912 to 1949 65
  Chart 7—Family Benefits : Comparison of Index Numbers for Exempt
    Income and Nominal Wage Rate, 1930 to 1935 67
  Chart 8—Family Benefits : Number Granted and in Force Each Year,
    1928 to 1949 70
  Chart 9—Sickness and Unemployment Benefits : Number in Force at
    Four-weekly Intervals, 1939 to 1949 84
  Chart 10—Administrative Organization 102
  Chart 11—Cash Benefits : Number in Force by Type, 1940 to 1949 .. 114
  Chart 12—Expenditure : Proportion of Benefits Without Means Test to
    Benefits Subject to Means Test, 1940 to 1949 122

TABLES

1. Unemployment Relief : Expenditure from Employment Promotion Fund
   and by Other Government Departments, 1931–32 to 1938–39 .. 38
2. Age-benefits : Rate and Allowable Income at 1st June, 1949 .. 52
3. Comparison of Age-benefits in 1898, 1939, and 1949 53
4. Superannuation Benefits : Number Granted, Number in Force, and
   Expenditure, 1st April, 1939, to 31st March, 1949 53
5. Age Benefits : Number Granted, Number in Force, and Expenditure,
   1st April, 1939, to 31st March, 1949 53
6. Proportion of Population on Age and Superannuation Benefits for Ten
   Years to 31st March, 1949 55
7. Ages of Age-beneficiaries 57
8. Benefits for Aged : Number in Relation to Population Over Sixty Years
   of Age 59
9. Age-beneficiaries : Classification by Income and Property 60
10. Widows' Benefits : Particulars of Benefits Granted to Deserted Wives for
   Three Years to 31st March, 1949 64
11. Widows' Benefits : Rates and Allowable Income at 1st June, 1949 .. 64
12. Widow's Benefits : Number Granted, Number in Force, and Expenditure,
   1st April, 1939, to 31st March, 1949 64
13. Family Benefits : Legislative Changes Since 1927 66
14. Relation of Exempt Income for Family Benefits to Nominal Wage Rates
   for Adult Males, 1930 to 1946 67

CONTENTS—*continued*

15. Family Benefits : Payments to Post Office Savings-bank Accounts and *Page* Commissioner of Taxes From 1st April, 1946, to 31st March, 1949 .. 68
16. Family Benefits : Number Granted, Number in Force, and Expenditure, 1st April, 1939, to 31st March, 1949 69
17. Number of Family Benefits According to Size of Families, 31st March, 1947, to 31st March, 1949 70
18. Invalids' Benefits : Rates and Allowable Income as at 1st June, 1949 .. 72
19. Invalids' Benefits : Number Granted, Number in Force, and Expenditure, 1st April, 1939, to 31st March, 1949 73
20. Invalids' Benefits : Classification by Age, Sex, and Disease at 31st January, 1949.. 74
21 Miners' Benefits : Number Granted, Number in Force, and Expenditure, 1st April, 1939, to 31st March, 1949 75
22. Miners' Benefits : Diseases for Which Benefit Granted 76
23. Miners' Benefits : Occupation at Time of Claiming Benefit 76
24. Miners' Benefits : Age at Time of Claiming Benefit 76
25. Miners' Benefits : Years Engaged in Mining 76
26. Miners' Benefits : Age at Time of Claiming Benefit and Period Between Date of Ceasing Mining and Date of Claiming Benefit 77
27. Sickness Benefits : Rate and Allowable Income as at 1st April, 1939 .. 79
28. Sickness Benefits : Classification by Age, Sex, and Disease at 31st March, 1949 82
29. Sickness Benefits : Number Granted, Number in Force, and Expenditure, 1st April, 1939, to 31st March, 1949 85
30. Sickness Benefits : Reasons tor Cessation of Benefits Terminated During Year Ended 31st March, 1949 85
31. Sickness Benefits : Duration of Sickness of Beneficiaries Whose Benefits Ceased During Year Ended 31st March, 1949 85
32. Sickness Benefits : Private Income of Beneficiaries Who Received Benefit During the Year Ended 31st March, 1949 86
33. Unemployment Benefits : Number Granted, Number in Force, and Expenditure, 1st April, 1939, to 31st March, 1949 88
34. Emergency Benefits : Number Granted, Number in Force, and Expenditure, 1st April, 1939, to 31st March, 1949 92
35. Reciprocal Benefits With Australia : Comparison of Particulars at 1st July, 1949 95
36. Reciprocal Benefits With Australia : Number in Force at 31st March, 1944 to 1949 95
37. Comparison of Weekly Rates of War Pension, War Veterans' Allowances, and Social Security Benefits at 1st June, 1949 99
38. Rehabilitation Allowances : Number Granted, Number in Force, and Expenditure, 1st April, 1942, to 31st March, 1949 100
39. Cash Benefits : Number in Force, by Type of Benefit, 31st March, 1940, to 31st March, 1949 115
40. Cash and Health Benefits : Expenditure Per Head of Population, 1st April, 1939, to 31st March, 1949 116
41. Cash Benefits : Expenditure, by Type of Benefit, 1st April, 1939, to 31st March, 1949 117
42. Health Benefits : Expenditure, by Type of Benefit, 1st April, 1939, to 31st March, 1949 118
43. Comparison of National Income, Government Expenditure, Social Security Expenditure, and War Pensions Expenditure, 1940 to 1949 .. 119
44. Value of Production, Exports, Civil Pensions, and Social Security Benefits 120
45. Social Security Expenditure : Proportion With and Without a Means Test, 1940 to 1949 121
46. Comparison of Increases in Social Security Benefits and Cost of Living, December, 1939, to December, 1948 123
47. Civil Pensions : Expenditure, by Type of Benefit, 1899 to 1939 .. 124
48. Hospital Benefits : Expenditure on In-patient Treatment in Public and Private Hospitals, 1939–40 to 1948–49 134
49. Hospital Benefits : Expenditure on Out-patient Treatment, 1941–42 to 1948–49 137
50. Medical Benefits : Expenditure on General Medical Services, 1941–42 to 1948–49 139
51. Pharmaceutical Benefits : Number of Prescriptions, Expenditure, and Cost Per Prescription, 1941–42 to 1948–49 142
52. Medical Benefits : Expenditure, 1939 to 1949 156
53. Social Security Fund : Receipts by Source, 1st April, 1939, to 31st March, 1949 162

FOREWORD

SOCIAL SECURITY in New Zealand has a history behind it of beginnings and partial successes, and in presenting this survey an attempt has been made to fill a gap in New Zealand's social data by showing the growth and development of social security in New Zealand in so far as it relates to cash and health benefits. It is hoped that the pages which follow will satisfy the interest of those who are interested in social security as it has been applied in New Zealand.

This work has been compiled for the Minister of Social Security, with the co-operation of the Health Department, which was responsible for the Health Benefit Section of this book.

The publishers are specially indebted to the Land and Income Tax Department for contributing material for the financial section of this publication.

B. F. WATERS, Chairman,
Social Security Commission.

New Zealand.

HON. J. T. WATTS

Minister of Social Security and Minister of Health

PREFACE

NEW ZEALAND

LOCATION, AREA, BOUNDARIES

NEW ZEALAND is a small, comparatively isolated country in the South
Pacific Ocean, approximately 1,200 miles eastwards of Australia, the
nearest country, and 1,600 miles north of the Antarctic Continent. The
islands, with adjacent islets forming New Zealand, include the North
Island, with an area of approximately 44,000 square miles, the South
Island, approximately 58,000 square miles, Stewart Island, 670 square
miles, and Chatham Islands, 372 square miles, making a total area of
approximately 103,000 square miles, including inland waters. In
addition, there are outlying islands not regularly inhabited and other
islands annexed to New Zealand, the two main groups of annexed islands
being the Kermadec and Cook Islands, but these are not included in the
social security scheme in New Zealand.

The three main islands have a total length of 1,000 miles from north-
east to south-west and an average width of 100 miles, being 280 miles
across at the broadest point. Of the 66,000,000 acres, 43,000,000 acres
could be brought into production, and the remaining 23,000,000 acres
consist of urban areas, native communal land, mountains, forests, and
scrub lands. Less than one-quarter of New Zealand's land surface is
below 650 ft. contour. Of the land suitable for farming, about 20,000,000
acres is sown in English grasses, field crops, plantations, orchards, and
gardens, while the other 23,000,000 acres is unimproved land covered
with tussocks, native grass, fern, scrub, and second growth. Most of
the rivers are swift-flowing and unsuitable for navigation.

CLIMATE

The climate varies from sub-tropical in the north to sub-temperate
in the south, the average temperature being between 50° and 60° F. As
the winters are mild, there being no continuous snow on low country,
stock do not need to be kept under cover during the winter, although
pastures are supplemented by fodder crops. The rainfall of 45 in. a
year is adequate and evenly distributed throughout the year, falling on
147 days, or on an average of every two and a half days. The average
duration of sunshine is about 2,000 hours a year.

11

New Zealand is primarily a grazing country, with its economy evolving around dairy, meat, and wool production. The live-stock population at 31st January, 1948, amounted to almost 32½ million sheep and 4¾ million cattle, including over 2½ million dairy cattle.

Butter plays an important part in New Zealand's economy, production amounting to over 150,000 tons annually.

Factory production is playing an increasing part in New Zealand's economy. The total value of production in 1947 was £230·9 million of which 57 per cent. was farming and 27 per cent. factory production.

New Zealand's overseas trade per head is one of the biggest in the world. Total external trade for 1948 amounted to £276 million, being £147·8 million exports and £128·2 million imports.

13

POPULATION

New Zealand is sparsely populated, there being about 18 people to the square mile. This amounts to about 35 acres a person, of which about 11 acres are under production. The population at 31st March, 1949, was estimated at 1,870,000, including about 112,600 Maoris. The last available figures, based on the 1945 census, show that over 93 per cent. of the population are European, less than 6 per cent. Maori, and less than 1 per cent. race aliens. The predominant group of the race aliens is Chinese. Between 1936 and 1945 the relative rates of increase in the population for the various groups were European, 7·3, Maoris, 19·9 ; and race aliens, 53 per cent. Between 1936 and 1945 the number of people over sixty years of age increased by 66,289, and this ageing population is a material factor in the social security structure. The increasing percentage of people over sixty years of age to the total population was as follows :—

			Percentage of Population (Excluding Maoris) over Sixty Years of Age.
1874	..	..	.. 2·33
1926	..	..	.. 7·84
1936	..	..	.. 10·42
1945	..	..	.. 13·83

In 1881 about 60 per cent. of the population lived in the South Island but when old-age pensions were introduced in 1898 the population was more or less evenly distributed between the two main Islands. By 1945 the census showed that 65 per cent. of the people were living in the North Island, thus reversing the earlier position.* This same census also showed that about half of the people lived in towns of 10,000 population or over†, while 41 per cent. of the total population lived in the four main cities, Auckland, Wellington, Christchurch, and Dunedin.

PRODUCTION

New Zealand is primarily a grazing country with its economy evolving largely around sheep and cattle, but factory production is playing an increasing part in the country's economy. In the year ended 31st March, 1929, the value of production was £(m.)126·2, of which 65 per cent. was from farming and 19 per cent. factory production. In the year ended 31st March, 1947, production was £(m.)230·9, of which only 57 per cent. was farming and 27 per cent. was factory production. The value of production in the principal groups for 1946–47 was as follows :—

				£(m.)
Pastoral	..	..	..	64·9
Dairy, poultry, and bees		..	..	50·9
Agriculture	..	..	..	15·6
				———
Total farming		..	..	131·4
Factory	..	..	..	61·7
Building and miscellaneous		..	..	23·8
Forestry	..	..	..	6·6
Mining	..	..	..	6·4
Fisheries	..	..	..	1·0
				———
Total	..	..	...	230·9

* N.Z. Official Year-Book, 1946, page 27.   † N.Z. Official Year-Book, 1946, page 28.

Of the farm production, almost 50 per cent. in value was from pastoral farming, 39 per cent. from dairy, poultry, and bees, and 12 per cent. from agriculture. The live-stock population at 31st January, 1948, amounted to almost 32,500,000 sheep, 4,700,000 cattle, including over 2,500,000 dairy cattle, just over 500,000 pigs, and 204,000 horses.

The main items of farm production are as follows :—

	Approximate Volume.		Exported. Per Cent.
Wool ..	.. 365 million lb.	..	.. 96
Mutton	.. 128,700 tons	..	.. 61
Lamb ..	.. 185,500 ,,	..	.. 97
Butter	.. 151,400 ,,	..	.. 86
Cheese	.. 89,000 ,,	..	.. 93
Beef ..	.. 168,000 ,,	..	.. 49
Wheat	.. 4,500,000 bushels	..	.. Nil
Oats ..	.. 2,800,000 ,,	..	.. Nil
Barley	.. 2,000,000 ,,	..	.. Nil
Peas ..	.. 1,250,000 ,,	..	.. Nil
Apples	.. 2,250,000 ,,	..	.. 45
Pears ..	.. 363,638 ,,	..	.. 40
Stone-fruits	.. 557,615 ,,	..	.. Nil
Lemons	.. 97,875 ,,	..	.. Nil

The wheat production is insufficient for the country's requirements and is supplemented by importing approximately 2,000,000 bushels a year, mainly from Australia. Two-thirds of the gross farming income is derived from exports, which account for 86 per cent. of the income from pastoral produce, 62 per cent. of the income from dairying, poultry, and bees, and 16 per cent. of the income from agricultural produce.

Apart from tropical or sub-tropical products such as tea, sugar, cotton, bananas, &c., practically all the domestic requirements of agricultural produce are grown within the country. The main crops are wheat and oats grown in the eastern and southern districts of the South Island. Much of the oats is chaffed for stock feeding, and turnips are grown extensively for winter feed and stock fattening, particularly in the South Island. In rural and urban areas home gardening supplies a very considerable proportion of family requirements of vegetables, and there is a substantial area of market gardens. Indigenous timber for homes is being worked out gradually, and the Government has gone in for afforestation to supply future needs.

OVERSEAS TRADE

New Zealand's overseas trade per head is one of the biggest in the world. The principal exports for the year ended 31st December, 1948, were wool, 188,000 tons, valued at £(m.)44·5, butter, 135,600 tons, worth £(m.)33·8 ; frozen meat, 343,500 tons, worth £(m.)28·6 ; cheese, 75,600 tons, worth £(m.)11·2 ; and hides, pelts, or skins, £(m.)9·5. The principal imports were textiles, fibres, and yarns £(m.)24·7 ; machinery, £(m.)21 ; metals and manufactures, £(m.)16·9 ; food, drink, and tobacco, £(m.)14·3 ; vehicles and accessories, £(m.)11·7 ; oils, fats, and waxes, £(m.)9·7 ; paper and stationery, £(m.)6·9 ; drugs, chemicals, and manures, £(m.)5·3 ; and apparel, £(m.)3·3.

Total external trade for the year amounted to £(m.)276, being £(m.)147·8 exports and £(m.)128·2 imports.

PUBLIC DEBT

The public debt in New Zealand at 31st March, 1948, amounted to approximately £(m.)598·9, or about £327 per head of population, including Maoris. In the past New Zealand has relied mainly on overseas borrowing, but, apart from minor fluctuations, the proportion of the debt domiciled overseas has shown a steady decrease. In 1907 only 14·8 per cent. of the debt was domiciled in New Zealand, but by 1948, 82·5 per cent. of the debt was so domiciled.

With a healthy climate, an abundance of meat, butter, cheese, grain, fruit, and vegetables, a surplus of wool for clothing, and an adequate timber-supply for homes, New Zealand has the three essentials, and was in a fortunate position to develop a social security scheme to ensure that every one was provided with at least a minimum standard of comfort in the matter of food, clothing, and shelter. After these requirements have been met the surplus commodities are exported to meet interest payments on overseas loans and to import machinery and other amenities of life, giving a high standard of living.

New Zealand has its social security problems, but is much more fortunately placed than the thickly-populated countries of the world, which depend on imports for the primary necessities of life. The small size of the country and the homogenity of the population have enabled eligibility requirements and benefit levels to be standardized and also permits a simple administration of the scheme.

N.B.—Information used in this preface has been obtained from the *New Zealand Official Year-Book*, 1946, and the *Monthly Abstract of Statistics* for November, 1948, January and March, 1949.

INTRODUCTION

" I want to know why people should not have decent wages, why they should not have decent pensions in the evening of their days or when they are invalided. What is there more valuable in our christianity than to be our brother's keepers in reality ? . . . I want to see people have security . . . I want to see humanity secure against poverty, secure in illness or old age." *

THESE were the words of Michael Joseph Savage, Prime Minister of New Zealand, when the Social Security Act, 1938, under which the present social security scheme is administered, was placed on the statute-book.

Ten years have now passed since social security as we know it to-day came into our social life, and it is fitting that at the end of a decade a stocktaking should be taken to assess the real worth of this legislation, and the manner in which it has been welded into the frame-work of our economic, social, and national life.

New Zealand has an unequalled record of half a century of progressive social legislation. A small but important start was made in 1898 with the Old-age Pensions Act, where the predominant thought was to make provision for the needy in their old age. This was largely brought about by the realization that the earnings of wage-earners were never sufficient to enable them to provide for old age, and that it was the duty of the State, and not any particular community group, to make provision for them, not on the basis of poor relief or charity, but as wages for past services.

The conception of the responsibility of the State to make provision for the aged, invalided, sick, widowed, orphaned, and unemployed showed steady realization through forty years of slow but sure progress, culminating in 1938, with the passing of the Social Security Act.

In New Zealand the responsibility for social services has naturally devolved on the State, for being a young country there were no established organizations, guilds, or other community movements which are associated with older countries, and the individual had to look to the community as a whole to provide the help which was so often necessary.

* *Hansard*, 1938, Volume 251, page 649.

17

RT. HON. M. J. SAVAGE
Prime Minister of New Zealand from 1935 to 1940, Who Launched New Zealand's Social Security Scheme

As social reforms frequently arise out of periods of national stress and hardship, it is not surprising that the two great advances in social legislation arose, the first the Old-age Pensions Act, from the depression of the 1880's and the Social Security Act out of the depression of the 1930's. Both these catastrophies showed the limitations of individual effort with the consequent and inevitable failure of the individual to provide for his economic security when the wages of the breadwinner were affected.

The Old-age Pensions Act, 1898, providing non-contributory pensions, was the earliest pensions legislation in New Zealand and the first statutory provision made by any British country for old-age pensions. The first country to introduce non-contributory old-age insurance was Denmark in 1891, followed by New Zealand in 1898. In the same decade New Zealand extended the franchise to women, introduced legislation providing for improved working conditions, established machinery for arbitration of labour disputes, introduced life, accident, and fire insurance, and finance for housing and settling on the land under Government auspices. Although New Zealand was among the first counties to introduce such progressive social legislation, this initial pre-eminence was lost until the social legislation of the 1930's again brought New Zealand to the fore in this sphere.

The term " social security " has passed into the political vocabulary of the English-speaking world, and the ideal of social security is now accepted by almost all democratic governments. The problem of bringing about social security has a different background in different countries and is being solved by different methods. It is clear also that the term " social security " means somewhat different things in different countries. In the following chapters, therefore, an attempt has been made to explain and demonstrate what " social security " means as applied to New Zealand, and the progress that has been made over the years to make that ideal a reality.

RT. HON. R. J. SEDDON

*Prime Minister of New Zealand From 1893 to 1906, Who Pioneered
Security for the Aged by the Old Age Pension Act,
1898—New Zealand's First Social Security*

PART I—CASH BENEFITS

CHAPTER I—EARLY DEMAND FOR PENSIONS

BECAUSE of the system of colonization adopted in New Zealand, large numbers of assisted immigrants from the British Isles were brought to the colony primarily to work for wages and form a wage-earning class of settlers. The majority of immigrants had limited capital and little opportunity to provide out of current wages for periods of unemployment, sickness, or old age. Economic insecurity and the irregularity of employment of many of the settlers led to a demand for strong measures to provide security. For a time the New Zealand Company paid immigrants an inadequate relief when work could not be found, but there were no poor laws, labour laws, pensions, or sustenance, while charitable aid by hospitals was limited through lack of funds.

Regulations were issued in 1846 * placing the responsibility for the care of the destitute on near relatives, and in 1877 the Destitute Persons Act extended the term " near relative."

Owing to the Maori Wars, the collapse of the alluvial-gold boom in the South Island and the unstable economy of the Colony, dependent as it was on the overseas price of wool, the primary export, unemployment became serious in the 1860's. The Vogel policy of public works and assisted immigration attempted to solve this unemployment problem, but was curtailed by lack of finance during the long depression of the " eighties." There was little accumulated capital in New Zealand to meet this and later depressions, and the problem grew too big for the existing voluntary organizations to handle. One of the effects of the resulting realization that public funds would have to be used to relieve poverty was an agitation for old-age pensions.

Public thought was inevitably moving in the direction that it was the community's responsibility to protect the people from the risks of destitution, and during 1882 and 1883, Atkinson, the Colonial Treasurer, strongly advocated a scheme of social insurance, and put forward proposals for insurance against sickness, accident, old age, widowhood, and orphanhood on an actuarial insurance basis. Atkinson's proposals came before the House of Representatives during two consecutive years, but were not taken seriously, as it was argued that the scheme would encourage idleness and thriftlessness, would undermine the self-reliance of the people, and break up families. His philosophy can best be summed up in his own words :—

> We have to consider in what way we can provide against destitution without demoralizing the people. I think it must be evident to all that private thrift is quite useless in this matter because it must take considerable time to ensure any result, and it is absolutely powerless to provide against premature sickness or death. The only effectual remedy against pauperism seems to me to be not private thrift or saving, but co-operative thrift or insurance, and that to be thoroughly successful . . . it must be national and compulsory.

* Ordinance for the support of destitute families and illegitimate children 26th October, 1846.

The idea of social insurance was developing, and the introduction of social insurance in Germany between 1883–89, followed by the first non-contributory old-age pension Act in Denmark in 1891, showed that pensions were a practical proposal. Realizing that there was a growing strong public sentiment in favour of more sympathetic and discriminating treatment of the aged poor, the Liberal Government, on 26th June, 1894, appointed a Select Committee of ten members of the House of Representatives to examine into and report on the question of making provision for old age.

The Committee did not advocate any particular scheme, but suggested an inquiry into the position by a Royal Commission.

The recommendations of the Committee were :—

   (i) That a system for the provision of pensions for the old of both sexes should be established by the State if a practicable method for providing the necessary funds could be devised.

  (ii) That, though for many reasons it would be desirable to fix the age for commencement at sixty years, the Committee were of the opinion that it would not be within the scope of practicable finance to fix it below sixty-five years :

 (iii) That all applicants for a pension must have resided in the colony for at least twenty years immediately previous to their application.

 (iv) No pension to be granted to any applicant who had been convicted of an indictable offence, unless he or she had received a free pardon from the Governor, or to anyone who had been convicted of drunkenness three times during the last seven years previous to his or her application.

  (v) That every male and female pensioner should be entitled to a weekly sum of 8s., and in the case of a husband and wife the joint allowance should be 15s. a week.

An indication of the unsatisfactory conditions prevailing at this time was given by the Chairman of this Committee, Mr. William Hutchison, who remarked :—

" Looking at the precarious nature of the employment of working-men in the colony—one week in work and another out of it—only the smallest number of this class could contribute regularly to the establishment of any pension fund." Furthermore, the Committee added for the information of members " every year upwards of 1,500 children under fifteen years of age are left fatherless—how many without adequate means of support it is not possible to say."

At this time old-age pensions were becoming even more necessary, as the speeding up of industry was forcing older men out, while the establishment of minimum wages in awards prevented their employment at lower rates.

Prior to the 1896 general elections the Prime Minister, Rt. Hon. R. J. Seddon, introduced an Old-age Pension Bill. This Bill provided for a pension of 10s. a week for all people over sixty-five years of age whose income, excluding earnings and pension, was not more than £50 a year. The scheme was to be financed from the proceeds of one or more special taxes.* In face of the demand for the abolition of the means test, Seddon abandoned the Bill.

* These taxes included primage duty on imports, increased excise duty, graduated income-tax, increased graduated land-tax, increased death duty by graduation, increased stamp duty, and taxes on mortgages, entertainment, and totalizators.

In order to ascertain what claims there would be for a pension without means test, the Registration of Peoples' Claims Act was passed in October, 1896. Not every one who could apply for old-age pension registered, but 8,010 people, including a very large proportion of women, paid 2s. 6d. fee and registered their claims. The main occupational groups were labourers, miners, farmers, gardeners, shoemakers, nurses, and a few professional men. Many were in their seventies and eighties and some over ninety years of age, but only about one in twenty had proof of age. Of the 8,010 claims 5,584 established proof of eligibility.

Old-age pensions were one of the main issues of the 1896 general election, and the victory of the Liberal Party increased the prospects of pension legislation. In 1897 another Old-age Pension Bill was introduced proposing a payment from general revenue of 6s. 11d. a week at sixty-five years of age to all those whose earnings were not more than £36 a year. This was not as generous as the 1896 Bill. Objections to the Bill were based on the grounds that it might result in higher taxation and would demoralize society. The Opposition party thought that workers should contribute to the scheme, while some members contended that as wage-earners paid most of the taxes, the scheme was in fact contributory.

The Bill passed the second reading by a large majority, but the House in Committee decided against a means test. The Prime Minister, Mr. Seddon, again threatened to drop the Bill, but this was not necessary as it was rejected by the Legislative Council on its second reading.

In July, 1898, the Liberal Government once again introduced an Old-age Pensions Bill, and in the face of considerable opposition it was finally passed and received the Governor's assent on the 1st November, 1898.

In reading the provisions of the Old-age Pension Act, 1898, one can hardly understand the reasons for the opposition and uproar the measure created. The Act provided for a pension of £18 a year on a means-test basis for persons sixty-five years of age and over who had been in New Zealand for twenty-five years. The pension was reduced by £1 for each £1 of income in excess of £34, and by £1 for each £15 accumulated property over £50. Pensions were paid out of general revenue with no direct contributions. Maoris receiving money under the Civil List Act, aliens, naturalized subjects who had been naturalized for less than five years, Chinese, and other Asiatics were excluded from pension.

In order to distinguish between the deserving and undeserving poor, the following people were not entitled to pension :—

    (i) Those imprisoned for four months during the past twelve years or for five years during the past twenty-five years :

    (ii) Those who had deserted wife, husband, or children at any time for six months or more :

    (iii) Those who had not led a sober and reputable life for the past five years, and those who had deprived themselves of property to qualify for a pension.

During the debate on this Bill the Prime Minister promised, if possible, to introduce additional legislation providing for contributory insurance on the lines of that of the British Post Office.* Thus all classes would be covered, the better off by the contributory scheme, the deserving poor by old-age pensions, and the undeserving poor by charitable aid. It

* *Hansard*, 1898, Volume 103, page 540.

was claimed by the Prime Minister that not more than 5,000 would qualify for pension the first year, that 500 would be added to the roll each year, and that the cost would increase from £90,000 the first year to £126,000 after the fifth year.*

In his second reading speech on the Bill, Mr. Seddon said :—

> I consider it would be impossible, much as I would like it for us to give a pension to all persons who are over sixty-five years of age. . . . Let us make a commencement . . . if we find we have funds at our disposal, the principle being admitted, we could expand the operation and scope of the measure.†

> . . . in twenty years the progress this colony will have made with its increased wealth and its increased population will be such that the burden cast upon the people then will be no greater than I would ask to have placed on them now.‡

The core of the Opposition argument to the pension scheme was that it would demoralize society, and is neatly summed up in the speech of one member of the House :—

> You cannot by any means take away from the people the principal incentive to thrift and that feeling of self-reliance which is the basis of self-respect without in the end injuring the people.§

The importance of the Old-age Pensions Act lies not so much in the provision of the pension to individuals at £18 a year (an amount which seems very meagre now, and was so hedged around with restrictions that it was said that a man must be a saint to earn a pension in New Zealand), but that it recognized the principle that the State had some responsibility for those citizens whose efforts were not enough to keep them from poverty in their old age.

CHAPTER II—PENSIONS LEGISLATION, 1900 TO 1930

DURING the next thirty years the scope of the scheme was gradually expanded with the inclusion of widow pensions in 1911, Maori War pensions in 1912, pensions for miners in 1915, provision for the blind in 1924, and family allowances in 1926.

OLD-AGE PENSIONS

From 1898 onwards the old-age-pensions legislation remained relatively static, but later Governments amended the Act with a view to liberalizing its provisions to make more people eligible for assistance. The rate of pension was increased to 10s. a week in 1905, 15s. a week in 1917, and 17s. 6d. a week in 1925. In 1911 a variation in the age limits was introduced. The qualifying age for parents who had to maintain two or more children under fourteen years of age was reduced to fifty-five years for women and sixty years for men. In such cases the age pension was increased by £13 a year. Two years later the qualifying age for

---

* *Hansard*, 1898, Volume 103, page 537–8. (Actual expenditure for three months ended 31st March, 1889, was £3,124, for the first complete year (ended 31st March, 1890), £157,342, and for the fifth year (ended 31st March, 1903) £210,140.)

† *Hansard*, 1898, Volume 103, page 538.

‡ (1) *Hansard*, 1898, Volume 103, page 540. (It is interesting to note that forty years later, when Rt. Hon. W. Nash, Minister of Finance, was introducing the Social Security Bill, he pointed out that exports had increased from £9,300,000 in 1896 to £66,713,000 in 1937, or from £12 9s. per head of population to £41 19s. per head.)

§ *Hansard*, 1898, Volume 103, page 541.

women was reduced to sixty, but the pension was reduced by £1 for each year by which the age of the applicant was less that sixty-five years. If, however, the pensioner was the parent of two or more children under fourteen years of age, the reduction did not apply. In 1924 an additional pension of 2s. 6d. a week was provided for old-age pensioners who had no income or property, but this was withdrawn in 1925 when the rate of pension was increased to 17s. 6d. Also a supplementary pension not exceeding 5s. a week was granted to those old-age pensioners who saw service in the South African War, 1899 to 1902, as members of the New Zealand contingent, provided their total income and pension did not exceed £91 a year.

Although through the years certain minor classes of income were exempted for income purposes, the general income exemption, which was originally £34, was finally stabilized at £52 in 1924. The accumulated property exemption originally began at £50 and remained so all this period, except that legislation for including or excluding the home property had a relatively chequered career. Originally the value of the home was included in the £50 property exemption, and if the home and other property exceeded £50 in value the pension was reduced accordingly. As could be imagined, very few applicants owning a home could qualify for pension.

In order to enable aged persons with their own home but with limited resources to obtain the pension, provision was made in the 1902 Pensions Amendment Act to enable a pensioner, if he wished to do so, to transfer to the Public Trustee a home valued at not more than £300. Any property transferred on this basis was excluded from the accumulated property of the pensioner, who was allowed to reside on the property rent-free for life.

On the death of the pensioner, a surviving husband or wife eligible for pension carried on occupancy of the property under the same conditions, and during occupation the pensioner or survivor was responsible for repairs, rates, and other charges in respect of the property. On the death of the pensioner or survivor, or where the pensioner was no longer entitled to pension, the Public Trustee sold the property and refunded to the Treasury the amount of the pension paid since the transfer, together with interest at 4 per cent. Any balance was paid to the person entitled to it. If the pensioner wished the Public Trustee to return the property to him, this was done on payment by the pensioner of the additional pension, plus commission and interest. In such cases the home property was again charged as accumulated property and the pension adjusted accordingly.

In 1908 the limit of value of the home property which could be transferred to the Public Trustee was increased to £650, and the next year the limit was removed. The year 1910 saw another change. Where previously the concession regarding home property applied only to those who transferred the property to the Public Trustee, the Amendment Act of this year exempted all home property and furniture up to £340.

These provisions remained stationary until in 1920 the value was raised to £390 and to £520 in 1924, and finally the culminating point was reached in 1925 when all restrictions on the value of home property were removed and the total value of such property, including furniture in the possession of the pensioner, was exempted for pension purposes.

WIDOWS' PENSIONS

Widows' pensions were first introduced in 1911. So small were these grants that it can well be said that they were for the very poor widows. The pension was £12 a year for widows with one child and a further £6 a year for each additional child under fourteen years, up to a maximum of £30 a year. The pension was subject to a deduction of £1 for each £1 income in excess of £30 after exempting personal earnings and pension (combined) up to £100. Income included receipts from all sources, including " constructive " income, calculated at 5 per cent. of all property producing no income or income of less than 5 per cent. Aliens and Asiatics were excluded from pension, and illegitimate or adopted children and children born out of New Zealand or less than six months after the arrival of the mother in New Zealand were not covered by the Act. The next year the income provisions were varied to deduct personal earnings up to £100 and pensions from income. At the same time children born out of New Zealand were brought within the legislation if they were born during the temporary absence of the mother or if the mother subsequently resided in New Zealand for ten years. Also the legitimation of illegitimate children was dispensed with if the parents subsequently inter-married. A year later step-children and children legally adopted during the lifetime of the husband were included in the Act. In 1919 the special exemption of personal earnings up to £100 was removed.

Rates of pension and conditions of grant were gradually expanded over the following years until, in 1924, a widow with one child was paid 20s. a week, plus 10s. a week for each of the next six children. The qualifying age for a child was raised to fifteen years in 1925. Wives of mental patients were also entitled to these pensions from 1912.

On the death of a widow the pension in respect of the children could be paid to the guardian of the children. This was an important provision as it was the forerunner of the orphans' benefit established under the Social Security Act, 1938. Until that Act was passed there was no general provision for orphaned children, help being entirely restricted to those children of a widow who had been on pension herself prior to her death, and children of a deceased serviceman who were provided for under the war pensions legislation. All other orphans had to rely on assistance from relatives, guardians, or charitable institutions.

MAORI WAR PENSIONS

A military pension of £36 a year in lieu of an old-age pension to any ex-soldier who had served in any war under the Crown was provided for by the Military Pensions Act, 1911. Next year this Act was repealed and the pension was restricted to veterans of the Maori Wars. Only ten year' continuous residence in New Zealand was required, as against twenty-five years at that time required for old-age pensions. As with other pensions, there were income and property qualifications comparable with the then existing age pensions. The means-test provisions, however, were removed in 1913. The rate of pension was increased to £49 a year in 1920 and to £58 10s. a year in 1936.

(Relatively few men qualified for this pension and grants were made to only 1,698 of these veterans from the inception of the pension. The last grant was made in 1931, and only 20 of these pensions were in existence when the Social Security Act, 1938, came into operation. The rate then was £78 a year, and this was increased subsequently by steps to £117 a year. With the death of the only surviving veteran in 1948 the need for this pension has eventually passed into history. The total cost of this pension from inception was £615,553.)

MINERS' PENSIONS

The need to provide for miners incapacitated by industrial accident was recognized in 1908, when pneumoconiosis was included in the schedule of disabilities in the Workers' Compensation Act passed that year. However, because miners commencing work at the mines were unwilling to undergo a medical examination required by the insurance companies in connection with compensation, pneumoconiosis was removed from the schedule.

The Mining Amendment Act, 1910, established the Gold-miners' Relief Fund for the benefit of miners injured while working or for the families of miners killed or injured. This fund, administered by the Public Trustee, was financed by a special duty of 3d. an ounce on gold produced in quartz-mines. In 1911 legislation provided that relief from the fund should be available to miners suffering from pneumoconiosis, so the cost of supporting disabled miners was thus borne by the industry in which the men had been employed ; men incapacitated by accident, or pneumoconiosis could receive either 12s. 6d. a week or a lump-sum settlement of £50. A widow could receive £50 and a grant of £25 for funeral expenses.

Within a few years it became clear that the fund was not strong enough to meet the demands on it, for when the fund was established many men who had contracted miners' phthisis in the previous fifteen years claimed assistance and swamped the fund. Also the revenue of the fund was greatly reduced, mainly on account of the failure of the Great Waihi Mine to produce as much gold as in the past. As a result, many miners applying for relief could not be assisted or had to wait months before relief was available.

In 1912 the sum of £1,000 was credited to the Minister of Public Works to use to provide relief for extreme cases where no assistance was available from the Gold-miners' Relief Fund. This unsatisfactory state of affairs continued until the passing of the Miners' Phthisis Act, 1915, which provided pensions for miners totally incapacitated by pneumoconiosis contracted while working as a miner in New Zealand. This Act also provided that any moneys to the credit of the Gold-miners' Relief Fund and any future revenue from gold duty should be paid into the Public Account for the Consolidated Fund. The rate of duty on gold produced from quartz-mines was increased to 6d. an ounce in 1916.

Pensions were granted only to British subjects by birth or naturalization for one year who had resided in New Zealand for five years immediately prior to application for pension and had been employed as a miner in New Zealand for two and a half years. The original rate of pension was £52 a year for a married man or widower with children to support and £39 for a single man. If a miner entitled to pension died, his widow received a pension of £32 10s. a year for two years, and funeral expenses up to £20 were paid.

During the debate in Parliament on the Bill many Members stressed the need for a higher rate of pension than that proposed, but because the financial resources of the country were strained by war expenditure, the

Government could not agree to any increase. The Prime Minister (Right Hon. W. F. Massey) promised that if it was found that less people applied than was expected, and if the revenue from gold duties was more than anticipated, he would do his utmost to increase the benefits of the Bill.

As the industry through the gold duty was still partially responsible for financing the scheme, no means test was applied to miners or their widows. In 1919 the Finance Act authorized miners' widows' pensions to be continued during widowhood instead of for two years only.

By 1920 the rates of pension had increased to £91 a year for a married man and £65 a year for a single man. In 1929 an additional £26 a year was provided for each dependent child under fifteen years of age, but a maximum pension of £4 5s. a week was imposed. Where it had been a pension granted without means test, now, however, an income restriction was introduced, in that the portion of the pension paid in respect of the children was reduced by any income of the *miner* (not his wife) over £104 a year.

The Act later extended the term " miners' phthisis " to include tuberculosis of the lungs and any other disease of the respiratory organs commonly associated with or following pneumoconiosis. The requirement of total incapacity was relaxed provided that serious incapacity was proved.

EPIDEMIC ALLOWANCE

Following the influenza outbreak of November, 1918, Parliament voted allowances to relieve distress arising throughout the country from the epidemic. These allowances were paid without statutory authority in terms of a Cabinet decision, and provision was made in the Government Budget from year to year for the current expenditure. The maximum allowance paid to a widow with a child or children, whose husband died of influenza during the epidemic and before 31st January, 1919, was 25s. a week, plus 10s. 6d. for each boy up to sixteen years and each girl up to eighteen years of age. Also an allowance up to 25s. a week was paid to widowers with children to enable them to employ a housekeeper and so keep the home together. As a general rule, no payment was made to a widower whose income was £3 10s. a week or more. No payment, however, was made where relatives were able to assist financially.

Originally these allowances were decided and administered by local Hospital Boards subject to the control of the Health Department, but this method of administration resulted in a lack of uniformity in the treatment of persons applying for relief. In some cases widows received an epidemic allowance in addition to a civil widow's pension, while in many cases relief was granted at a lesser rate than the rate which could have been granted. It is interesting to note that this allowance was much more generous than a widow's pension at that time, which was only 7s. 6d. for the widow, plus 7s. 6d. for each child.

The control of these allowances was handed over to the Pensions Department in 1920.

In 1919 epidemic allowances were being paid to 828 widows with 2,323 children and 89 widowers with 366 children. Each succeeding year showed a decrease in the number receiving this relief, until they finally disappeared in 1938.

The total expenditure on these allowances was £474,101.

BLIND PENSIONS

The year 1924 saw the introduction of a new class of pension for those unfortunate individuals suffering from blindness. Apart from the economic relief it afforded the blind recipients, the importance of this pension lies in the fact that it was the forerunner of the invalids' pension which was introduced twelve years later, and it established the principle of State assistance for those adults who were unable to obtain a livelihood through physical disablement or illness, irrespective of age.

Originally the blind pension was paid only to people twenty years of age or over who became blind in New Zealand and who had resided in New Zealand for ten years, but in 1925 it was extended to include those losing their sight out of New Zealand provided they had ten years' residence in New Zealand before the 29th October, 1924, or alternatively, twenty-five years' residence. The pension, which was originally £39 a year (later increased to £45 10s.), was subject to the same income and property qualifications as old-age pensions, except that earnings were subsidized by the State by 25 per cent. where the total income, including pension, did not exceed £182 a year.

FAMILY ALLOWANCES

New Zealand was one of the first, if not the first, country to adopt the principle embodied in the Family Allowances Act, 1926, of the State bearing to some extent the responsibility for the well-being of the families of those who were in poorer circumstances. It was generally recognized in most democratic countries at that time that those people who were not in good financial circumstances and who were in bad health, or otherwise handicapped were entitled to some help in bringing up their families. Some European countries had already somewhat similar schemes operating, but these were generally of a voluntary contributory nature and formed as a result of agreements and arrangements between workers and employers in trade groups.

The New Zealand allowance was non-contributory and granted subject to a means test. These allowances were small, but the principle underlying the Act was an important advance in the social legislation of the country. The Act provided 2s. a week for each child in excess of two under fifteen years of age where the family income did not exceed £4 a week, so that a man earing £4 a week and having three children would receive 2s., one with five children 6s. a week, or eight children 12s. a week. Illegitimate, alien, and Asiatic children were excluded, but the allowance for invalid children could be continued beyond the age of fifteen years. The allowance was generally paid to the mother of the children and was to be used for their maintenance and education.

Until the social security legislation of 1938 there was no increase in these allowances, but during the years of the 1930–35 depression the income limit was reduced to £3 5s. a week, but later restored to the original £4 a week in 1936.

CHAPTER III — DEPRESSION, 1930-35

Across the gradual and continuous growth of the State's interest in the well-being of its poorer citizens cut the slump of 1930–35 during which New Zealand, like the rest of the world, was confronted with an unemployment problem on a scale which proved conclusively that economic disaster was beyond the range of individual control and thrift. There was no appreciable change and no advance in social legislation during these years, the Government's attention being inevitably focused on ways and means to combat the increasing unemployment.

PENSIONS REDUCTIONS

Pensions, like wages and salaries, were reduced by 10 per cent. in 1932. A slight improvement in the economic condition of the country enabled old-age pensions to be increased by 5 per cent. in 1934, and the next year the rates of all pensions were restored to the amounts payable prior to the 1932 cuts.

UNEMPLOYMENT RELIEF

PRE-DEPRESSION DEVELOPMENTS

Prior to the depression of the early " thirties " there was little permanent effective legislation to cope with the problem of unemployment. The Department of Labour was founded in 1891, and through its employment bureaux endeavoured to find employment for those who registered with them. The responsibility for relieving unemployment was shared between the Government and local bodies, and in 1926 legislation was passed enabling local bodies to raise money by loans to carry out work for the relief of unemployment without taking a poll of ratepayers. Further legislation in 1927 allowed the Government to set aside funds to subsidize expenditure by local bodies on relief works.

No special organization to deal with unemployment on a national basis had been set up at this stage, but unemployment had been combated by accelerated public-works programmes, the institution of State forestry works, and by local authorities creating work, often of a wasteful nature, to meet the problem in their particular districts. There was no statutory provision for the relief of hardship due to unemployment.

DEPRESSION MEASURES

The Unemployment Act, 1930, provided for the establishment of an Unemployment Fund, an Unemployment Board, and a national registration of all men twenty years of age or over. The Board was to establish labour exchanges, co-ordinate employment to reduce seasonal fluctuations, encourage training and promotion of employment in industries, and provide sustenance to the unemployed.

Lack of finance and limited knowledge at the time regarding trade recessions restricted the Board's activities, and there was no comprehensive policy for providing full employment, the relief measures adopted being in the nature of improvization to alleviate the worst features of unemployment.

As a matter of policy the Board decided that work should be performed in return for relief granted and payment without work avoided as long as suitable work could be provided. For nearly three years after the passing of the Unemployment Act no relief was given except in return for the performance of work which was provided through the agency of private individuals, firms, companies, local authorities, or Government Departments.

Various schemes were introduced to alleviate unemployment, and the Board was immediately faced with the question of the rate of wages to be paid to the men employed thereunder. After careful consideration it was decided that the determination of the rates of wages was not a function of the Board, but was a matter for agreement between employers and employees. The Board adhered strictly to this attitude in all its schemes for relief work, but ruled that for skilled work which ordinarily would be subject to Arbitration Court awards, the award rates should operate. While adhering to this principle, the Board insisted that its subsidies and refunds of wages should never exceed the rate of pay on public works.

The rates of sustenance and relief varied between main towns, secondary towns, smaller centres, and rural areas, different scales being adopted to meet different conditions. Cash assistance was not always granted as there was a system of rationed work and benefits in kind. Married men received relief according to the number of children.

Preliminary Schemes

Among the early emergency schemes introduced to relieve unemployment were Scheme 1, providing subsidies to local bodies for capital work or special maintenance ; Scheme 2, providing subsidies for approved work such as draining, fencing, or clearing noxious weeds, &c.; and Scheme 3, consisting of a grant to local bodies to provide two days' work as a Christmas relief measure.

Farm and Land Settlement Schemes

Subsidies for work on farms were provided by Scheme 4A, which assisted people working on their own farms ; Scheme 4B, which subsidized farm-development work ; and Scheme 4F, which subsidized farm labour.

Legislation was introduced in 1932 providing for the settlement of unemployed men and their families on small leased holdings of ten acres or more in strategic positions where casual employment might be obtained on surrounding farms. The cost of establishment, including the erection of cottages, provision of the necessary improvements, and the transport of personal effects, was met out of a special vote and was recoverable by way of amortized rent. The cost of transport of the families to the location and payment of sustenance during the initial period of occupation was borne by the Unemployment Fund. In addition to the settlement of small areas, the scheme was varied to enable land-owners to establish share-milkers on their property under definite contracts with the Crown. Under this variation of the scheme cottages and sheds were erected by the Crown subject to employment of the unemployed worker and his family.

Attention was also given to the problem of unemployment among youths, and as a result of special grants and the activities of voluntary organizations many youths were absorbed in farming occupations. The Board also authorized the payment of £25 each in respect of New Zealand soldiers' sons admitted to a special farm training institution.

Scheme 5

Notwithstanding the launching of earlier schemes, it was obvious that they could not cope with the alarming increase in the number of unemployed registered at all centres, and it was necessary to make additional arrangements for immediate relief. Accordingly, in close co-operation with all local bodies who were in a position to provide work near the homes of the workers, a scheme of rationed work was introduced early in 1931.

Apart from various special schemes for providing certain classes of useful work for a section of the unemployed, this scheme developed into the mainstay of the Board's efforts to relieve unemployment and was the first attempt in New Zealand to find some work for practically all genuinely unemployed male wage earners.

Under this scheme work of a national or local character was undertaken by local bodies which provided the material, tools, transport, and supervision, &c., while the Unemployment Board provided the wages. Later on this scheme was extended to development work on private property (usually approved farms), the local employing authorities generally being the County Councils. Work was rationed to two, three, or four days a week according to family responsibilities.

Expenditure under this main scheme assumed such proportions that the Board was reluctantly compelled in April, 1931, to effect a drastic curtailment in the amount of relief by reducing the rate of relief pay, providing rationed work for only three out of four weeks, and reducing the number of days work for married men or widowers with two dependent children from four to three days. In addition, there was a general tightening-up of the rules regarding eligibility for relief.

Additional revenue became available following the introduction of the emergency unemployment charge in 1931, and the maximum scale of unemployment relief in the four main centres was revised. The rate of relief pay was reduced, but to compensate for this reduction rationed work was provided for each week instead of for three weeks in every four. At the same time the Board assumed responsibility for the issue of relief in the form of food rations formerly granted by Hospital Boards.

Towards the end of September, 1932, the new rates of relief pay were applied to all districts outside the four main centres.

In this scheme the Local Unemployment Committees played an important part advising the Unemployment Board periodically of the number of men employed, the estimated weekly wages to be paid and the number for whom employment could not be found, &c.

HOSPITAL BOARD RELIEF

Prior to July, 1932 the relief activities of the Unemployment Board were supplemented by Hospital Boards which under normal conditions were responsible for the relief of distress due to indigence. The abnormal distress, due to unemployment, created a problem beyond the capacity of Hospital Boards, and it became necessary to define the responsibility of the Boards. Following a conference between the Unemployment and Hospital Boards, it was agreed that applicants should be classified by hospital doctors as fit for any class of work, fit for light work only, or unfit for work. From the 4th July, 1932, the Unemployment Board assumed full responsibility for relief to able-bodied men who were formerly assisted to some extent by the Hospital Boards, while the Hospital Boards cared for those who were unfit for work or fit for light work in the towns only.

CLEARING RABBIT-INFESTED LANDS

Subsidies were paid to owners or occupiers of land who employed relief workers to destroy rabbits. Employers supplied camp equipment, food, implements, rabbit poison and materials, and had to insure the workers. All rabbit-skins remained the property of the workers. A similar scheme operated on unoccupied Crown lands.

Single Men's Camps

Because sufficient useful work for the large number of unemployed could not be found in the towns, the Board embarked on a new policy of transferring groups of single men to useful works in rural districts. The work selected for the initial experiment was the improvement of roads, mostly secondary highways. The Main Highways Board provided the camps, utensils, and food, while the Unemployment Board provided transport and paid the men an average of 10s. a week according to a contract scale based on individual effort.

Later the camp scheme was extended to land improvement, especially drainage and other forms of development work, such as sand-dune reclamation, irrigation, and afforestation. The Unemployment Board and the State Forest Service co-operated in the employment of considerable numbers of unemployed in tree-planting. This proved an excellent means of absorbing relief labour as the busy planting season was during the winter and the work was productive.

Alluvial-gold Mining

Under Scheme 15 arrangements were made with the Mines Department to subsidize the employment of specially-selected men under experienced miners in gold mining and prospecting in approved localities, the men providing the equipment and retaining the proceeds from the gold won. Sometimes it was necessary to advance the cost of fares, tents, &c., which were recovered by withholding 10 per cent. of the gold won until the amount owing was offset. These schemes met with a fair measure of success, and an appreciable quantity of gold was recovered that otherwise would not have been found.

Maori Land Development

Because of the high proportion of unemployed Maoris (over one-half of the male Maori population between twenty and sixty years of age), grants were made to the Department of Maori Affairs for developmental schemes on Maori lands. This relief was in addition to the benefits of the main relief scheme in which Maoris could participate.

Building Subsidies

When reviewing the unemployment problem in 1932 the Board found that the most important single factor contributing to unemployment was the collapse of the building industry. To stimulate building activity, the Board evolved a scheme (Scheme 16) whereby it subsidized labour costs of approved works. The scheme was not to interfere in any way with wages or conditions of employment under industrial awards for the workers concerned, and wherever possible New Zealand materials and products were to be used on subsidized work. This scheme was the most successful of the experiments, and from almost complete inactivity in 1932 the building industry experienced a mild boom during the latter part of 1933. At the peak of the activities of the scheme some 3,250 men were employed on a subsidy basis.

The success of the scheme led to an extension of subsidies to other building activities, but these additional subsidies were withdrawn early in 1936 as they were no longer necessary. The main scheme ceased on 30th September, 1936.

3—Soc. Sec.

Issue of Boots, Blankets, and Food Rations

An innovation during the winter of 1933 was the issue of working-boots to part-time workers under the Board's relief schemes, camp workers (except where standard wages were paid), and gold-prospectors. In pursuance of the Board's policy of requiring work to be performed in return for relief, part-time workers who received boots were required to work an extra day. Meat was distributed to necessitous cases at half price through unofficial relief organizations.

In 1934 a second issue of boots was made, and there was also an issue of blankets to men in relief camps, the blankets becoming the property of the men after a month in camp.

With the general improvement in conditions during the year ended 31st March, 1935, it was possible to grant a considerable number of benefits to relief workers in the way of extra payments and relief in kind, such as working-boots and blankets. The introduction of the amended scale of relief payments and the general economic improvement reduced the necessity for the issue of extra relief in the form of food rations in the four main centres, and this supplementary relief was therefore limited generally to the issue of milk orders, the provision of special foods before and after confinement of a relief worker's wife, and to other special assistance to meet individual needs.

Provision of Full-time Work

During 1934 there was a general economic improvement in New Zealand, and the Board's efforts to encourage employing authorities in industry (Scheme 16A) and local bodies, &c. (Scheme 13) to provide additional full-time employment at standard rates of pay met with some success. The success of the building scheme resulted in an improvement in employment which was not confined to the workers employed on subsidized building jobs, but affected other avenues of employment. At the same time local bodies and Government Departments were encouraged to undertake permanent work justifying the use of loan-money assisted by a subsidy from the Unemployment Fund. This full-time work was paid for at standard wages as an alternative to the principal scheme of rationed work. However, it was found that local bodies and Government Departments were reluctant to undertake work even with a subsidy slightly in excess of the cost to the Fund of paying unemployment relief. Most of the work under this scheme, classed as suitable for employment of labour not required in ordinary industry, was such that the return was insufficient to justify the use of loan-moneys. To overcome this the Board agreed to meet the difference between the economic value of the work and the total cost of approved works. In many cases this meant providing the full labour cost from the Unemployment Fund.

A review of the unemployed in 1934 showed that between 10,000 and 15,000 men were unfit for normal industrial employment and another 10,000 were fit for ordinary industrial employment but incapable of earning standard rates of pay on public works carried out on a co-operative contract basis. There were thus 15,000 to 20,000 men on relief work unfit for the heavy manual work involved in the works being organized by the Public Works Department.

Difficulty was experienced on account of the reluctance of men to leave home and accept work in the country, and this reluctance was understandable. When the men were in receipt of sustenance or rationed work they received a fixed sum each week supplemented by relief in kind

34

such as free boots, blankets, food, clothing, and also what they could earn from casual employment. On the other hand, the acceptance of work in the country incurred all the financial responsibility of a worker in ordinary industry, the payment of wages tax, and usually after a lengthy spell of unemployment relief, the liquidation of debts contracted while on relief. However, the increasing of the daily rates of pay on public-works standard jobs overcame this to some extent.

SUSTENANCE WITHOUT WORK

By 1934 many local bodies were experiencing difficulty in arranging sufficient suitable work for unemployment relief as much of the useful work coming within the scope of the Board's rules was nearing completion. It was not intended that relief workers should be used for essential maintenance work, which, of course, should be done by labour at standard rates of pay, and the Board was forced to review its policy of no sustenance without work.

Sustenance without work was granted mainly to men over fifty years of age or unfit for manual work who could not be placed on approved relief schemes. Every effort was made to rotate work and sustenance so that men would not be penalized by circumstances over which they had no control. Because of the high proportion of men who were unfit for the class of work offering on account of age, physique, or previous experience the position was still unsatisfactory, and a new scale of payments covering the four main centres and the secondary centres was brought into use in August, 1934. No worker received more by way of sustenance than he would have been eligible for as a relief worker.

ASSISTANCE FOR WOMEN

Although women contributed to the Unemployment Fund they could not receive sustenance, but because of the difficulty in placing them in suitable work and of subsidizing female employment without prejudicing normal employment, Women's Unemployment Committees were set up in the four main centres and later in some of the smaller centres. These committees, which received grants from the Unemployment Board, established placement centres and training centres for instruction in domestic work. Some free meals and clothing were provided and 10s. a week paid for the work done. Accommodation was provided where required and efforts made to place the girls in private domestic employment, if necessary the wages being subsidized by the Board.

CHAPTER IV — RECONSTRUCTION PERIOD, 1936–39

A LABOUR Government followed the general election of November, 1935, and took office on the 6th December, 1935. Immediate plans for improving the social legislation were put in train, two important steps in this direction being the passing of the Employment Promotion Act, 1936, and the Pensions Amendment Act, 1936.

PROMOTION OF EMPLOYMENT

During the depression efforts were made to find work for the unemployed, but unemployment relief was dealt with largely as an emergency measure with rationed relief work and sustenance playing an important part. From 1936 on, however, the promotion of employment was emphasized rather than the provision of temporary relief.

This changed approach was evident in the Employment Promotion Act, which consolidated legislation dealing with unemployment relief and was one of the new Government's preliminary moves in implementing its policy of providing a comprehensive social security scheme. Under this Act the Employment Division of the Labour Department, which was made responsible for the administration of the Act, undertook the promotion of work and industries for absorbing surplus labour, the placement of unemployed in industry through the State Placement Service operating as a labour exchange, and the administration of relief for the unemployed. The Unemployment Board was abolished, and the Unemployment Fund replaced by the Employment Promotion Fund, financed by receipts from an employment tax and money appropriated by Parliament. Uniform sustenance payments and rates of pay for work were established throughout New Zealand, and the divisions into main towns, secondary towns, country areas, &c., were abolished. Sustenance rates and payments under the system of rationed relief were increased from 30th November, 1936. As far as possible employment on public works was provided in place of part-time relief work.

Under the authority contained in the Employment Promotion Act, 1936, payment of sickness allowances could be made in certain cases. For a time these allowances were restricted to men registered as unemployed, but later they were extended to men who, although not registered, were in necessitous circumstances.

In June, 1937, a scheme was begun with the help of local bodies to provide full-time work up to four months for 7,000 fit men who were receiving relief, and the local bodies were offered subsidies up to the full labour costs.

As far as practicable unemployed Maoris were engaged on the development of Maori lands, and it was only when such work was not available that rationed relief was approved. Sustenance payments to Maoris were avoided as much as possible, but when necessary were made by way of one-third payment in cash and two-thirds in orders for rations. When Maoris were employed as relief workers on contracts through the Department of Maori Affairs such contracts were based on the public-works rate of pay for full-time work. At the end of the contract the men were required to stand down for a period, so that their earnings over the whole period (including the stand-down) would average 30s. for single men and rates up to 66s. 6d. a week for married men with seven or more children.

The payment to unemployed women and girls through the Women's Employment Committees was increased where the recipient was living away from home, and substantial assistance was granted by way of free meals, clothing, &c. However, at this stage unemployment among women and girls was not serious, and there was a distinct shortage of certain types of female labour.

The employment of labour in industry was kept under constant review, particular interest being taken in the gold-mining, tobacco-growing, flax, steel, and kauri-gum industries. In the gold-mining industry the object of the Department's scheme was to prove areas for subsequent enterprise. This work was carried out almost wholly on a contract basis under arrangements that enabled an average worker to earn at least the equivalent of public-works standard rates of pay for the class of work involved. By 1937 the flax industry, which was assisted by an export subsidy on hemp, provided direct and indirect employment for over 250 people. An interest was also taken in the development of the woolpack industry, which uses native flax in the manufacture of its products. In the kauri-gum industry a survey of the remaining gumfields was undertaken, and a process developed for the purification of the gum in order to increase its competitive strength.

Among the activities of the Labour Department to promote employment were the provision of grants, and financial or labour subsidies for the eradication of noxious weeds, rabbit extermination, fireblight control and eradication, general land development, development of " pakihi " land, irrigation projects, river clearing, afforestation, and aerodrome construction. Assistance was also granted to the gold-mining, coal-mining, and fruit growing industries.

During 1937, when there was a shortage of experienced labour in skilled trades, it was found that schools and colleges were being drained of employable boys by employers who preferred the younger boys to unskilled youths in the older age-groups. This was probably due to the desire to obtain young apprentices and to the fixing of a basic wage for people aged twenty-one years, making it uneconomic to employ unskilled adults. At the middle of 1937 it was estimated that there were 5,500 unemployed men between eighteen and twenty-five years of age with little prospect of work. A campaign to interest young men in farming was undertaken, and apprenticeships, particularly in the carpentry and bricklaying trades, were arranged by the Labour Department for youths from eighteen to twenty-five years of age. By the end of May, 1938, about a thousand young men were placed in positions with good prospects, and subsequently most of the youths in the above age-group obtained private employment. The shortage of skilled labour in the building and certain engineering trades was still apparent in 1938 and 1939, by which time a shortage had developed in some of the manufacturing industries which were expanding.

In 1938 the maximum amount of relief pay and sustenance for unemployed men (including Maoris) with large families were increased to £4 for those employed on rationed relief and £3 19s. for those on sustenance.

Number Receiving Unemployment Relief

The number of registered unemployed males increased from 51,000 in June, 1931, to a peak of 79,435 in September, 1933, and then decreased. By March, 1939, the number of registrations was down to 32,069.

From 1931 most of those registered as unemployed were assisted by the No. 5 Scheme (rationed work). In 1933 sustenance without work was paid to a few of those registered as unemployed, and by 1936 there were more men receiving sustenance than there were on rationed work under Scheme 5. The number of men working in industry and assisted from the Employment Promotion Fund rose from approximately 6,000 in 1931 to 30,000 in 1933. With the emphasis given to employment promotion rather than unemployment relief from 1936 on, the number of men working full time in industry with assistance from the Fund increased in relation to those receiving other forms of relief, and in 1938 and 1939 the majority of the registered unemployed were assisted by means of full-time work.

Year Ended 31st March,	Expenditure From Employment Promotion Fund.	Expenditure by Other Government Departments.
	£(m.)	£(m.)
1932	2·2	1·0
1933	3·7	0·41
1934	4·1	0·54
1935	3·8	0·68
1936	4·7	0·83
1937	4·3	0·91
1938	4·0	0·99
1939	6·2	1·06

IMPROVEMENT IN PENSIONS LEGISLATION

As a preliminary to the comprehensive social security scheme introduced in 1939 the newly-elected Government passed the Pensions Amendment Act, 1936, the most comprehensive measure of its kind which had been passed by the New Zealand Parliament for many years. Pensions were introduced for invalids and deserted wives, and existing pensions were improved.

Invalidity Pensions

Up to 1924 there were no pensions for invalided persons apart from miners. The Pensions Amendment Act, 1924, made an important beginning by providing a pension for blind persons over the age of twenty years.

The invalidity pensions of the 1936 Act, however, made provision for people sixteen years of age and over who were permanently incapacitated for work because of accident, illness, or congenital defect. Blind people were also covered by the new pension, which incorporated all existing blind pensions.

Ten years' residence preceding application was required, and a pension was not paid for self-induced incapacity or where there was an outstanding claim for compensation or damages. The rate of pension was £52, plus £26 for a wife and £26 for each child under sixteen years of age, with a maximum pension of £208 a year. Married pensioners or widowers with children were allowed other income of £104 and other pensioners £52 a year without affecting the benefit. Deductions on account of property were made as for old-age pensions. The subsidy of 25 per cent. on personal earnings of blind pensioners was retained in the Act. All applicants for pension were required to undergo a medical examination to determine eligibility for pension. If an application was refused on the ground of not being permanently incapacitated for work or totally blind, the aggrieved person had a right of appeal to a Board of three medical practitioners.

DESERTED WIVES' PENSIONS

Another new class of pension introduced at this time provided pensions for women with children who had been deserted by their husbands. These were paid on the same basis as widows' pensions, and it was necessary for an applicant to show that maintenance proceedings had failed or that a maintenance order was not being complied with, and also that the wife was not aware of her husband's whereabouts.

OLD-AGE PENSIONS

Substantial improvements were made in respect of old-age pensions in 1936 and 1937. The residential qualification was reduced from twenty-five years to twenty years, and for those people who were resident in New Zealand on 15th March, 1938, the period was further reduced to ten years. The disqualification in respect of past imprisonment was removed. Previously a person disqualified from pension because of past imprisonment was in effect being punished a second time for the same offence.

Pensions were increased to £58 10s. and deductions from this rate in respect of women under sixty-five years of age were removed. The income exemption remained at £52, but the property exemption of £50 which had remained stable at that figure for some decades was increased to £500. The exemption from property of the pensioner's home and furniture was extended to include an interest in any land, thus eliminating the majority of deductions from pensions formerly made in respect of property which produced in actual practice little or no income. The effect of this legislation was to make the actual income of an applicant largely the determining factor in assessing a pension.

WIDOWS' PENSIONS

Widows' pensions were increased from £26 plus £26 for each child to £52 plus £26 for each child, and the family income limit was increased to £234. The arbitrary assessment of income at 5 per cent. on property other than the home was abolished and actual income charged. The restriction on the granting of a pension in respect of illegitimate children was removed.

RESTRICTION ON ASIATICS

The restrictions applicable to Asiatics and people naturalized less than one year were removed so that the only classes not covered by the Pensions Act were aliens, and, in so far as old-age and widows' pensions were concerned, Maoris receiving money from the Civil List Act, 1920.

CHAPTER V—FINANCING OF PENSIONS AND UNEMPLOYMENT RELIEF TO 1939

PENSIONS

BEFORE the introduction of the social security scheme in 1939 pensions were financed from general revenue, there being no special contribution or tax earmarked for pensions apart from a portion of the revenue from national endowment lands for old-age pensions.

In July, 1899, the newspaper *Clutha Leader* suggested that a tax sufficient to meet the cost of old-age pensions without a means test be levied on some article of daily use, used by all people to about the same extent—for example, sugar and molasses. This suggestion was referred to the Colonial Treasurer, but not adopted.

A later suggestion was for a tax on amusements, but on the 26th July, 1905, when replying to a question in the House of Representatives, the Government stated that it did not intend to place a tax on amusements or specially earmark any revenue for old-age pensions.

The idea of having some special revenue set aside towards the cost of old-age pensions was not forgotten entirely, and following consideration of the matter of reserving land as endowments for charitable aid, hospitals, mental hospitals, old-age pensions, and education the Government indicated in August, 1906, that it intended to introduce legislation to set aside as an endowment all the ordinary Crown lands not then sold or leased, the net proceeds from the endowment to be available solely for the above purposes. Until the endowment became self-supporting it was to be supplemented by ordinary appropriations, but it was confidently anticipated that with the expansion of the Colony the fund would grow until in time it would meet all the charges.*

The following year the National Endowment Act, 1907, was passed and set aside 9,000,000 acres of Crown land as a permanent endowment for education and old-age pensions. The land set apart could not be sold, and continued to be administered as Crown land. From 1st April, 1908, all revenue from national-endowment land was paid into the National Endowment Account of the Public Account, the money available, after meeting the cost of administration of national-endowment land and existing statutory commitments from Crown lands to local or public authorities, was applied to education, which received 70 per cent., and old-age pensions, which received 30 per cent. Until 1932 money available for old-age pensions was paid into the Post Office Account to be applied in payment of old-age pensions, but from 1932 was credited direct to the Pensions Account.†

The first credit for old-age pensions amounting to £20,143 was made in the year ended 31st March, 1910, and after five years the sum of £95,155 had been made available from national endowment. The total amount credited to 31st March, 1939, when the credits ceased, was £946,644 ; or less than 3 per cent. of the cost of old-age pensions to that date. With the passing of the Land Amendment Act, 1939, on the 6th October of that year, the reservation of national-endowment land was cancelled and these lands became ordinary Crown land.

Apart from the above, the cost of pensions was met from the Public Account out of general revenue.

UNEMPLOYMENT RELIEF

As with pensions, funds for unemployment relief were also originally derived from general revenue, but during the depression of the 1930's it was found necessary to introduce special taxation to raise funds for unemployment relief.

The Unemployment Act, 1930, established an Unemployment Fund to be financed by a registration fee of £1 10s. a year from December, 1930, on all males aged twenty years or over, with certain exceptions, and by a subsidy from the Consolidated Fund of half the expenditure from the Unemployment Fund. This subsidy was withdrawn in 1932.

* Source : Financial Statement, 1906 (in Committee of Supply, 28th August, 1906).   † Section 2, Finance Act (No. 2), 1932.

The registration fee was reduced to £1 a year from July, 1931, when an emergency unemployment charge of 3d. in the pound was imposed on all salaries and wages irrespective of the taxpayer's age and on income other than salary and wages of all people living in New Zealand who were twenty years of age or over. Women with income less than £250 a year were not liable for the charge on income other than salary or wages. Although Maoris were exempt from payment of the registration fee unless they elected to become liable, they were required to pay the charge on wages and other income.

These provisions were amended from time to time, and the rate of charge fluctuated, until by October, 1935, it was payable at 8d. in the pound on all income of people twenty years of age or over. Women did not pay the charge on income other than salary or wages unless their income exceeded £50 a year. The registration fee remained at 5s. a quarter.

In 1936 the Employment Promotion Act consolidated legislation dealing with unemployment relief and taxation, but did not vary the registration fee and employment charge, which remained at the same rate until replaced by the social security contribution in April, 1939.

CHAPTER VI — ADMINISTRATION OF PENSIONS AND UNEMPLOYMENT RELIEF TO 1939

PENSIONS

THE Pensions Department was established on the passing of the Old-age Pensions Act, 1898, which came into force on 1st November, 1898, and for the first thirteen years was concerned only with the administration of old-age pensions. In November, 1898, a Registrar of Old-age Pensions was appointed as head of the Department, and a month later old-age-pension districts were constituted and Deputy Registrars appointed.

Most of the staff was attached to other Departments, the administration of pensions being a part-time duty, and the Registrar himself being an officer of the Treasury. Many of the seventy-five Deputy Registrars appointed were Clerks of Court who received no remuneration from the Pensions Department for the additional work.

The first annual reports of the Department show that the administration of pensions was smooth and effective. Claim forms were obtainable at all post-offices, and pensions were paid through money-order offices. Detailed preliminary work in connection with the applications was done by the Deputy Registrars, who then arranged for applicants and their wives to appear before a Stipendiary Magistrate in open Court. The Magistrates granted or declined the claims according to the evidence before them without verification of the answers given by each applicant in evidence.

Within three or four years it was found that pensions had been obtained by fraud or misrepresentation, and to remedy this a new claim form was introduced. Applicants were required to appear before the Deputy Registrar if physically fit to do so, and the answers given were then verified by a set of inquiry forms. When this had been done the applicant appeared before the Magistrate, who decided the application. This verification of particulars threw additional work on the Head Office in Wellington and on the various Deputy Registrars. An interesting indication of the circumstances giving rise to the new method of carefully investigating claims which was adopted in 1903 is shown by the following extract from the Department's annual report, 1904 :—

. . . the original Act of 1898 provides for no corroborative proof of age, except in the case of the Native, and the sworn declarations of people holding responsible positions in the community have very naturally been accepted as proof of age in a great number of cases, but I very much regret to have to state that these self-same declarations (and this applies to declarations made in regard to other important matters affecting the eligibility of claimants) have, from the point of view of correctness, been proved absolutely valueless. Pensioners who have been drawing for years have been found even now to be short of the required age . . .

The same report also referred to the " gross misstatements " of pensioners in regard to residence and the difficulty experienced in obtaining convictions under the penal clauses of the Act because often little or no evidence could be found on the Court papers of the questions asked and the answers given.

The extent to which pensions had been wrongfully obtained is indicated by the fact that with the introduction of the new claim form and more complete investigation of applications the proportion of new pensions granted to population becoming eligible for pension by age and residence dropped from 43 per cent. in 1902, to 37 per cent. in 1903, and 27 per cent. in 1904.

By 1905 the staff in Wellington had been increased to take over much of the detail work formerly done by the various Deputy Registrars.

An amendment to the law in 1908 altered the designation of the head of the Department from " Registrar " to " Commissioner," and that of the district officers from " Deputy Registrars " to " Registrars."

As an economy measure during a period of financial depression it was decided by the Government in 1909 to merge the old-age pensions organization into the Post and Telegraph Department. The Head of the Post and Telegraph Department became also Commissioner of Old-age Pensions, and the former Old-age Pensions Department became a section of the Accountant's branch of the General Post Office. Later on this section was elevated to the status of a division of the General Post Office, and the officer in charge was designated the " Deputy Commissioner." Economies were also effected in the district offices, and postal officers were utilized for duties formerly performed by Registrars only.

The scope of the Department's work was increased in 1912 by the introduction of widows' pensions and military pensions. On assuming office in March, 1912, the Mackenzie Government announced its intention to recreate the Pensions Department, and this was done from the 14th November, 1912.

The granting of military pensions (in 1912) was vested in the Commissioner of Pensions instead of a Stipendiary Magistrate as with old-age and widows' pensions, and as it was thought that veterans might be reluctant to apply to an old-age pension office, the organization of the Defence Department was used to record and investigate military pension claims.

In 1913 the Pensions Act abolished the system of investigating claims in open Court. Originally all applications were investigated in open Court, then in 1905 it was left to the discretion of Magistrates, but the 1913 Act made it mandatory for claims to be investigated in Chambers.

At the outbreak of the Great War in 1914 there were less than thirty officers on the staff of the Department, but the introduction of war pensions and miners' pensions in 1915 added to the work of the Department. War pensions were administered by the Department, and the Commissioner of Pensions was also Secretary of the War Pensions Board of three members.

On the 1st April, 1920, the Department assumed control of just under one thousand epidemic pensions, which, since the influenza epidemic of 1918, had been administered by the Health Department and paid through local Hospital Boards. On the 1st October of the following year the Department's activities were further extended, when approximately two thousand Imperial pensions of all classes were taken over from the Treasury Department. In 1922 the branch of the Defence Department dealing with medical treatment of ex-members of the New Zealand Expeditionary Force was amalgamated with the Pensions Department, necessitating the creation of the position of Medical Administrator of Pensions, and also involving the running of an artificial-limb factory from 1922 to 1925.

On the 1st April, 1923, the administration of Boer War pensions, the Civil Service Act pensions, other sundry pensions, and annuities was transferred to the Department. The introduction of blind pensions in 1924 and family allowances from 1st April, 1927, further increased the scope of the Department's operations.

In 1931 the Department was made responsible for the administration of the Disabled Soldiers' Civil Re-establishment Act, 1930, the object of which, as the title suggests, was the rehabilitation of disabled soldiers in civil life. These activities were transferred from the direct control of the Department to the Soldiers' Civil Re-establishment League on 1st October, 1934.

The remaining years of the Pensions Department's activities saw a further rapid increase in the volume of business and the introduction of legislation which made greater demands on the administrative machinery than at any other period of its history apart from the war period. In 1935 the scope of the war-pensions legislation was widened by the introduction of war veterans' allowances, while in 1936 the Pensions Amendment Act of that year enlarged the field of civil pensions legislation.

The passing of the Social Security Act, 1938, brought to a close the activities of the Pensions Department, which, after forty years, lost its identity from the 31st March, 1939, its staff and records merging into the Social Security Department the following day.

UNEMPLOYMENT RELIEF

Before the establishment of the Unemployment Board in 1930 unemployment relief was administered mainly by local bodies assisted by Government subsidies. The Unemployment Act, 1930, established an Unemployment Board of eight members representing the Government, primary and secondary industries, employers and workers' organizations, and the Returned Soldiers' Association, Inc., and the first meeting of the Board was held on the 25th November, 1930. It was intended as far as possible to avoid the creation of a separate Department of State and to use existing Government organizations whenever these were suitable. The Government Statistician was appointed Executive Officer of the Board with the title of Unemployment Commissioner.

The Labour Department and the Post and Telegraph Department dealt with registration of the unemployed and payment of wages and subsidies, while the services of other Departments were also availed of in connection with relief works—*e.g.*, the land-development schemes of the Department of Maori Affairs. At an early stage the Board realized the necessity for co-operation with some local-body organizations to carry out relief work, and as a result of an appeal by the Board to Mayors of all cities and boroughs some 165 local unemployment relief committees were functioning by the end of March, 1931. Some of these committees had sub-committees operating in outlying districts under their jurisdiction. Each local committee had a small executive with a Government officer from the Labour Department or Post and Telegraph Department acting with the committee or with its executive in dealing with applications for relief and the approval and supervision of relief works being carried out in the district.

The Unemployment Board was reconstituted by the Unemployment Amendment Act, 1931, which provided five members, instead of eight as previously. The Board consisted of the Minister of Labour, three members appointed by the Governor-General, and the Commissioner of Unemployment.

In 1936 the Employment Promotion Act abolished the Unemployment Board and made the Labour Department responsible for the administration of the Act, except that the Commissioner of Taxes was responsible for the assessment and collection of employment tax. Unemployment Relief Committees were disbanded with the exception of the Women's Employment Committees, which remained in operation. The administration was reorganized on a permanent basis instead of the emergency atmosphere in which unemployment relief began. Local offices of the Labour Department were established and the Department took over services previously rendered by other Departments.

Following the success of the State Placement Service established in 1936, Dominion Committees with employer and worker representatives were established in all principal towns.

Early in 1938 youth centres were established to provide vocational guidance for boys from school leaving age up to eighteen years of age and for girls from such time as they left school until they were twenty-one years of age. In this work the vocational officers of the Education Department co-operated with the Secretaries of the youth centres under the Labour Department.

From the 1st April, 1939, administration of unemployment relief was taken over by the newly-formed Social Security Department, although the State Placement Service in the four main centres still operated as part of the Labour Department.

44

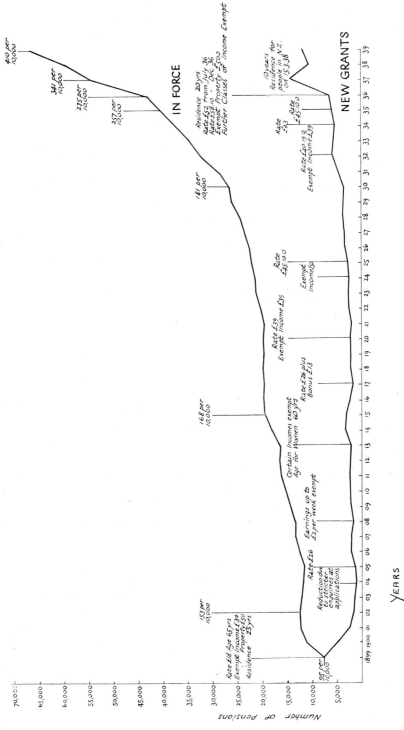

45

CHAPTER VII — PRELIMINARY CONSIDERATION OF THE SOCIAL SECURITY SCHEME

In March, 1938, the Government set up a select Parliamentary Committee to examine its proposals to establish a National Health and Superannuation Scheme.

The proposals set before the Committee for consideration were divided into two main sections—

    (1) Health Services ; and
    (2) National Superannuation and Social Security Benefits.

Details regarding the Health Service proposals are set out on page 128 under the Health Benefit section of this publication.

The Government's proposals in so far as cash benefits and the financing of the scheme were concerned are as follow :—

NATIONAL SUPERANNUATION AND SOCIAL SECURITY BENEFITS

INVALIDITY BENEFITS

(a) That a payment of 30s. per week be made to invalids when certified as permanently unfit for employment ; with supplementary payments to the wife and each dependent child of the invalid of 10s. per week, with a maximum benefit of £4 per week ; this benefit to supersede the existing pension of 20s. per week.

SICKNESS BENEFIT

(b) That sickness benefit of appropriate amounts be paid to men and women during periods when they are prevented from earning a livelihood by reason of sickness or accident ; provision to be made for the payment of this benefit to the members of friendly societies through these societies.

DISABILITY BENEFIT

(c) That disability benefits be made available for persons who could not qualify for invalidity, sickness, or sustenance benefit or State superannuation, but who were otherwise physically or mentally disabled from earning a livelihood.

SUSTENANCE BENEFITS

(d) That sustenance benefits be paid to persons who were capable of and available for work, but for whom work could not be found ; that the rates of benefit be 20s. plus, if married, 15s. for wife, with 5s. for each dependent child, in lieu of the present rate of 4s.

WIDOWED MOTHERS' BENEFIT

(e) That a social security benefit be paid to widowed mothers at the rate of 25s. per week and 10s. per week for each dependent child ; the benefit to continue until the child reaches the age of sixteen years (instead of fifteen years as at present), and, in special circumstances, until the age of eighteen years, so long as the child was still at school ; this to replace the existing widows' pension of 20s. per week. Wives of inmates of mental hospitals and deserted wives with dependent children to qualify as at present.

WIDOWS' BENEFIT

(f) That widows' benefit be payable—
(i) At any age to widow who has previously drawn a widowed mother's benefit and whose youngest child has reached the age at which the benefit ceased ;
(ii) To a widow who had not previously drawn a widowed mother's benefit—
    (a) If she was widowed before age fifty and had been married for not less than fifteen years, the benefit to be payable from age fifty ;
    (b) If she had been widowed after age fifty and had been married for not less than five years, the benefit to be payable from the date of commencement of widowhood.

ORPHANS' BENEFIT

(g) That orphans' benefit be payable to relatives or guardians who had been approved as foster-parents at the rate of 15s. per week in respect of orphans under age of sixteen years.

Family Allowance

(*h*) That the family allowance be paid at the rate of 4s. per week in respect of the third and subsequent children ; the maximum allowable income to be £5 per week plus the allowance (instead of the present provision of £4 per week plus the allowance) ; the allowance to continue to be payable in respect of eligible children until they reach the age of sixteen years.

Miners' Phthisis

(*i*) That superannuation at the rate of 30s. per week be paid to miners suffering from miners' phthisis, with a supplementary benefit of 10s. for the wife and 10s. for each dependent child up to the age of sixteen years.

State Superannuation

(*j*) That State superannuation be payable at the rate of 30s. per week on the attainment of the age of sixty years, with the qualifications set out in the present legislation ; the superannuation benefit not to be reduced so long as the income of the superannuitant, if a single person, or the joint income of a married couple (in addition to superannuation) does not exceed £1 per week ; this will supersede the existing old-age pension of 22s. 6d. per week.

Finance

That the necessary funds should be provided by—

(*a*) A social security contribution of 1s. in the pound on the wages and other income of all persons :

(*b*) Continuance of the present registration fee of £1 per annum for males over twenty years of age :

(*c*) Subsidy from the Consolidated Fund.

Commencement

That all benefits and services be made available and contributions be payable as from 1st April, 1939.

Recommendations of Select Committee

In regard to cash benefits the evidence submitted to this Committee showed that public opinion demanded provision for those unable to support themselves as it was realized that too many people were outside the scope of friendly societies or other similar voluntary organizations, and that only a national scheme of social security would be effective.

The Committee considered that the proposed benefits were a logical development of the social services that had been a fixture of the legislature of New Zealand for many decades and that they represented the embodiment of public conscience as to the community's responsibilities for those who had been deprived of the means of fending for themselves.

As far as sickness benefits were concerned, the Committee recommended that instead of a flat rate which was the usual method employed in sick pay, the rate of benefit should vary according to the domestic circumstances and family responsibilities of the individual.

Those witnesses who appeared before the Committee agreed that the whole community should bear the cost of old-age pensions, but some thought that if superannuation was treated separately only those who benefited should contribute. However, the Committee pointed out in its report that no portion of the contribution or subsidy from the general revenue of the country, or, as it is called, the Consolidated Fund, was earmarked for any particular benefit. The scheme was an insurance against disaster analogous to fire and accident insurance which prudent people undertook as a matter of course, hoping, nevertheless, that they would not be so unfortunate as to have to make a claim for a cash return.

While the Committee recognized the desirability of paying benefits without a means test, it realized that the available money was limited and that the needs of some were so great as to require the application of all that money, leaving nothing for those otherwise adequately provided for. To exempt from contributions those not to benefit from superannuation would have increased the rate of contribution or reduced the benefit to an impossible degree.

The Committee recommended that the Government should adopt the proposals and consider an extension of the scheme to provide a gradual increase in allowable income until universal superannuation was achieved. It also recommended provision for wives under sixty years of age and for children of men eligible for superannuation.

In his report placed before the Committee the Actuary estimated that the total cost of the proposed benefits and health service, including administration expenses, would be £17,850,000 for the first full year and that under the proposed method of finance four-ninths of the scheme would be borne by the special contributions and approximately five-ninths by the Consolidated Fund. While most schemes in other countries relied on a flat-rate contribution as a method of finance it was thought that such a method threw an unduly heavy burden on the low-income group. The Committee therefore considered that the proposed method of levying a contribution assessed on a percentage of the income of each individual, augmented by a State subsidy from general taxation, was a much more efficient and fairer way of raising funds. Furthermore, as the contributions would be such that public opinion would feel a sense of responsibility and control over the future development of the scheme that would be absent if the cost were met from the Consolidated Fund, the Committee was satisfied that the proposed method of financing the scheme was a sound one.

Evidence was submitted which endeavoured to show that the cost of the scheme was beyond the resources of the Dominion, but the Committee was confident that the Dominion could extend production sufficiently to carry out the scheme and believed that it might contribute largely to more rapid development of the country. The Committee also considered that the scheme was simply a more equitable distribution of the national income and that all of the expenditure would be available for consumption of foods available in the Dominion's markets. It felt certain that such a redistribution would stimulate production, particularly for those goods which were produced in New Zealand and should tend to expand primary and secondary production. It also considered that any increase in the rate of taxation would be accompanied by a redistribution of the national income, which would represent no loss whatever to the community.

CHAPTER VIII—SOCIAL SECURITY, 1939 TO 1949

SCOPE OF THE SOCIAL SECURITY ACT, 1938

THE Social Security Act, which was passed in September, 1938, and came into operation on the 1st April, 1939, followed closely the Government's preliminary proposals which had been investigated and reported favourably upon by the Parliamentary Committee. It embodied in a comprehensive plan State assistance by a system of cash benefits and a universal health service designed to provide subsistence to the people of New Zealand who through various misfortunes of age, sickness, widowhood, orphanhood, unemployment, or other exceptional conditions came to want, and to maintain and promote the health and the general welfare of the community. The scheme was not regarded as the ultimate achievement in social security legislation, but as a basic plan which could be extended as required.

The scheme was to be financed through a special Social Security Fund, into which was to be paid—

(1) Proceeds from a tax of 5 per cent. levied on all salaries, wages, and other income.

(2) Registration fees of 5s. a year paid by males sixteen to twenty years, and all females over sixteen years, and 20s. a year paid by all males over twenty years of age. Thus every one sixteen years of age and over was liable for payment of a social security contribution.

(3) Money specially appropriated by Parliament to make up the amount by which the above taxes were short of requirements.

To the extent that almost half the cost was to be met by specially earmarked taxes, to which every one over the age of sixteen years contributed, the scheme was a contributory one.

The basic principle of the Act was that people should contribute according to their means and receive benefits from the fund according to their needs, so that the amounts received by beneficiaries have no relation to the amount they had contributed. Those whose need was the greatest would receive the greatest assistance.

All existing legislation relating to pensions and unemployment relief was consolidated into this Act, and the term " benefits " was used in place of the previous term " pensions." The Act was divided into three main parts—cash benefits, health benefits, and financial provisions.

Superannuation benefits, which were to come into operation from the 1st April, 1940, Maori War benefits, and miners' benefits, including benefits for wives and widows of miners, were paid irrespective of financial circumstances, but all other cash benefits were subject to a means test.

Health benefits were available to all people ordinarily resident in New Zealand irrespective of their financial position. The health benefits included maternity benefit (free hospital and domiciliary care), medical attention, and free or partial private-hospital services. Public hospitals were available free of charge to any patient, and there was provision for the initial payment of fees in respect of services afforded in licensed private hospitals, while treatment in State-owned mental hospitals was also free. Details for the provision of a free general practitioner service with medicine, drugs, materials, and appliances ordered by them, together with supplementary benefits as were thought necessary to ensure effective operation of the health benefits or to maintain and promote public health were still under consideration when the rest of the Act came into operation from the 1st April, 1939.

49

BENEFITS IN RESPECT OF AGE

SUPERANNUATION BENEFIT

The superannuation benefit can be treated in brief compass because of its extreme simplicity.

The qualifying age is sixty-five years, and the only other condition is the residential qualification. These residential qualifications are set out in detail below under the heading of " age-benefits."

A gradual start was made in implementing this class of benefit by the payment of £10 a year from 1st April, 1940. This amount was to be increased progressively by £2 10s. a year until the equivalent rate of age-benefit was reached. With the rate of age benefit at £78 a year from the 1st April, 1939, the superannuation benefit was designed to be paid at an equivalent rate in 1968. Although age-benefits, along with other clases of benefits, have increased in amount during the last ten years, no actual increase in pay out has taken place in respect of super-annuation benefit other than the yearly increment of £2 10s. These successive increases in age-benefit have had the effect of postponing the date on which the superannuation benefit would reach parity with the age-benefit. With the age-benefit now at £130 a year the superannuation benefit will not be paid at that rate until 1988.

AGE-BENEFITS

To claim an age-benefit a person must be sixty years of age. Pre-viously old-age pensions had been paid at that age for women, but at sixty-five years for men.

Residence

The residential requirements for both age and superannuation benefits are the same as those set out in the former old-age-pensions legislation. For those who were in New Zealand on the 15th March, 1938, it is necessary to establish ten years' residence, with allowable absence of twelve months plus six months for every year of residence over ten years ; others must show a twenty years' residence and may have allowable absence of two years plus six months for every year of residence over twenty years. Where the absence exceeds one year or two years respectively the appli-cants are required to have actually resided in New Zealand for the year preceding application Beneficiaries leaving New Zealand and returning within five years are not required to again comply with the residential qualifications.

Character

Applicants for benefit are required to be of good moral character and sober habits. The period during which a married applicant for age-benefit must not have deserted his wife or wilfully failed to provide for his children for six months, or during which a married woman must not have deserted her husband or children for the same period was reduced to five years, compared with the period of twelve years for old-age pensions.

Rates of Benefit

With the passing of the Social Security Act, 1938, the old-age pension of £58 10s. a year was replaced by the age-benefit of £78 a year. Successive increases have now raised the basic rate of benefit to £130 a year.

Additional Benefits

Dependent Wife

Under previous legislation there was no provision for the wife of an age-beneficiary if she was not eligible for a pension in her own right. The Social Security Act, however, provides an additional benefit for a wife under sixty years of age or otherwise ineligible for benefit.

The allowance was small to commence with, being only £13 a year, but it is now paid at the same rate as the basic rate of £130 a year, so that to-day a man sixty years of age with a wife of, say, fifty-five years may receive a combined benefit of £260 a year and is placed in the same relative position as a married couple both over sixty years of age and each receiving the basic benefit of £130 a year in their own right.

Dependent Children

An old-age pensioner who was the parent of two or more children under the age of fifteen years received an additional allowance of £13 a year. This extra allowance for children was continued in the social security scheme at the same amount as previously, but it applied to each child under sixteen years of age and included any child being maintained by the beneficiary. The rate was later increased to £26 a year, and from the 1st October, 1945, children have been paid for by way of family benefit and not included in the parents' benefit. This principle was adopted in respect of all benefits and has made for easier administration.

South African War Veterans

The additional payment of £13 to a veteran who served with a New Zealand Contingent in the South African War was retained in the Social Security Act. These grants have been extended to include, in addition to those who served in a New Zealand unit, any age-beneficiary who had served in that war as a member of His Majesty's Forces other than a New Zealand Contingent who was either born in New Zealand or domiciled in New Zealand at the start of the war.

The allowance has been increased to £13 13s. a year, with a limit of income including benefit of £182 a year.

Income and Property

The income and property qualifications for age-benefit remain the same as for old-age pension. In addition to an age-benefit, a single beneficiary is allowed a yearly income of £52 from any other source. A married couple both on benefit is allowed the same amount, and where there is excess income each benefit is reduced by 10s. for every £1 of excess. Where only one of the couple receives the benefit a greater income exemption is allowable so as to bring the total income, including benefit, to the same amount as would be applicable to a married couple both on benefit.

TABLE 2—AGE-BENEFITS : RATE AND ALLOWABLE INCOME AT 1ST JUNE, 1949

Applicant.	Basic Rate.		Allowable Income.		Total Benefit and Allowable Income.	
	Weekly.	Yearly.	Weekly.	Yearly.	Weekly.	Yearly.
	£ s. d.	£ s. d.	£ s. d.	£ s. d.	£ s. d.	£ s. d.
Single, widowed, separated, or divorced	2 10 0	130 0 0	1 0 0	52 0 0	3 10 0	182 0 0
Married persons (husband or wife not eligible)	2 10 0	130 0 0	3 10 0	182 0 0	6 0 0	312 0 0
Married persons (both eligible)	2 10 0 (each)	130 0 0 (each)	1 0 0	52 0 0	6 0 0	312 0 0

The amount of the income exemption has not altered in the last ten years, and the classes of income not taken into account are referred to in detail in Chapter XI, page 106.

The property exemption of £500 also has not been altered, and benefits are reduced by £1 for every complete £10 of property in excess of the exemption.

No reduction in benefit is made in respect of both income and the property from which income is derived, but the benefit is reduced by whichever results in the greater reduction.

During the 1939–45 world war it was found that some age-beneficiaries who were physically fit for work were sometimes reluctant to do so because they feared when they again ceased work there would be difficulty or delay in securing restoration of benefit. As a concession to those wishing to work regulations were issued in 1942 under which the earnings of an age-beneficiary during a period in which payment of benefits was withheld could be exempted from income. This enabled beneficiaries to surrender their benefits in order to take up wartime employment, knowing that as soon as they ceased work payment of age-benefit would be resumed without taking into account earnings during the period no benefit was paid. Many beneficiaries took advantage of this concession and resumed employment during those critical years.

Because of the higher-income exemption combined with the subsidy on the earnings of blind people, blind invalid beneficiaries sometimes suffered a reduction in benefit when they reached age sixty, and, thereby becoming ineligible for invalids' benefit, were arbitrarily transferred to age-benefit. To remove this anomaly the law was altered in 1943 so that payment of age-benefit could be made at a rate not less than the amount the beneficiary would have received as an invalid beneficiary. From 1948 this provision was further extended to include blind people who were not on invalids' benefit at the time they qualified for age-benefit.

Previously old-age pensions had not been paid to Maoris receiving money from the Civil List appropriation for Native purposes. This restriction was removed under the Social Security Act, and Maoris are now treated in exactly the same manner as all other sections of the community in regard to social security legislation.

TABLE 3—COMPARISON OF AGE-BENEFITS IN 1898, 1939, AND 1949

Age-benefit.	1898 : Old-age Pensions First Introduced in New Zealand.	1939 : Social Security Scheme Introduced.	1949 : After Ten Years of Social Security.
Basic rate	£18	£78	£130
Dependent wife not eligible in own right	Nil	£13	£130
Dependent children	Nil	£13 each child	£26 each child. (Family benefit.)
Qualifying age (men and women)	65 years	60 years	60 years.
Income exemption	£34	£52	£52
Property exemption	£50 (deduction of £1 for each £15 in excess of £50)	£500 (deduction of £1 for each £10 in excess of £500)	£500 (deduction of £1 for each £10 in excess of £500).
Home property	Taken into account as property	Excluded as property	Excluded as property
Residential qualifications	25 years	10 years if in New Zealand on 15th March, 1938; otherwise twenty years	10 years if in New Zealand on 15th March, 1938; otherwise twenty years.

TABLE 4—SUPERANNUATION BENEFITS : NUMBER GRANTED, NUMBER IN FORCE, AND EXPENDITURE, 1ST APRIL, 1940, TO 31ST MARCH, 1949

Year Ended 31st March,	Number of Benefits.		Rate of Benefit Per Annum.	Expenditure.	
	Granted During Year.	In Force at End of Year.		Year Ended 31st March.	Grand Total Expenditure.
			£ s. d.	£	£
1941	38,938	36,602	10 0 0	240,336	240,336
1942	7,796	41,021	12 10 0	445,686	686,022
1943	8,023	44,448	15 0 0	603,124	1,289,146
1944	8,599	49,289	17 10 0	778,758	2,067,904
1945	8,771	53,679	20 0 0	995,035	3,062,939
1946	9,017	56,181	22 10 0	1,185,508	4,248,447
1947	8,729	57,992	25 0 0	1,349,689	5,598,136
1948	9,425*	61,612	27 10 0	1,593,757	7,191,893
1949	10,030*	65,839	30 0 0	1,850,079	9,041,972

TABLE 5—AGE-BENEFITS : NUMBER GRANTED, NUMBER IN FORCE, AND EXPENDITURE, 1ST APRIL, 1939, TO 31ST MARCH, 1949

Year Ended 31st March,	Number of Age-benefits.		Expenditure.	
	Granted During Year.	In Force at End of Year.	Year Ended 31st March.	Grand Total Expenditure.
			£	£
1940	33,208	93,262	6,517,899	6,517,899
1941	12,553	97,606	7,101,346	13,619,245
1942	9,852	99,152	7,190,694	20,809,939
1943	8,443	99,671	7,783,084	28,593,023
1944	9,927	102,530	8,101,668	36,694,691
1945	9,993	104,653	8,492,015	45,186,706
1946	12,832	110,060	9,817,615	55,004,321
1947	12,835	115,287	11,881,119	66,885,440
1948	10,728*	117,161	12,976,286	79,861,726
1949	9,351*	116,254†	13,790,971	93,652,697

* The reduction in the number of age-benefits granted in 1948 and 1949 is counterbalanced to a certain extent by the increase in the number of persons over sixty-five years of age coming on to superannuation benefit during those years.

† The reduction in the number of age-benefits in force at the 31st March, 1949, compared with the previous year is partly accounted for by the removal from the age-benefit roll of cases where benefit had been suspended for some time because the beneficiaries had resumed full-time employment.

CHART 2—AGE-BENEFITS : NUMBER GRANTED EACH YEAR, 1935 TO 1949

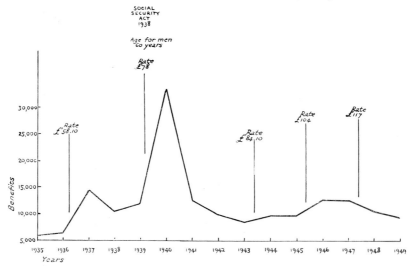

CHART 3—AGE-BENEFITS : NUMBER IN FORCE EACH YEAR, 1935 TO 1949

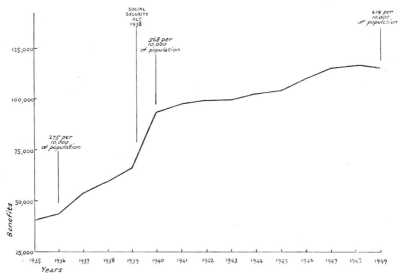

Year.	Population, Including Maoris.			Age-benefit (Payable Sixty Years, Subject to Means Test).			Superannuation Benefit (Payable Sixty-five Years, no Means Test).			Age and Superannuation Combined.		
	Total at 31st March.	Aged Sixty Years and Over.	Percentage of Population Aged Sixty and Over to Total Population.	Number in Force at 31st March.	Percentage to Total Population.	Percentage to Population Aged Sixty and Over.	Number in Force at 31st March.	Percentage to Total Population.	Percentage to Population Sixty Years and Over.	Number in Force at 31st March.	Percentage to Total Population.	Percentage to Population Sixty Years and Over.
1940	1,640,901	186,550	11·37	93,262	5·68	49·99	..	..	..	93,262	5·68	49·99
1941	1,636,230	193,750	11·84	97,606	5·96	50·38	36,602	2·24	18·89	134,208	8·20	69·27
1942	1,634,338	200,525	12·27	99,152	6·07	49·45	41,021	2·51	20·45	140,173	8·58	69·90
1943	1,634,094	205,100*	12·55	99,671	6·10	48·60	44,448	2·72	21·67	144,119	8·82	70·27
1944	1,643,900	211,350*	12·86	102,530	6·24	48·51	49,289	3·00	23·32	151,819	9·24	71·83
1945	1,679,972	218,025*	12·98	104,653	6·23	48·00	53,679	3·19	24·62	158,332	9·42	72·62
1946	1,758,004	225,998*	12·86	110,060	6·26	48·70	56,181	3·20	24·86	166,241	9·46	73·56
1947	1,793,225	233,725*	13·03	115,287	6·43	49·33	57,992	3·23	24·81	173,279	9·66	74·14
1948	1,834,270	236,525*	12·89	117,161	6·39	49·53	61,612	3·36	26·05	178,773	9·75	75·58
1949	1,873,244	244,725*	13·06	116,254	6·21	47·50	65,839	3·51	26·90	182,093	9·72	74·40

* At previous 31st December.

N.B.—Population figures do not include members of the Armed Forces serving outside New Zealand.

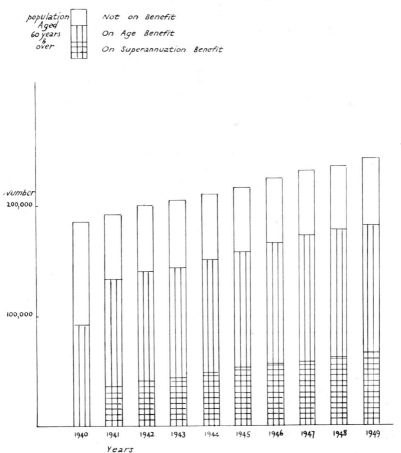

When the Social Security Act came into operation on 1st April, 1939, 66,694 old-age pensioners, representing 410 per 10,000 of the population, were brought under the new legislation. At this time there were still many unemployed persons in New Zealand, and among those receiving assistance were some men aged sixty or more.

The lower qualifying-age of sixty years compared with sixty-five years as previously for old-age pensions resulted in many of these men coming on to age-benefit. In addition, the more generous qualifying conditions, together with the higher rate of benefit, encouraged many new applications, and during the year ended 31st March, 1940, over 33,000 new benefits were granted, bringing the total number of age-benefits in force up to 93,262, or 568 per 10,000 of population, an increase of 35 per cent.

Following this sudden increase and the abnormal demand for employment which the World War created, the number of benefits continued to increase at a much slower rate, and by the 31st March, 1949, after ten years of social security, there were 116,254 age-benefits being paid, representing 621 per 10,000 of population.

At the 1st April, 1939, 37 per cent. of the population aged sixty years and over were receiving age-benefit, and a year later the number had increased to 50 per cent. of the population sixty years and over. Since then the percentage has been relatively static and has not varied more than 2 per cent.

The amount spent on age-benefits for the first year of social security was £6,517,899, compared with £3,577,129 spent on old-age pensions the previous year, an increase of 84 per cent. Within five years the expenditure on age-benefits had exceeded the total amount paid out on old-age pensions for the previous forty years.

Voluntary Withdrawal From Employment to go on to Age-benefit

In order to ascertain if there is a tendency for people to prefer retiring on age-benefit in preference to continuing in employment beyond the age of sixty years the following analysis has been made of the ages of persons on age-benefit as at 30th September, 1948.

TABLE 7—AGES OF AGE-BENEFICIARIES

Age at 30th June, 1948.	Males.			Females.			Grand Total.
	Married.	Unmarried.	Total.	Married.	Unmarried.	Total.	
60	610	247	857	679	1,487	2,166	3,033
61	1,322	402	1,724	1,306	1,793	3,099	4,823
62	1,602	527	2,129	1,414	1,785	3,199	5,317
63	1,704	607	2,311	1,543	1,844	3,387	5,699
64	1,866	683	2,549	1,680	2,161	3,841	6,390
Sub-total ..	7,104	2,466	9,570	6,622	9,070	15,692	25,262
65	2,091	762	2,583	1,759	2,151	3,910	6,763
66	2,072	874	2,946	1,679	2,075	3,754	6,700
67	2,018	865	2,883	1,654	2,231	3,885	6,768
68	2,211	994	3,205	1,627	2,380	4,007	7,212
69	1,956	1,063	3,019	1,501	2,260	3,761	6,780
70	2,028	1,086	3,114	1,372	2,224	3,596	6,710
71	1,724	1,064	2,788	1,155	2,074	3,229	6,017
72	1,640	1,119	2,759	1,152	2,195	3,347	6,106
73	1,422	1,016	2,438	917	1,944	2,861	5,299
74	1,279	952	2,231	768	1,811	2,579	4,810
75	989	923	1,912	587	1,747	2,334	4,246
76	886	875	1,761	513	1,567	2,080	3,841
77	735	797	1,532	422	1,411	1,833	3,365
78	698	775	1,473	415	1,467	1,882	3,355
79	599	600	1,199	276	1,090	1,366	2,565
80	421	550	971	221	1,020	1,241	2,212
81	331	466	797	136	872	1,008	1,805
82	267	428	695	120	862	982	1,677
83	209	354	563	83	701	784	1,347
84	157	299	456	58	609	667	1,113
85 and over ..	376	961	1,337	126	2,094	2,220	3,557
Sub-total	24,109	16,823	40,932	16,541	34,785	51,326	92,258
Grand total	31,213	19,289	50,502	23,163	43,855	67,018	117,520

Summary

Age-group.	Males.		Females.		Totals.		Grand Total.
	Married.	Unmarried.	Married.	Unmarried.	Males.	Females.	
60–64 ..	7,104	2,466	6,622	9,070	9,570	15,692	25,262
65 and over ..	24,109	16,823	16,541	34,785	40,932	51,326	92,258
Totals ..	31,213	19,289	23,163	43,855	50,502	67,018	117,520*

* Included in the above figures are widows of sixty years of age and over without dependent children who have not been transferred to age-benefit from widows' benefit.

The analysis shows that only 3,033 persons aged sixty years are on benefit, and the numbers rise progressively until in the sixty-eight years' age-group there are 7,212 beneficiaries. The peak numbers in the sixty-eight years' age-group would undoubtedly be influenced by the fact that there was an extraordinary influx of age-beneficiaries during 1939–40, when the social security scheme came into operation, and no doubt many were sixty years of age on application and would fall into the sixty-eight years' age-group at 30th September, 1948, when the analysis was made. However, apart from this factor, the data indicates that a considerable proportion of persons who are eligible on age grounds delay applying for benefit for some years, and many of these will have been continuing in employment.*

Of the 3,033 sixty-year-old beneficiaries an appreciable number will have been automatically transferred from invalids' benefit to age-benefit on attaining sixty years of age in accordance with the law, and also there will be included in that figure a number of married women who were previously included as " under age " wives in their husbands' benefit. Then, again, a number of females were in receipt of widows' benefit prior to attaining the age of sixty years and would probably not have been engaged in employment for many years if at all.

Having regard to all these factors it would appear that the number coming on the age-benefit roll when reaching sixty years of age and being withdrawn from remunerative employment is considerably below the 3,033 actually on benefit.

A proportion of those coming on to benefit for the first time in their sixty-first year will have reached the end of their working-days through ill health or other causes, and consequently it would appear that the drain on the labour pool through the attractions of benefit is almost negligible, particularly at this period when there is an abnormal demand for labour at attractive rates of remuneration.

* An analysis of a proportion of men granted age-benefit for the first time in 1949 showed that the average age at grant of benefit was 64·76 years.

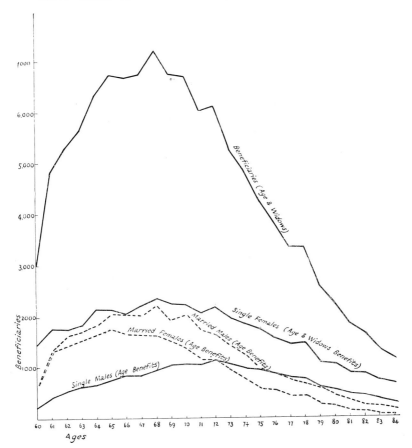

Benefits for Aged

TABLE 8—NUMBERS IN RELATION TO POPULATION OVER SIXTY YEARS OF AGE

Age-group.	Population.	On Age or Widows' Benefit.	On Superannuation Benefit (Available at Sixty-five Years of Age).	Numbers Not on Benefit.
60–64	79,575	25,262	..	54,313
65 and over	156,950	92,258	63,814	878
Total	236,525*	117,520†	63,814†	55,191

* At December, 1947. † Denotes number of benefits in force as at 30th September, 1948.

Although 33·6 per cent. of the population aged sixty years or more is in the 60–64 age-group, only 21·1 per cent. of the total age-beneficiaries were included in the same group. Only 31·7 per cent of the population in the 60–64 age-group is in receipt of age-benefit, but there is almost complete coverage in the sixty-five years and over group, as practically all who are not on age-benefit are in receipt of the superannuation benefit.

The percentage of age-beneficiaries to the population in the sixty-five and over age-group is 58·8 per cent. as against 31·7 per cent. in the 60–64 year age-group. Only 18·9 per cent of the male and 23·4 per cent. of the female age-beneficiaries are included in the 60–64 age-group.

Of married males 22·4 per cent. and of unmarried males 12·8 per cent. are within the 60–64 age-group. Of married females, 28·6 per cent. and of unmarried females 20·7 per cent. are within the 60–64 age-group.

Private Resources of Age-beneficiaries

An analysis of 118,323 age-benefits, the result of which is tabulated below, showed that the great majority of age-beneficiaries have little or no private resources.

TABLE 9—AGE-BENEFICIARIES : CLASSIFICATION BY INCOME AND PROPERTY

	Income.			Property.		
Chargeable Income of Beneficiaries.	Number of Beneficiaries.	Percentage of Total Age-beneficiaries.	Value of Chargeable Property.	Number of Beneficiaries.	Percentage of Total Age-beneficiaries.
£				£		
Nil	42,187	35·7	Nil	35,813	30·3
1–52	64,676	54·6	1–250	57,223	48·4
53–104 ..	8,451	7·1	251–500	17,964	15·2
105–156 ..	2,084	1·8	501–1000	6,511	5·5
157–208 ..	496	0·4	1001–1500	752	0·6
209–286 ..	429	0·4	1501–1670	60	..
Total ..	118,323*	100·0	..	118,323*	100·0

* Wives who are not eligible for benefit in their own right but who are included in their husband's benefit have been counted as separate benefits.

N.B.—Property of a married beneficiary is half total property of husband and wife.

The above table discloses that over a third of the age-beneficiaries have no other income and are entirely dependent on their benefits. Over half of them have income amounting to from £1–£52 a year and depend mainly on the age-benefits for their livelihood. Thus about 90 per cent of the age-beneficiaries have little or no income, being in receipt of the maximum rate of age-benefit and not affected by the means test. While income taken into account in the above table includes practically all money and the value of benefits received, there are some items such as funeral benefits, insurance, and capital receipts which are not taken into account as income. For a further explanation of these items the reader is referred to page 106.

The position regarding the proportion of beneficiaries with little or no property is much the same. Almost a third have no accumulated property, and over half own property but within the property exemption of £500. About 94 per cent. of the beneficiaries either have no property or own property the value of which does not exceed £500. Many of these beneficiaries, however, have property such as a home, furniture, an interest in land, life insurance, or personal effects which are excluded from the chargeable property taken into account for age-benefit purposes. A further explanation of the classes of property not included in " accumulated property " is shown on page 107.

WIDOWS' BENEFITS

A distinction is made between widows who have borne children and childless widows, and this class of benefit falls into two main groups:—

(a) Widows with child or children under sixteen years of age.
(b) Widows without dependent children.

In addition, the following two classes of women (although not legally widows) may be granted benefit as though they were widows:—

(1) Wives of mental patients who are the subjects of reception orders or are inmates of mental hospitals.
(2) Wives who have been deserted by their husbands and have taken proceedings under the Destitute Persons Act, 1910, for maintenance.

WIDOWS WITH CHILDREN

Residence

The residential requirements have not varied during the last ten years and are the same as for the former widow's pension. If the child by virtue of which the widow qualifies for a benefit is born in New Zealand the widow is entitled to receive benefit irrespective of the period of residence of the family in New Zealand. However, if the child is not born in New Zealand the widow does not qualify for benefit unless she was only temporarily out of New Zealand at the time of the birth or unless both parents had lived in New Zealand for the three years immediately before the death or desertion or the making of a reception order in respect of the husband.

Character

As with widows' pensions, applicants for widows' benefit are required to be of good moral character and sober habits.

Rates

Widows' pensions of £52 plus £26 for each child under fifteen years of age were replaced from 1st April, 1939, by a widow's benefit of £65 plus £26 for each child under sixteen years of age.

The basic rate has increased at various times in later years, and the present rate, which has been ruling since 1st October, 1947, is £130 a year for the widow. In addition to the benefit a mother's allowance of £78 a year is granted to assist in the maintenance of the children, for whom she also receives a family benefit of £26 a year for each child.

Income and Property

The income exemption for widows with children is £78 and has not been altered over the last decade. These benefits are payable irrespective of any property possessed by the widow.

WIDOWS WITHOUT CHILDREN

Assistance for widows without children was provided for the first time by the Social Security Act, 1938. These benefits are divided into two classes:—

(a) A widow who has borne children.
(b) A childless widow.

Prior to 1945 benefits for these two classes were restricted to women whose husbands were dead, but since 1st October, 1945, these benefits have been paid to deserted wives and wives of mental patients.

A widow who has borne children, but at the time of application has no children under sixteen years of age, can be granted a widow's benefit so long as she has been married fifteen years or the total period of the marriage and the subsequent period she has had the care and control of at least one of her children under sixteen years of age is not less than fifteen years. Under the previous pensions legislation a widow's pension ceased at the end of the pension year during which the child died or attained fifteen years. The social security legislation, however, provides that a benefit granted to a widow with children ceases when, because of death or otherwise, there ceases to be a child in respect of whom a benefit is payable, but these widows are entitled to a benefit as widows without children if not less than fifteen years has passed since marriage.

A widow who has never borne a child qualifies for benefit if she became a widow after she reached fifty years of age and had been married for at least five years ; or if she, being not less than fifty years of age, became a widow after she reached the age of forty years. In addition, she must have been married for ten years and at least fifteen years must have elapsed since the date of her marriage.

Residence

For widows without dependent children three years' residence of both husband and wife up to the time of the husband's death is necessary to enable the widow to qualify for benefit.

Rates of Benefit

The rate of benefit for widows without children was £52 a year at 1st April, 1939, and subsequent increases have raised the basic rate to the present figure of £130 a year as part of the Government policy to have a standard basic rate for all adult benefits.

Income and Property

Originally all benefits for widows were reduced by the amount of income over £52 a year. From 1st October, 1945, the exemption was raised to £78 a year, and still remains at that figure. When a widow without dependent children turns sixty years of age the benefit is assessed on the same basis as age-benefits, and both property and income are taken into account.

GENERAL

Application for Widows' Benefit

Normally the onus of applying for a social security benefit is on the individual. It has been realized that on the death of her husband a widow will not usually be in a state of mind to immediately concern herself with financial affairs. The Social Security Department therefore comes to her aid and takes the initiative by getting in touch with women whose husbands have just died unless it is known that financial help is not required.

Through death notices in newspapers and the co-operation of funeral directors, Public Trust Office, and many legal firms every possible method is used to locate the widows needing assistance. Contacts by correspondence, telephone through near relations, or personal visits by officers of the Department have generally enabled speedy assistance to be given when most needed.

Where a widow is in straitened circumstances and there may be delay in completing an application for widow's benefit a temporary emergency grant is made by district officers to the widow.

This small service has enabled claims for widow's benefit to be assessed with a minimum of delay, and the Department's interest and desire to help have been greatly appreciated.

Number of Beneficiaries

The limitation of assistance to widows with children under previous legislation inferred that unless a widow had children she must earn her own living, irrespective of whether or not she was capable or had the opportunity of suitable employment. By the inclusion of benefits for widows without children under the Social Security Act a large number of women in this category were granted benefits, and by the 31st March, 1940, after one year's operation of the social security legislation the number of widows receiving benefit had increased to 10,174, double the number for the previous year under the old legislation.

The number receiving benefit at 31st March, 1949, was 14,883, with 4,683 receiving the mothers' allowance in supplementation thereto.

DESERTED WIVES

" Deserted wives," in order to qualify for widows' benefits, must satisfy the main provisions of the Act applicable to widows whose husbands have died, and, in addition, satisfy the Social Security Commission that they have been deserted by their husbands and have taken proceedings against the deserting husbands for maintenance orders under the Destitute Persons Act, 1910.

Previously this class of assistance was confined to women with children in cases where the whereabouts of the husband was unknown or if there was a maintenance order in force which was not being complied with. Since October, 1945, the benefit has been available to women without children in the same way as other widows' benefits.

Recovery of Maintenance

On the granting of a benefit any maintenance paid under the Court maintenance order is credited to the Social Security Fund to offset the benefit paid. In this way wives of husbands who are erratic in the payment of maintenance are provided with a regular income by way of widows' benefit. At the end of each year, if the amount of maintenance credited to the Social Security Fund is greater than the amount paid to the wife by way of widows' benefit, the credit balance is paid over to the wife by the Department, if the maintenance order is paid up to date.

From the time a benefit is granted to the wife the Department takes over the enforcement of the maintenance order and if the husband is dilatory in his payments legal action is taken to ensure that the order is being complied with.

A close check is kept on the husbands' earnings to ensure that if his financial circumstances materially improve an increase in the maintenance order is applied for. If the parties subsequently cohabit or become reconciled the widow's benefit is cancelled, and usually no action is taken to recover maintenance arrears from the husband. Benefits for deserted wives, while not numerous, have relieved a great deal of genuine distress.

TABLE 10—WIDOWS' BENEFITS : PARTICULARS OF BENEFITS GRANTED TO DESERTED WIVES FOR THREE YEARS TO 31ST MARCH, 1949

Year.	Deserted Wives' Benefit.		Maintenance.		
	Number in Force at 31st March.	Expenditure, Year Ended 31st March.	Number of Maintenance Orders in Force at 31st March.	Amount Collected, Year Ended 31st March.	Percentage of Amount Collected to Orders in Force.
		£		£	
1947	1,102	161,368	959	44,554	40·5
1948	1,096	170,444	899	60,996	53·0
1949	1,140	180,758	926	64,104	54·4

TABLE 11—WIDOWS' BENEFITS : RATE AND ALLOWABLE INCOME AT 1ST JUNE, 1949

Class.	Maximum Benefit a Year.	To Widow With Dependent Child or Children : Mothers' Allowance.	Allowable Other Income.	Amount of Income and Benefit a Year.
	£	£	£	£
1. Widow *with* dependent children under sixteen years of age (N.B.—For each child the widow also receives 10s. a week by way of family benefit.)	130	78	78	286
2. Widows *without* dependent children	130	..	78	208

TABLE 12—WIDOWS' BENEFITS : NUMBER GRANTED, NUMBER IN FORCE, AND EXPENDITURE. 1ST APRIL, 1939, TO 31ST MARCH, 1949
(Includes benefits paid to deserted wives and wives of mental hospital patients)

Year.	Number of Benefits.		Expenditure, Year Ended 31st March.
	Granted, Year Ended 31st March.	In Force at 31st March,	
			£
1940	6,310	10,174	785,952
1941	2,089	10,569	836,368
1942	1,845	10,765	844,928
1943	1,712	10,589	866,597
1944	1,987	10,836	949,099
1945	1,859	10,965	985,452
1946	2,187	11,507	1,043,593
1947	2,407	13,133	1,529,010
1948	2,075	14,145	1,770,622
1949	2,067	14,883	1,911,134

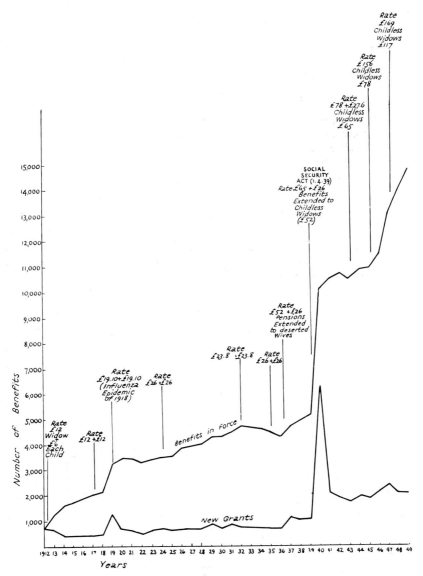

ORPHANS' BENEFITS

Benefits for orphans were one of the Social Security Act's original contributions. Although the Widows' Pensions Act, 1911, had authorized pensions in respect of children of widows who had died while receiving widows' pensions, prior to 1939 no general provision had been made for specific assistance to orphaned children.

Children under sixteen years of age who are either born in New Zealand or whose last surviving parent lived in New Zealand for three years immediately preceding death are entitled to an orphan's benefit.

65

The rate was originally £39 a year, but has since been raised to £65 a year ; within the limit of £65 the actual rate is fixed by the Social Security Commission having regard to the income and property of the orphan. In actual practice no regard is taken of the property of the child, but the benefit is reduced £1 for £1 in respect of all income. Benefits are not paid to children who are being maintained in a State institution, but where children are granted this benefit the payments are made to the person having the care and control of the orphan or some other reputable person and is to be used for the maintenance, education, and benefit of the child.

For the purpose of assisting in the further education of children this benefit may be continued up to the end of the year during which the children turned eighteen years of age. Although the benefit is initially for orphans under sixteen years of age the benefit may be granted in respect of children who become orphans when they are over sixteen years of age provided they are still continuing at school. In such cases it may be continued for their further education up to the end of the year in which they turn eighteen years.

It is pleasing to note that there are relatively few of these benefits, only 431 being granted in the first year. The average number of benefits being paid is approximately four hundred a year. At 31st March, 1949, there were actually 371 in force in respect of 518 children.

FAMILY BENEFITS

Family benefit legislation since 1939 has developed from the original concept of providing allowances to parents with large families who were in the lowest income bracket to a system of universal coverage with the payment of family benefit for all children of the family unit irrespective of the income of the parents.

The gradual progress which has been made over the last twenty years to the ultimate goal of universal coverage is shown in the following table.

TABLE 13—FAMILY BENEFITS : LEGISLATIVE CHANGES SINCE 1927

Legislation Changes.	Weekly Rate of Allowance or Benefit.	Children Paid for.	Qualifying-age of Children.	Weekly Allowable Exempted Income of Family.
	s. d.			£ s. d.
1927 ..	2 0 a child for			4 0 0
1931 ..	2 0 ,,	Third and subsequent children	Under fifteen years	3 12 0
1932 ..	2 0 ,,			3 5 0
1936 ..	2 0 ,,			4 0 0
1939 ..	4 0 ,,	Third and subsequent children	Under sixteen years	5 0 0
1940 ..	4 0 ,,	Second and subsequent children	Ditto ..	5 0 0
1941 ..	4 0 ,,			5 0 0
1942 ..	6 0 ,,			5 5 0
1943 ..	7 6 ,,	All children of family	Under sixteen years	5 5 0
1944 ..	10 0 ,,			5 10 0
1945 ..	10 0 ,,			6 10 0
1946 ..	10 0 ,,			No means test.

Calendar Year.	Family Benefit Exempt Income.	Index No. for F.B. Exempt Income (1930 = 1017).	Index No. for Nominal Wage Rate, Adult Males.*
1930	80/-	1017	1017
1931	72/-	915	942
1932	65/-	826	864
1933	65/-	826	833
1934	65/-	826	839
1935	65/-	826	858
1936	80/-	1017	950
1937	80/-	1017	1036
1938	80/-	1017	1081
1939	100/-	1271	1100
1940	100/-	1271	1130
1941	100/-	1271	1170
1942	105/-	1335	1222
1943	105/-	1335	1261
1944	110/-	1398	1274
1945	130/-	1653	1381
1946	All income exempt from 1/4/46	..	..

* Taken from 1946 Year-Book, page 608.

CHART 7—FAMILY BENEFITS: COMPARISON OF INDEX NUMBERS FOR
EXEMPT INCOME AND NOMINAL WAGE RATE, 1930 TO 1945

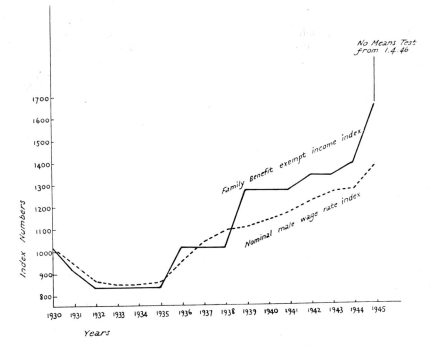

To qualify for benefit the children must have been born in New
Zealand or lived in New Zealand for not less than one year. Until
recently family benefit was not paid for children born out of New Zealand

during the temporary absence of the mother until the twelve months' residence of the child had been completed, but from December, 1948, this restriction has been removed, and now children born during the temporary absence of the mother are eligible for benefit immediately they arrive in New Zealand.

Children not being maintained as members of the family of an applicant or receiving any other social security benefit or war pension are not included in a family benefit.

When a child reaches the age of sixteen years the benefit normally ceases, but payment may be continued beyond that age for any child physically and mentally incapable of earning a living. Also for the purpose of assisting in the further education of any child the benefit may be continued until the end of the year in which the child reaches eighteen years of age.

Either parent may apply for the benefit, but payment is usually made to the mother, and while the benefit may be regarded as an accretion of total family income the law emphasizes that it is to be used exclusively towards the maintenance or education of the children. If it is not being properly applied for this purpose, the Social Security Commission has power to withhold payment of the benefit until it is satisfied that the parent or guardian is prepared to use the money for the benefit of the children.

When the means-test restrictions were lifted it was realized that many mothers with very young children might often find it inconvenient to collect benefit instalments in cash each month, and since April, 1946, when universal coverage was instituted, it has been possible for mothers to have the benefit paid into their private post-office savings-bank accounts by arrangement with the Social Security Department and Post Office authorities. Approximately a third of the mothers take advantage of this provision. Also with the consent of the mother, part or whole of the family benefit may be diverted to the Commissioner of Taxes to meet the income-tax payments of the husband.

The extent to which these facilities are availed of is illustrated by the following table :—

TABLE 15—FAMILY BENEFITS : PAYMENTS TO POST-OFFICE SAVINGS-BANK ACCOUNTS AND COMMISSIONER OF TAXES FROM 1ST APRIL, 1946, TO 31ST MARCH, 1949

Year.	Total Number of Family Benefits at 31st March.	Number of Benefits Paid Direct to Post-office Savings-bank Account at 31st March.	Number of Benefits Paid Direct to Commissioner of Taxes at 31st March.	Amount to Post-office Savings-bank Accounts Year Ended 31st March.	Amount to Commissioner of Taxes, Year Ended 31st March.
				£	£
1947	230,021	58,960	6,602	3,073,406	248,072
1948	243,137	63,975	5,520	3,379,675	227,535
1949	248,726	74,534	4,737	3,705,398	198,874

TABLE 16—FAMILY BENEFITS: NUMBER GRANTED, NUMBER IN FORCE, AND EXPENDITURE FROM 1ST APRIL, 1939, TO 31ST MARCH, 1949

| Year. | Number of Benefits. | | Expenditure for Year Ended 31st March. |
	Granted, Year Ended 31st March.	In Force at 31st March.	
			£
1940	6,410	11,053	252,562
1941	7,075	16,626	411,811
1942	5,730	18,316	539,183
1943	3,443	14,190	790,719
1944	5,746	15,950	876,858
1945	10,784	24,251	1,405,113
1946	21,679*	42,637	2,611,759
1947	194,313	230,021	12,680,778
1948	24,422	243,137	13,798,638
1949	19,979	248,726	14,242,202

* Includes family benefits previously paid as child allowances in conjunction with benefits being paid to parents.

The easing of the qualifying conditions from 1939 resulted in a large number of new applications for benefit during the first year of operation of the social security scheme. For several years previously the number of allowances granted and in force had been dwindling, and only 5,606 allowances paid in respect of 15,780 children were absorbed into the new scheme. Within a year the number of families receiving this benefit had doubled, and as the legislation was extended the benefits increased. When the means-test restrictions were lifted from 1st April, 1946, there were 42,637 benefits being paid, and this number jumped to 230,021 when universal coverage was granted. At 31st March, 1949, there were 248,726 family benefits being paid in respect of 548,330 children. Included in the total number of children are 9,958 over sixteen years of age whose benefits have been extended for their further education.

CHART 8—FAMILY BENEFITS: NUMBER GRANTED AND IN FORCE EACH
YEAR, 1928 TO 1949

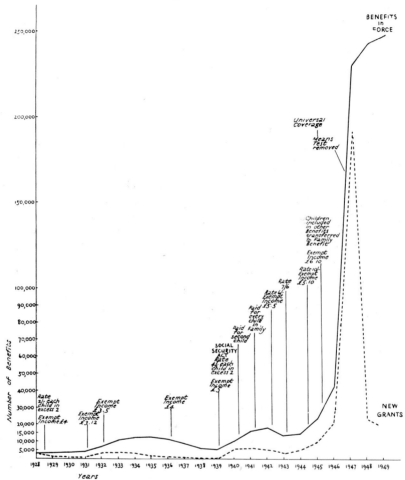

TABLE 17—NUMBER OF FAMILY BENEFITS ACCORDING TO SIZE OF FAMILIES,
31ST MARCH, 1947, TO 31ST MARCH, 1949

31st March,	Number of Families to Which Benefit is Paid for—										Total Number of Benefits.	Total Number of Children.
	One Child.	Two Children.	Three Children.	Four Children.	Five Children.	Six Children.	Seven Children.	Eight Children.	Nine Children.	Ten Children or More.		
1947	94,163	68,292	36,171	17,722	7,252	3,430	1,576	797	401	217	230,021	490,260
1948	101,325	68,883	38,871	18,552	8,048	3,737	1,984	988	462	287	243,137	521,394
1949	95,681	75,178	41,488	19,741	8,586	3,975	2,088	1,098	531	360	248,726	548,330

70

INVALIDS' BENEFITS

The provisions of the old invalids' pensions legislation were not materially changed by the corresponding provisions in the Social Security Act relating to invalids' benefits.

QUALIFYING CONDITIONS

This benefit is payable to every person between sixteen and sixty years of age who is totally blind or permanently incapacitated for work as a result of accident, illness, or congenital defect.

RESIDENCE

To qualify for a benefit the applicant must have resided continuously in New Zealand for not less than ten years immediately preceding the date of application.

An aggregate allowance of one year for absence is permitted plus a further allowance of one month for every year of residence in excess of ten years.

CHARACTER

The requirement that applicants for invalidity pension should be of good moral character and sober habits applies also to invalids' benefits under the Social Security Act.

RATES OF BENEFIT

The basic rate for adult invalids is uniform with age-benefits and has increased from £78 a year in 1939 to the present figure of £130, which has operated from 1st June, 1949.

The rate of benefit for unmarried persons under twenty-one years of age was £52 in 1939, but has increased gradually to £104 a year in later years. The class to whom this rate applies has now been narrowed to those sixteen years but under twenty years of age.

ADDITIONAL BENEFITS

For Dependent Wife

For a dependent wife the annual rate of benefit has increased from £26 a year to £130 a year.

For Dependent Children

When all benefits for dependent children were paid for by way of family benefit from 1st October, 1945, the additional invalid's benefit of £26 a year in respect of children was withdrawn.

For the Blind

The 25-per-cent. subsidy on personal earnings of blind beneficiaries was retained in the Social Security Act and these beneficiaries now have a limit of income, subsidy, and benefit of £286 a year.

INCOME EXEMPTION

Married Men and Widowers with Dependent Children

The income exemption which had been £104 a year under previous legislation was reduced under the Social Security Act to £78 a year, and from October, 1945, the exemption for married men was further reduced to £52 a year.

Married Women

In cases where a married woman is the invalid beneficiary, her husband not being on benefit, the income exemption has been increased from £104 a year to £182 a year.

Special Assistance for Married Women Invalids

In special cases, where owing to the incapacity of a married woman nursing or domestic assistance is paid for, a higher limit of income, including benefit, has been provided in the Social Security Act. Although the beneficiary may only receive up to the maximum benefit of £130 a year the combined allowable income and benefit is £416 a year, of £7 8s. a week, and the advantage of a higher income exemption helps to offset to some degree the additional nursing expenditure.

Others

The income exemption for all other persons is £52 a year, and in addition no account is taken of the personal earnings of blind beneficiaries up to £156 a year. The property exemption is standard for all classes of invalids, being the same rate and applied in the same manner as for age-benefits.

Medical Examination

To determine the extent of incapacity of an applicant a medical examination is required and is arranged and paid for by the Department, the registered medical practitioner being nominated by the Department.

If the application is declined or a current benefit cancelled on medical grounds, there is a right of appeal to a board of three medical practitioners nominated by the Department. This right of appeal must be exercised within three months of the decision being conveyed to the person concerned.

Table 18—Invalids' Benefits : Rates and Allowable Income as at 1st June, 1949

Class of Person.	Rate of Benefit.		Allowable Other Income.		Total Allowable Income and Benefit (Year's Rate).
	Weekly.	Yearly.	Weekly.	Yearly.	
	£ s. d.	£ s. d.	£ s. d.	£ s. d.	£ s. d.
1. Single under twenty years	2 0 0	104 0 0	1 0 0	52 0 0	156 0 0
2. Widower with dependent children	2 10 0	130 0 0	1 10 0	78 0 0	208 0 0
3. Married—					
Man	2 10 0	130 0 0	} 1 0 0	52 0 0	312 0 0
Wife	2 10 0	130 0 0			
4. Married woman ..	2 10 0	130 0 0	3 10 0	182 0 0	312 0 0
5. All other persons ..	2 10 0	130 0 0	1 0 0	52 0 0	182 0 0

N.B.—Dependent children are paid for by way of family benefit at 10s. a week.

GENERAL

During the past ten years the number of invalids' benefits has varied only a little from the 12,489 pensions absorbed into the social security scheme on 1st April, 1939, to 10,051 benefits being paid for on 31st March, 1949.

TABLE 19—INVALIDS' BENEFITS : NUMBER GRANTED, NUMBER IN FORCE, AND EXPENDITURE, 1ST APRIL, 1939, TO 31ST MARCH, 1949

Year.	Number of Benefits.			Expenditure for Year Ended 31st March.
	Granted During Year Ended 31st March.	In Force at 31st March.	Per 10,000 of Total Population.	
				£
1940	3,746	11,811	72	942,196
1941	2,514	11,936	73	999,648
1942	2,248	12,107	74	1,011,375
1943	2,085	11,938	73	1,036,373
1944	2,255	12,126	74	1,067,409
1945	2,093	12,205	73	1,072,619
1946	2,079	12,164	69	1,183,537
1947	2,103	12,466	70	1,328,485
1948	1,249	10,682	58	1,367,300
1949	1,022	10,051	54	1,348,616

There is a noticeable variation in the number of new grants during 1947–48 brought about by a change in policy concerning people suffering from tuberculosis. Although invalids' benefits are intended for permanent invalids, benefits were granted up to 1947 to people suffering from tuberculosis who while not necessarily permanently incapacitated for work were, however, unfit for work for at least twelve months or more. As invalids' benefits prior to 1945 were paid at a higher rate than sickness benefits, which is the appropriate benefit for temporary sickness, the arrangement worked in favour of beneficiaries.

From October, 1945, sickness benefits were paid at the same rate as invalids' benefits, and from then on sufferers from tuberculosis were granted invalids' benefits only if their disease was considered incurable.

This has meant that young and early-middle-aged people suffering from tuberculosis are rarely granted a permanent invalid's benefit, but are more appropriately granted a temporary benefit for the duration of their incapacity. It is hoped in this way to avoid any possible harmful effect on these people if they feel that they are branded as permanent invalids with no ultimate hope of recovery.

TABLE 20—INVALIDS' BENEFITS : CLASSIFICATION, BY AGE, SEX, AND DISEASE, AS AT 31ST JANUARY, 1949

Disease Category	Age at 31st January, 1949, and Sex														Total		Grand Total	Percentage
	16–19		20–25		26–29		30–34		35–39		40–49		50–					
	M	F	M	F	M	F	M	F	M	F	M	F	M	F	M	F		
1. Infectious and parasitic diseases—																		
Tuberculosis of the respiratory system	4	5	51	95	28	53	44	46	57	42	142	65	122	65	448	371	819	8·1
Other forms of tuberculosis	3	3	13	14	7	6	10	6	12	6	20	16	17	18	82	69	151	1·5
Acute poliomyelitis and sequelæ	2	1	17	14	14	25	24	19	36	28	30	46	24	35	147	168	315	3·1
Other infectious and parasitic diseases	..	3	4	7	2	3	7	10	8	4	29	7	40	20	90	54	144	1·4
2. Neoplasms—																		
Malignant neoplasms	1	..	1	1	..	..	3	..	3	1	4	4	18	8	30	19	49	0·5
Non-malignant neoplasms	1	1	1	1	..	..	..	..	1	..	4	4	8	11	15	18	33	0·3
3. Rheumatic fever, diseases of the endocrine glands and nutrition and other general diseases—																		
Rheumatic fever	1	1	4	2	1	1	3	..	3	3	9	6	4	6	25	19	44	0·4
Diabetes mellitus	..	1	1	2	1	3	3	3	4	1	7	7	21	25	37	41	78	0·8
Diseases of the thyroid and endocrine glands	4	..	8	15	3	15	7	10	5	12	5	15	10	37	42	104	146	1·4
Other nutritional and general diseases	..	..	..	3	..	1	..	..	..	..	2	3	3	12	5	19	24	0·2
4. Diseases of the blood and blood-forming organs	..	1	2	3	2	1	1	1	1	..	2	3	17	17	25	26	51	0·5
5. Chronic poisoning and intoxication	..	..	..	..	..	..	..	..	..	..	..	..	..	..	Nil	Nil	Nil	..
6. Diseases of the nervous system and sense organs, including mental disorders—																		
Residuals of other and unspecified paralysis	12	10	27	34	24	30	24	26	26	36	50	35	69	31	232	202	434	4·3
Mental deficiency	56	71	198	233	141	157	149	150	98	136	177	253	127	212	946	1,212	2,158	21·3
Epilepsy	10	8	35	44	32	38	27	41	20	35	54	62	27	37	205	265	470	4·6
Diseases of the organs of vision	6	12	19	16	21	17	26	14	39	8	77	32	137	62	325	161	486	4·8
Other diseases of the nervous system and sense organs, including mental disorders	13	15	21	36	20	36	41	46	35	52	128	129	222	261	480	575	1,055	10·4
7. Diseases of the circulatory system—																		
Diseases of the heart	2	3	12	19	6	10	10	16	18	18	87	73	502	316	637	455	1,092	10·8
Diseases of the arteries	1	..	1	1	2	..	1	1	1	1	6	4	50	22	63	31	94	0·9
Varicose veins and hæmorrhoids	..	..	..	..	..	..	..	..	1	..	..	3	14	16	16	19	35	0·3
Other diseases of the circulatory system	..	..	1	..	1	..	1	..	..	..	1	2	11	7	14	10	24	0·2
8. Diseases of the respiratory system—																		
Bronchitis	..	1	1	..	..	1	1	..	3	..	14	13	57	24	78	46	124	1·2
Asthma	..	1	11	12	6	9	9	12	11	12	47	26	96	59	180	131	311	3·1
Other diseases of the respiratory system	..	..	..	..	..	..	..	1	..	..	9	2	33	10	42	19	61	0·6
9. Diseases of the Digestive system—																		
Ulcer of the stomach and intestines	..	..	..	..	..	..	1	..	1	..	6	2	28	6	35	8	43	0·4
Hernia	1	..	..	..	..	..	..	..	..	..	..	2	10	7	11	9	20	0·2
Other diseases of the digestive system	1	1	..	3	2	3	3	5	4	3	12	14	25	33	47	57	104	1·0
10. Diseases of the genito-urinary system	1	1	1	3	1	..	2	1	2	1	11	16	24	29	43	55	98	1·0
11. Diseases of the skin	1	1	..	5	..	1	..	..	..	2	8	3	13	12	25	23	48	0·5
12. Diseases of the bones and organs of movement—																		
Arthritis and rheumatism	1	2	7	14	4	3	17	12	28	21	98	97	230	239	385	388	773	7·6
Other diseases of the bones and organs of movement	1	4	16	10	9	13	13	16	19	18	44	21	53	36	155	118	273	2·7
Other deformities due to previous disease or injury, including amputations	2	2	4	3	7	5	3	8	14	4	24	16	35	26	89	64	153	1·5
13. Congenital malformations	2	9	16	14	8	11	9	11	20	13	29	23	47	23	131	104	235	2·3
14. Other and ill-defined diseases	..	1	..	2	1	1	..	2	..	5	10	11	22	35	32	61	93	0·9
15. Injuries and poisoning	2	..	1	2	..	1	7	8	3	..	20	6	50	15	85	33	118	1·2
Totals	125	156	473	610	351	447	446	475	474	467	1,168	1,024	2,165	1,775	5,202	4,954	10,156*	100

* Includes 28 Emergency Invalids' Benefits.

74

MINERS' BENEFITS

There has been relatively little change in conditions applicable to miners' benefits since their inception.

Over the last ten years there has been a gradual decline in the number of men covered by this class of benefit, due principally to the fewer quartz-mines in operation, and consequently there are less men contracting the diseases associated with mining pursuits.

The legislation as it stands to-day covers miners who are either permanently and seriously incapacitated for work as a result of miners' phthisis or permanently and totally incapacitated for work as a result of any other occupational or heart disease contracted while engaged as a miner in New Zealand. " Miners' phthisis means pneumoconiosis, and includes tuberculosis of the lungs and any other disease of the respiratory organs commonly associated with or a sequel to pneumoconiosis."

Five years' residence in New Zealand immediately preceding application and a total of two and a half years' work in the mines is necessary.

BASIC RATE

The basic rate has risen from £78 in 1939 to the present rate of £130 a year, and the corresponding benefit for a dependent wife has increased from £26 a year to £130.

The benefit is paid without a means test, and a married miner with, say, two dependent children would receive £2 10s. a week for himself plus £2 10s. for wife and 10s. by way of family benefit for each of the children, a total of £6 a week and paid without regard to the income and property of the whole family.

BENEFIT FOR WIDOW

The benefit for the widow of a miner who dies on benefit is now payable at £104 a year, compared with £45 10s. in 1939, and no account is taken of any income or property she may have. On the miner's death a reasonable amount is paid towards the funeral expenses, provided application for a grant is made within one year of the date of death.

MEDICAL EXAMINATION

As in the case of an invalid's benefit, a medical examination is required, and if the application is declined or benefit cancelled on medical grounds there is a right of appeal to a board of three medical practitioners.

TABLE 21—MINERS' BENEFITS: NUMBER GRANTED, NUMBER IN FORCE, AND EXPENDITURE, 1ST APRIL, 1939, TO 31ST MARCH, 1949.

Year.	Granted, Year Ended 31st March	Number of Benefits in Force at 31st March.			Expenditure for Year Ended 31st March.
		Widows.	Miners.	Total.	
					£
1940	60	152	836	988	92,653
1941	40	137	794	931	88,656
1942	36	133	755	888	83,258
1943	24	118	723	841	80,100
1944	33	106	689	795	76,652
1945	30	108	675	783	74,367
1946	29	91	645	736	88,359
1947	45	84	634	718	105,416
1948	29	81	604	685	110,106
1949	25	85	575	660	113,659

ANALYSIS OF MINERS' BENEFITS CURRENT AS AT 30TH SEPTEMBER, 1948

The information contained in the five following tables numbered 22 to 26 was obtained from an analysis of miners' benefits current at the end of September, 1948.

TABLE 22—MINERS' BENEFITS: DISEASES FOR WHICH BENEFIT GRANTED

Disease.	Disease Contracted in—		Total.
	Coal-mines.	Gold (Quartz mines).	
Miners' phthisis	46	451	497
Heart-disease	15	34	49
Other associated diseases	10	28	38
Total	71	513	584

TABLE 23—MINERS' BENEFITS: OCCUPATION AT TIME OF CLAIMING BENEFIT

Mining quartz	239
Mining coal	48
	287
General labouring	158
Agricultural and pastoral	33
Waterfront industry	13
Building trade	10
Prospecting	8
Engine-driving	6
Miscellaneous occupations	69
Total	584

TABLE 24—MINERS' BENEFITS: AGE AT TIME OF CLAIMING BENEFIT

Type of Mining.	Age, in Years.										Total.
	26–30.	31–35.	36–40.	41–45.	46–50.	51–55.	56–60.	61–65.	66–70.	Over 70.	
Coal-mining	..	..	..	3	12	8	28	14	6	..	71
Quartz-mining	2	5	16	37	79	104	126	93	42	9	513
Total	2	5	16	40	91	112	154	107	48	9	584

TABLE 25—MINERS' BENEFITS: YEARS ENGAGED IN MINING

Type of Mining.	Up to 5 Years.	6–10 Years.	11–15 Years.	16–20 Years.	21–25 Years.	26–30 Years.	31–35 Years.	36–40 Years.	Over 40 Years.	Total.
Coal-mining	5	2	12	10	12	11	6	5	8	71
Quartz-mining	11	82	112	103	70	64	27	24	20	513
Total cases	16	84	124	113	82	75	33	29	28	584

TABLE 26—MINERS' BENEFITS: AGE AT TIME OF CLAIMING BENEFIT AND PERIOD OF YEARS BETWEEN DATE OF CEASING MINING AND DATE OF CLAIMING BENEFIT

Legend: C = Coal; Q = Quartz; T = Total

Number of Cases Within Each Age-group.

Benefit Claimed After Leaving Mining Employment.	Age 26-30			Age 31-35			Age 36-40			Age 41-45			Age 46-50			Age 51-55			Age 56-60			Age 61-65			Age 66-70			Age Over 70			Total			Percentages (Approximate).		
	C	Q	T	C	Q	T	C	Q	T	C	Q	T	C	Q	T	C	Q	T	C	Q	T	C	Q	T	C	Q	T	C	Q	T	C	Q	T	Of Total C.	Of Total Q.	Of Grand Total.
Claimed within first year	..	2	2	..	4	4	..	12	12	..	25	25	8	38	46	8	51	59	18	51	69	7	34	41	1	13	14	..	2	2	42	232	274	60	45	47
Claimed within second year	..	..	..	..	1	1	..	1	1	..	2	2	1	5	6	..	3	3	2	5	7	2	2	4	..	1	1	..	..	..	5	20	25	19	10	11
Claimed within third year	..	..	..	..	..	..	..	1	1	..	2	2	1	2	3	..	3	3	2	2	4	..	2	2	..	1	1	..	..	..	7	11	18			
Claimed within fourth year	..	..	..	..	..	..	..	..	..	..	1	1	..	2	2	..	3	3	..	4	4	..	2	2	1	2	3	..	..	..	1	13	14			
Claimed within fifth year	..	..	..	..	..	..	..	..	..	..	..	..	..	1	1	..	2	2	1	1	2	1	4	5	1	2	3	..	..	..	1	8	9			
Claimed between sixth and tenth years	..	..	..	..	..	..	..	2	2	1	7	8	..	11	11	..	10	10	3	13	16	..	4	4	2	10	12	..	1	1	4	51	55	6	10	9
Claimed between eleventh and twentieth years	..	..	..	..	..	..	..	..	..	1	..	1	2	16	18	..	16	16	2	20	22	2	14	16	..	11	11	..	2	2	8	79	87	11	15	15
Claimed between twenty-first and thirtieth years	..	..	..	..	..	..	..	..	..	1	..	1	..	4	4	..	13	13	..	26	26	..	18	18	..	1	1	..	2	2	..	74	74	..	15	13
Claimed between thirty-first and fortieth years	..	..	..	..	..	..	..	..	..	..	..	..	..	..	..	..	3	3	..	4	4	2	11	13	1	1	2	..	2	2	3	19	22	4	5	5
Claimed after fortieth year	..	..	..	..	..	..	..	..	..	..	..	..	..	..	..	..	..	..	..	..	..	..	2	2	..	..	..	..	..	..	..	6	6			
Totals	..	2	2	..	5	5	..	16	16	3	37	40	12	79	91	8	104	112	28	126	154	14	93	107	6	42	48	..	9	9	71	513	584	100	100	100

77

SICKNESS BENEFITS

Until the Social Security Act came into operation there was no provision in New Zealand's social legislation for compensation to individuals for loss of earnings arising out of periods of temporary sickness.

The Workers' Compensation Act provided protection for the injured worker, and payments under this Act resulted from the statutory liability of an employer to compensate a worker for personal injury by accident arising out of and in the course of his employment.

For a short period prior to 1939 unemployed workers who were unfit for employment were granted sickness allowances as distinct from unemployment relief allowances, but to a large extent any worker incapacitated through ordinary sickness had to maintain himself and his family out of his own resources or rely on charitable aid. Some workers were members of friendly societies and contributed regular sums towards the funds of these mutual-aid bodies so as to be assured of some measure

In New Zealand, social security aims to provide for all who, through misfortune beyond their control, need help

of financial protection if they lost wages due to periods off work on account of sickness. The majority of workers, however, were not members of friendly societies, and although some employers and employing authorities had sickness-benefit schemes for their employees the large bulk of workers were left to fend for themselves.

It can be seen, therefore, that the sickness benefits provided for under the Social Security Act fulfilled a real need in the community and were designed to meet the temporary situation which sickness ordinarily creates where the income of the breadwinner is reduced or lost by inability to work.

The Act provides that sickness benefits are available to people who have been resident in New Zealand for a year and are aged sixteen years and over and who have suffered a loss of salary, wages, or other earnings through being temporarily incapacitated for work by sickness or accident. People aged sixty years or more may qualify for sickness benefit, but these cases require careful investigation to ensure that the incapacity is only temporary and that the person intends to resume work. If they do not intend to resume work, they are more appropriately placed on age-benefit.

If a person is in business on his own account and is forced to employ a substitute, the latter's wages are regarded as a loss of earnings. A married woman is not entitled to a sickness benefit unless the Social Security Commission is satisfied that her husband cannot maintain her.

The sickness benefit, it will be noted, does not necessarily make good the earnings lost, but, as with other benefits, a specific maximum amount is allowed and benefit is payable subject to a means test, with the added stipulation that the amount of benefit will not be greater than the loss of earnings due to sickness.

RATE OF BENEFIT

The basic rates of benefit have altered considerably since the benefit was introduced in 1939. Originally benefits were payable on a scale providing a limit of benefit and other income graded according to the marital status and number of children of the beneficiaries, but with a limit of benefit of £4 a week.

The following table sets out the position as it was on 1st April, 1939.

TABLE 27—SICKNESS BENEFITS : RATE AND ALLOWABLE INCOME AS AT 1ST APRIL, 1939

Applicant.	Maximum Weekly Sickness Benefit.	Maximum Weekly " Other Income."	Maximum Allowable Income, Including Benefit.
	s.	s.	s.
Males and females under twenty years without dependants	10	20	30
Single men and women twenty years and over	20	20	40
Married women twenty years of age and over	20	20	40
Married man with wife only	35	25	60
Married man with wife and one child	40	25	65
Married man with wife and two children	45	25	70
Married man with wife and three children	50	25	75
Married man with wife and four children	55	25	80
Married man with wife and five children	60	20	80
Married man with wife and six children	65	15	80
Married man with wife and seven children	70	10	80
Married man with wife and eight children	75	5	80
Married man with wife and nine children and over	80	..	80

It will be seen, therefore, that the principle adopted was to distribute benefits in such a way that those in the greatest need received the largest share and the benefits payable were related to the need of the individual according to the size of the family of the incapacitated worker.

When the law was altered in 1945 to pay the children of beneficiaries by way of family benefit, the benefit maximum of £4 a week was removed, and the basic rates are now comparable with all other adult benefits.

The present rates are—

	Per Week.
	£ s. d.
To applicants sixteen and under twenty years without dependants	1 10 0
To all other applicants	2 10 0
In respect of the applicant's wife	2 10 0

Dependent children are paid for by way of family benefit at 10s. a week each.

INCOME EXEMPTION

Originally sickness benefits did not come within the definition of income applicable to other benefits, but the law provided that the Social Security Commission could, in its discretion, reduce the rate of benefit where the beneficiary received money from any source or owned property. As can be seen from Table 27 on page 79 the maximum weekly " other income " varied according to the domestic status of the individual.

The discretionary power of the Commission to reduce a benefit if the applicant received money from any source or was the owner of any property was removed in 1945, and from that date a statutory rate of " other income " has been provided and reductions in benefit have been on the basis of excess income only. Benefits are now reduced by 1s. for every 1s. of the total income of the husband and wife in excess of 20s. a week.

FRIENDLY SOCIETIES

It was appreciated when the Social Security Act was being drafted that the service given to members of friendly societies was of a very valuable nature and that receipt of a sickness benefit from such a source should not disqualify a sick person from receiving a similar benefit from the Social Security Fund. As a result the Act provided a maximum allowable income from all sources, including benefit, of £5 a week for sickness beneficiaries who were receiving sickness benefits from friendly societies. The effect of this was to increase by 20s. a week the " other income " scales applicable to each class of sickness benefit.

In addition, a similar concession was granted to other sickness-benefit schemes, and, although the organizations administering them are not registered friendly societies, authority is given for the Social Security Commission to regard and approve them as " like " societies.

Since October, 1945, when a definite exemption of 20s. was provided for sickness benefit generally, the exempted income of beneficiaries receiving payments from friendly societies and similar approved organizations has been 40s. a week. This concession therefore enables members of friendly or other " like " societies to have a total income of 20s. a week more than those who are not members. There are approximately one thousand registered friendly societies with a membership of approximately 83,000 in New Zealand, and the Social Security Commission has approved of sixty-eight organizations with a membership of approximately 41,000 workers being considered as " like " societies.

Waiting Period

A sickness benefit is not payable for the first seven days of any period of incapacity unless the Commission, having regard to the special circumstances of any case, decides that the benefit is to be paid for the whole or part of that period. The Commission exercises its discretionary powers in this direction very carefully, as this waiting period is considered to be an important factor in the administration of sickness benefits. In most countries where similar schemes are in operation a sick person who becomes unable to work cannot usually claim sickness benefit from the first day of incapacity, a waiting period being almost invariably imposed. It is usually contended that during the first few days of incapacity a person is able to support himself out of his own resources, especially if the indisposition is so soon over that he can resume work. Moreover, many workers are often entitled to sick pay for short periods of sickness, and little hardship is created by not paying a benefit for the first seven days. Where an unemployment beneficiary becomes temporarily unfit for work and is transferred to the sickness benefit roll, payment is continued without break and the seven days waiting period ignored.

Payment of Benefit

Normally incapacity is regarded as having commenced on the day on which the applicant is first examined by a doctor and certified unfit for work, although in certain cases the Commission may recognize a period of incapacity prior to medical examination if it is satisfied that the person ceased work on account of sickness.

Benefits continue for as long as incapacity lasts, unless in the meantime the beneficiary qualifies for another benefit (other than a family benefit).

Sickness benefits are granted even where there is an outstanding claim for compensation or damages, subject to recovery of the amount of benefit paid, if necessary, when compensation or damages are granted.

Miscellaneous

A married woman is entitled to a benefit only if her husband is unable to support her. A wife is not included in her husband's benefit if she is receiving a social security cash benefit (other than a family benefit) or a war pension in her own right. As a rule a wife is not included in her husband's benefit unless she is living with him, is maintained wholly or partly by him, or is entitled to maintenance under a deed of separation or Court order.

Where no payment is made for a wife an allowance not exceeding the rate for a wife may be paid in respect of any woman looking after the home of the beneficiary.

Every application has to be supported by a medical certificate, and the Social Security Commission can at any time require a beneficiary to be examined by a medical practitioner of its own choosing.

Usually medical certificates are required each four weeks during sickness, but in obvious cases of prolonged illness they are required at less frequent intervals, depending on the circumstances of each case. Medical certificates other than the first submitted with an application are not required while a beneficiary is in hospital.

81

TABLE 28—SICKNESS BENEFITS: CLASSIFICATION, BY AGE, SEX, AND DISEASE, AS AT 31ST MARCH, 1949

Age at 31st March, 1949, and Sex.

Disease Category.	16-19		20-29		30-39		40-49		50-59		60 and Over		Sub-total		Grand Total.	Per-centage.
	M.	F.	M.	F.	M.	F.	M.	F.	M.	F.	M.	F.	M.	F.		
1. Infectious and parasitic diseases—																
Influenza	19	41	151	76	196	28	235	24	180	18	95	5	876	192	1,068	4·0
Tuberculosis of the respiratory system	12	25	108	192	82	28	63	6	42	1	27		334	252	586	2·2
Other forms of tuberculosis	6	3	33	20	20	6	10	1	2	1		1	71	32	103	0·4
Acute poliomyelitis and sequelæ	11	9	42	18	30	2	4					1	87	29	116	0·4
Other infectious and parasitic diseases, not including above	46	46	203	108	166	11	73	10	54	9	41	5	583	189	772	2·9
2. Neoplasms—																
Malignant neoplasms	2	2	6	2	15	1	28	8	37	6	29	2	117	21	138	0·5
Nonmalignant neoplasms	7	12	62	73	21	28	42	35	29	18	25	4	186	170	356	1·3
3. Rheumatic fever, diseases of the endocrine glands and nutrition and other general diseases—																
Rheumatic fever	25	21	62	38	38	7	18	7	18	4	6		167	77	244	1·0
Diabetes mellitus	4	1	19	5	10		18	2	14	3	10		75	11	86	0·3
Diseases of the thyroid and endocrine glands	3	12	27	78	24	21	26	21	23	6	11	3	114	141	255	1·0
Other nutritional and general diseases		2	2	3	9	1	8	2	12	3	7		38	11	49	0·1
4. Diseases of the blood and blood-forming organs	3	14	13	64	10	12	15	13	8	5	6	5	55	113	168	0·6
5. Chronic poisoning and intoxication							6		1				7	Nil	7	0·1
6. Diseases of the nervous system and sense organs, including mental disorders—																
Neuritis	1	1	8	9	17	4	31	3	12	2	10		78	19	97	0·4
Sciatica	1	1	16	5	54	7	70	3	48	4	21		210	20	230	0·9
Psychoses and other mental diseases	19	73	220	311	216	146	231	86	131	57	42	9	859	682	1,541	5·8
Diseases of the organs of vision	17	10	47	21	62	5	44	10	46	3	30	1	246	50	296	1·1
Diseases of the ear and mastoid process	5	5	32	23	21	6	37	3	24	1	6	1	125	39	164	0·6
Other diseases of the nervous system and sense organs, including mental disorders	3		30	11	20	3	31	4	57	9	36		177	27	204	0·8
7. Diseases of the circulatory system—																
Diseases of the heart	11	6	37	24	74	17	163	28	323	48	255	19	863	142	1,005	3·7
Varicose veins and hemorrhoids	6	2	58	10	99	11	125	10	87	11	49	4	424	48	472	1·8
Other diseases of the circulatory system	13	13	46	41	44	11	28	10	36	6	28	3	195	84	279	1·1
8. Diseases of the respiratory system—																
Diseases of the nose and nasal fossæ (including sinusitis)	16	17	72	27	46	8	50	8	42	3	9	4	235	67	302	1·1
Diseases of the pharynx and larynx (including tonsilitis)	26	43	177	136	78	21	58	8	14	8	15		368	216	584	2·2
Bronchitis	12	20	101	57	93	30	162	21	227	19	136	4	731	151	882	3·3
Pneumonia	29	11	116	38	136	17	164	9	92	7	45		582	82	664	2·5
Pleurisy	9	7	80	65	66	10	62	8	48	5	27		292	95	387	1·5
Asthma	14	11	40	34	51	12	47	5	37	5	39	3	228	70	298	1·1

Cause of incapacity												Males	Females	Total	Per cent.
Other diseases of the respiratory system	3	4	24	12	21	2	23	1	18	4	12	1	101	24	125	0·5
9. *Diseases of the digestive system—*															
Ulcer of the stomach and intestines	..	1	55	7	106	9	140	5	131	4	58	..	490	26	516	1·9
Appendicitis	142	199	469	296	199	30	120	13	52	3	8	..	990	541	1,531	5·7
Hernia	27	7	129	15	140	3	175	5	139	9	82	..	692	39	731	2·7
Peritonitis	2	3	5	5	7	1	4	1	..	1	1	11	19	11	30	0·1
Other diseases of the digestive system	31	42	225	115	251	47	298	38	234	32	132	1	1,171	285	1,456	5·5
10. *Diseases of the genito-urinary system*	24	59	160	189	129	90	158	51	114	27	104	7	689	417	1,106	4·1
11. *Diseases of the skin*	72	60	405	153	358	29	313	32	212	26	111	16	1,471	317	1,788	6·7
12. *Diseases of the bones and organs of movement—*															
Arthritis and rheumatism (except rheumatic fever)	23	34	162	90	278	52	340	39	316	32	178	5	1,297	263	1,560	5·8
Other diseases of the bones and organs of movement	61	48	272	77	184	30	168	15	102	13	30	1	817	188	1,005	3·8
13. *Congenital malformations*	5	8	22	7	10	5	10	4	5	1	3	8	55	26	81	0·3
14. *Other and ill-defined diseases*	23	55	147	197	82	59	108	51	80	29	54	8	494	399	893	3·3
15. *Injuries and poisoning—*															
Fractures	172	33	778	54	303	15	198	16	134	18	80	1	1,665	144	1,809	6·8
Dislocations, sprain, or other joint injury without fracture	38	29	250	49	92	13	73	3	41	7	11	2	505	102	607	2·3
Other injuries and poisoning	124	38	703	80	335	19	261	11	175	11	93	..	1,691	161	1,852	6·9
16. *Other enumerated conditions without sickness—*															
Pregnancy	..	36	..	159	..	30	..	1	..	..	..	..	..	226	226	0·8
Other enumerated conditions without sickness	..	..	..	4	..	..	..	..	..	..	..	..	..	4	4	0·1
Totals	1,006	1,064	5,614	2,998	4,193	897	4,238	631	3,397	479	1,962	134	20,470	6,203	26,673	100

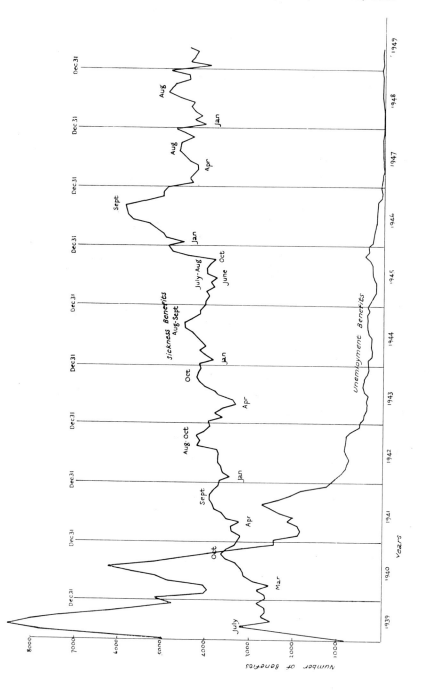

84

Year.	Number Granted, Year Ended 31st March.			Number in Force at 31st March.	Expenditure for Year Ended 31st March.
	Males.	Females.	Total.		
					£
1940	13,330	4,470	17,800	2,565	208,790
1941 .. .	17,189	6,236	23,425	3,452	279,581
1942	17,862	7,294	25,156	3,672	304,154
1943	18,936	7,807	26,743	3,699	362,088
1944	18,350	7,942	26,292	4,446	376,878
1945	18,489	8,433	26,922	4,233	351,866
1946	22,493	8,154	30,647	5,416	565,420
1947	28,232	8,479	36,711	4,273	853,328
1948	24,073	7,282	31,355	4,248	897,093
1949	23,150	7,271	30,421	4,945	911,107

TABLE 30—SICKNESS BENEFITS : REASONS FOR CESSATION OF BENEFITS TERMINATED DURING YEAR ENDED 31ST MARCH, 1949

Reason.	Males.	Females.	Total.
Recovered from incapacity	19,132	5,958	25,090
Benefit cancelled on account of excess income	125	56	181
Died	342	56	398
Granted war pension	278	1	279
Granted invalid's benefit	223	76	299
Granted age-benefit	309	28	337
Granted other social security benefits ..	61	28	89
Total	20,470	6,203	26,673

TABLE 31—SICKNESS BENEFITS : DURATION OF SICKNESS OF BENEFICIARIES WHOSE BENEFITS CEASED DURING YEAR ENDED 31ST MARCH, 1949

Period of Sickness.	Males.	Females.	Total.
1–4 weeks	7,939	1,913	9,852
5–12 weeks	7,864	2,380	10,244
13–25 weeks	2,763	1,047	3,810
26–52 weeks	1,418	594	2,012
Over 52 weeks	486	269	755*
Total	20,470	6,203	26,673

* Of the 755 beneficiaries who were on sickness benefit for over fifty-two weeks, 110 were eventually transferred to invalids' benefits, 35 to age benefits, 20 to other types of benefits, and 11 were granted war pensions

TABLE 32—SICKNESS BENEFITS : PRIVATE INCOME OF BENEFICIARIES WHO
RECEIVED BENEFIT DURING THE YEAR ENDED 31ST MARCH, 1949

Private Income of Beneficiaries While on Sickness Benefit (Amount).	Males.	Females.	Total.	Percentage to Total Beneficiaries.
Nil	12,023	4,866	16,889	63
One to twenty shillings a week ..	4,221	925	5,146	19
Over twenty shillings a week ..	4,226	412	4,638	18
Total	20,470	6,203	26,673	100

It will be seen from the above table that 82 per cent. of the beneficiaries had income of under 20s. a week and qualified for the full benefit. As the income exemption for members of friendly societies and " like " societies is 40s. a week, as against 20s. a week for non-members, some of the beneficiaries in the " over 20s. a week " group would qualify for full sickness benefit. Actually 4,237 members of these societies received sickness benefit during the year.

UNEMPLOYMENT BENEFITS

The primary object of unemployment relief under the Social Security Act is to enable the worker to tide himself over spells of unemployment due to trade and seasonal fluctuations and to maintain himself and family until he again obtains work. Thus the unemployment benefit provides assistance for those physically fit workers who are out of work for " frictional " causes and for whom no immediate work can be found. For those who may also be out of employment, but are in the " unemployable " class through permanent or temporary incapacity for work the other benefits under the Social Security Act provide the necessary relief.

Ever since the inauguration of national unemployment relief in New Zealand the granting of sustenance has been dependent on a test of means, and this principle was carried over to the Social Security Act, which provided unemployment benefit at fixed maximum rates with payments to the unemployed worker varying according to the private resources of the individual.

The qualifications as to age, and residence, and rates payable are the same as for sickness benefits, and by substituting " unemployment " for " incapacity " almost identical circumstances apply.

Applicants for unemployment benefit must be unemployed and capable and willing to undertake work. They must have taken reasonable steps to obtain employment, which from an administrative point of view requires enrolment at a local office of the Labour and Employment Department, which, through its State Placement Service, acts as a labour exchange and throughout the entire period the unemployed worker is on benefit endeavours to obtain suitable employment for the beneficiary.

In contrast with some unemployment insurance schemes operating in other countries, there is no limit on the duration of the benefit. A man who has worked steadily for many years does not exhaust his right to unemployment relief within a limited period. The unemployment benefit under the New Zealand legislation continues so long as the beneficiary is unemployed or unless he becomes eligible to receive another class of benefit.

INCOME AND PROPERTY

The law empowers the Social Security Commission at its discretion, having regard to circumstances, to reduce the rate of benefit where the applicant or his wife receives money from any source or owns property. The Commission in its administration of this section of the Act has largely provided income and property exemptions comparable with the other benefits which are subject to statutory provisions in the application of the means test. In formulating its policy it has had regard to the fact that an individual or a family is in need of assistance when cash cannot be found to provide the necessaries of life, and has considered it undesirable that an individual or family should be required completely to exhaust accumulated savings or all available resources before becoming eligible for an unemployment benefit.

Consequently the Commission has determined that, in so far as earnings of the husband and wife are concerned, the maximum rate of benefit is to be reduced by 1s. a week for every complete 1s. of earnings. For all other income, as distinct from earnings, a deduction of 1s. a week for every 1s. of income over 20s. a week is made from the maximum benefit. Also the benefit is reducable by 1s. a week for every complete £26 of accumulated property in excess of £500 for a single person and £1,000 in the case of a married person. The property not taken into account includes a home, furniture, personal effects, any interest in land, including a mortgage, or the present value of any annuity or life-insurance policy. Benefits are not reducible in respect of both property and the income from that property, but deductions are made on account of either income or property, whichever provides the greater deduction.

RATES OF BENEFIT

The rates of benefit have been identical with the rates provided for sickness since 1939, and the rates ruling at present are—

	£	s.	d.
Persons sixteen years and under twenty years without dependants	1	10	0
To all other applicants	2	10	0
In respect of the applicant's wife	2	10	0

DEPENDANTS

Benefit for children comes by way of family benefit, and where there is a deed of separation or Court order in existence the benefit for the wife does not exceed the rate provided in the deed or order. A married woman is entitled to a benefit only if her husband is unable to support her, and where no additional benefit is paid for a wife an allowance not exceeding the rate for a wife may be paid to the person who has care of the beneficiary's household.

GENERAL

An unemployment benefit is not paid for the first seven days of unemployment except in special circumstances. The Commission has power to postpone the commencement of an unemployment benefit for a period not exceeding six weeks or to terminate a benefit if the applicant—

(a) Has become voluntarily unemployed without good and sufficient reason.

(b) Has lost his employment through misconduct as a worker.

(c) Has failed without good and sufficient reason to accept an offer of suitable employment.

(d) Has received from seasonal employment earnings sufficient for the maintenance of himself and family, notwithstanding a period of temporary unemployment.

TABLE 33—UNEMPLOYMENT BENEFITS : NUMBER GRANTED, NUMBER IN FORCE, AND EXPENDITURE, 1ST APRIL, 1939, TO 31ST MARCH, 1949

Year.	Number of Benefits Granted During Year Ended 31st March.			Number in Force at 31st March.	Expenditure, Year Ended 31st March.
	Males.	Females.	Total.		
1940	32,560	2,202	34,762	4,053	£ 434,497
1941	21,720	1,191	22,911	1,906	299,161
1942	8,999	630	9,629	841	138,528
1943	2,052	317	2,369	373	49,639
1944	1,524	177	1,701	292	32,316
1945	1,151	99	1,250	198	27,822
1946	1,149	85	1,234	205	31,661
1947	790	51	841	35	24,332
1948	368	12	380	19	8,358
1949	330	14	344	30	8,948

Although 34,762 persons were paid unemployment benefits during the 1939–40 year the majority were on benefit for less than thirteen weeks, and succeeding years saw a rapid reduction in the number of beneficiaries. This reduction was largely brought about by the acute shortage of man-power due to wartime requirements and the relatively quick absorption into industry of the bulk of the pre-war unemployed.

EMERGENCY BENEFITS

Experience in the administration of pensions legislation prior to 1939 had shown that many people were denied assistance because they did not meet the requirements of the existing law and so could not qualify for State aid. There were therefore no means of assisting these people except by way of charitable aid or other relief even if their need was as great or greater than those who qualified by law for a pension. The bulk of the people concerned were those who were medically unfit, or unemployable, and unable to earn a livelihood.

Realizing that some legislative provision should be made for this wide and undefined class of person the Government placed before the 1938 Select Parliamentary Committee on National Health and Superannuation proposals for a " disability benefit " for those who for some reason or other could not qualify for a benefit but who were otherwise physically and mentally handicapped and unable to earn a living for themselves and their dependants. The Select Committee reported favourably on the Government's proposals and felt that the need of the individual within this class would vary so much that their cases could not be dealt with by a flat or standard rate of benefit. The Committee further pointed out that, quite apart from the relief of distress by the granting of assistance, the individuals coming within this benefit were in many cases those who for some reason or another, had not had a fair chance of establishing themselves in the economic life in the community and who without a special kind of assistance would have little chance in the future. This was such an important factor in the opinion of the Committee that it recommended to the Government that, where necessary, individuals applying for this benefit should be examined by a board of specialists in psychology, medicine, and social welfare, who would decide the form of assistance to be given, whether by way of individual training or the affording of special opportunities as well as monetary or other assistance.

The Committee's important recommendations to a large extent found expression in the Social Security Act, 1938, by the establishment of a class of benefit called an " emergency benefit."

The Social Security Commission is authorized to grant this special benefit on account of hardship to any person who by reason of age, or physical or mental incapacity, or of domestic circumstance, or for any other reason is unable to earn a sufficient livelihood for himself and his dependants and is not qualified to receive any other benefit under the Act.

The commencing date, rate of benefit, and condition of payment in any particular case is at the discretion of the Commission, but as far as possible the rate of benefit granted is the same as for the type of benefit for which the applicant most closely qualifies. The Commission is also empowered to grant an emergency benefit in lieu of a sickness or unemployment benefit even if the applicant qualifies for one of those benefits.

Further wide powers have also been granted to the Commission to transfer any person from any other class of benefit to an emergency benefit if it considered the beneficiary should undergo a course of training in any medical or psychological clinic or receive any medical or other treatment or undergo any course of training for the improvement of his physical or mental capacities or should do any work required of him. Furthermore, the Commission can make the grant or continuance of the benefit subject to the person complying with such conditions as it deems expedient.

The Social Security Commission has taken full advantage of the emergency portion of the Social Security Act to relieve many cases of genuine hardship.

The cases dealt with are many and varied, and the following types are quoted to illustrate the uses to which the benefit is put :—

(*a*) Pregnant single girls who enter special homes available for their confinement are granted benefit during their period in the home.

(*b*) Persons suffering from some form of disability which precludes them from employment but who cannot qualify for a sickness benefit are assisted until they are fit for employment.

(c) Some whose sickness is not of a temporary nature but of an indefinite duration, possibly extending over years, but who are not eligible for sickness benefit and whose degree of incapacity is not such that they can be classed as permanently incapacitated for work and so qualify for an invalid's benefit are granted an emergency benefit until their condition improves or they become eligible for a permanent benefit.

(d) The Commission receives a large number of applications from persons who for various domestic reasons remain at home or leave employment to go home to look after aged parents, invalid members of the family, or sick persons. In many cases, while the persons are " employable " in the general sense, the persons they are looking after cannot be left alone or cannot attend to their own requirements. Consequently, these applicants are not available for employment outside their own home either from necessity or from reluctance to temporarily desert persons under their care. In such cases where the Commission considers the circumstances are necessitous it grants an emergency benefit to the person caring for the home provided the care is considered indispensible. The amount of benefit depends on the surrounding general circumstances of the applicant and the persons in the home.

(e) Again, where families are in quarantine ordered by a medical officer of health and the earnings of the breadwinner cease an emergency benefit may be paid during the period of isolation, as happens in the case of an epidemic.

Where it is possible to establish specific conditions applicable to a special class of case the Commission does so, so that all cases of hardship arising out of similar circumstances are treated in a comparable manner.

This is illustrated by the Commission's action in establishing on a uniform basis the grant of emergency benefits to dependants of men serving a gaol sentence. Prior to the introduction of the Social Security Act the Prisons Department investigated the financial position of prisoners' dependants and determined the extent of maintenance that could be provided. The maximum payment that could be made was £1 6s. 8d. a week, which was totally inadequate for a married woman with a large family. Furthermore, no payment was made for the first month, and thereafter payments were made at monthly intervals so that it would be at least two months before the dependants received the first payment. The prisoners' state of health, weather conditions, &c., affected the amount of allowance that could be paid as this was determined by the prisoners' earnings. As a result of these circumstances the wives of prisoners applied to the Social Security Commission for assistance, so that some received grants from both sources and others from one Department only.

To establish assistance on a basis common to all in similar circumstances the Social Security Commission took over the full responsibility for payment of allowances to prisoners' dependants so that they would receive payments at frequent regular intervals and generally at much higher rates than could be provided by the Prisons Department and not subject to frequent variations in the rate of benefit. These allowances are now paid as a defined class of emergency benefit at rates equal to the full unemployment benefit for dependants.

An emergency benefit is often paid pending the settlement of a persons' application for a permanent benefit. For example, a widow may be in financial difficulties pending the settlement of her late husband's affairs and the granting of a widow's benefit. Until the position is clarified, and where financial hardship is present, the Commission initiates the action to grant emergency assistance.

During the 1939–45 war the emergency sections of the Act were put to many and varied uses to provide speedy and urgent assistance to persons who were the victims of the war itself, and although the people concerned would not have ordinarily been eligible for assistance from the Social Security Fund it was used as a convenient intermediate means of relieving urgent obvious cases of hardship. The expenditure in most cases was refunded to the Social Security Fund.

The classes of cases were :—

(1) Benefits were granted to the dependants of interned enemy aliens so that they did not suffer destitution or privation during the period of the war while the husband or father was interned.

(2) Payments were made to dependants of men who, as military defaulters, were detained in special detention camps for refusing to serve in the Armed forces.

(3) When a member of the Armed forces had deserted from his unit, pay and allowances for his dependants ceased after one month's illegal absence, and on his return to his unit service pay commenced immediately, but during the intervening period his family were without means of support. The Social Security Fund was used to bridge the gap and provide suitable monetary assistance to those deprived of the means of subsistence by the serviceman's action.

(4) When Japan came into the war on the side of the Axis Powers, numbers of British nationals were evacuated from Hong Kong, Malaya, and other British Pacific possessions. In view of its proximity to these areas New Zealand was called upon to give hospitality to the evacuees, who were forced by circumstances to give up most of their personal property as well as leaving, in many cases, husbands, sons, and brothers behind. On behalf of the Imperial Government the New Zealand Government, through the Social Security Fund, authorized grants to these people for their subsistence until permanent arrangements could be made for their maintenance by the Imperial Government.

The extent and nature of the investigation into each application which comes before the Commission for an emergency grant varies according to the individual case. Generally, more inquiries are necessary for emergency grants than for other types of benefit, but they are kept at a minimum, and the Commission endeavours to ensure that all investigations are carried out in as sympathetic a manner as possible with an absolute minimum of delay, as it realizes that cases of financial hardship require prompt and urgent treatment.

Circumstances of the war prevented the Commission from implementing that important section of the Act relating to the vocational training and occupational readjustment of beneficiaries who would benefit from this class of treatment. However, the training of disabled civilians has not been lost sight of. A Government Departmental Committee is exploring the possibility of establishing unified training for this class of person on a national basis

TABLE 34—EMERGENCY BENEFITS: NUMBER GRANTED, NUMBER IN FORCE, AND EXPENDITURE, 1ST APRIL, 1939, TO 31ST MARCH, 1940

Year.	Emergency Benefits Granted During Year Ended 31st March.	Number in Force at 31st March.	Expenditure for Year Ended 31st March.
			£
1940	3,223	1,043	86,711
1941	2,266	2,034	130,096
1942	2,010	2,170	126,718
1943	1,488	1,921	124,268
1944	1,554	1,915	115,574
1945	1,799	2,083	105,843
1946	1,547	2,094	121,959
1947	1,702	1,845	134,288
1948	2,518	2,141	227,857
1949	2,735	2,026	251,409

WAR SERVICEMEN'S DEPENDANTS' ALLOWANCE

The 1939–45 war brought forth a special allowance payable to certain beneficiaries who were parents of deceased servicemen who had lost their lives in the war. The 1943, 1945, and 1949 Social Security Amendment Acts gave discretionary power to the Social Security Commission to increase by an amount not exceeding £26 a year the rate of social security benefit payable to a beneficiary who was one of the parents of a deceased member of the New Zealand or other British Commonwealth forces and whose death was attributable to his service or who was one of the parents of a member of the New Zealand or other British Commonwealth mercantile marine whose death was attributable to the 1939–45 War.

The maximum allowance is £26 a year and in appropriate cases both husband and wife may qualify for war servicemen's dependant's allowance.

The number of allowances in force at 31st March in the last three years was as follows : 1947, 1,521 ; 1948, 1,639 ; 1949, 1,674.

92

CHAPTER IX—RECIPROCAL BENEFITS

ALTHOUGH the value of reciprocal arrangements in social services has long been recognized by various countries of the British Commonwealth, it is only comparatively recently that such arrangements have been brought into operation. At the present time New Zealand has no reciprocal arrangements with countries outside the Commonwealth, while arrangements within the Commonwealth are limited to reciprocity with Australia, covering most of the cash benefits available in New Zealand, and with Great Britain and Northern Ireland covering family benefits.

RECIPROCITY WITH AUSTRALIA

The first attempt to establish reciprocity between Australia and New Zealand was made in 1901, when the Premier of New South Wales wrote to the Premier of New Zealand pointing out that certain Australian States and New Zealand were providing old-age pensions, and suggesting that New Zealand amend its legislation to provide for reciprocity, the cost being borne in the proportion the residence in New Zealand or Australia bore to the total residence required. However, the Government of New Zealand was not prepared to take any action, mainly because it did not wish to add to the cost of New Zealand old-age pensions, which for the year ended 31st March, 1901, was £197,293.*

The matter was next raised in September, 1912, by the Commonwealth Government, which wished to amend its legislation to treat residence in New Zealand as residence in Australia for invalids' and old-age pensions. The New Zealand Government was not prepared to move immediately, but suggested that the matter be discussed at a projected conference in Australia of representatives of the Dominion. Following discussions at Albury, N.S.W., in May, 1913, between the Rt. Hon. Andrew Fisher, Prime Minister of Australia, and the Hon. F. M. B. Fisher, Minister in Charge of Pensions for New Zealand, an agreement was signed on 14th June, 1913, on behalf of the two Governments. This agreement was ratified in New Zealand by the Old-age Pensions Reciprocity Act, 1913, and was to be brought into operation by Proclamation after ratification by Act of the Commonwealth Parliament, but as the Australian Government never passed the necessary legislation the agreement lapsed.

The question of reciprocal old-age pensions was revived several times during the next eight years, and further efforts were made in 1927 and 1936, but it was not until 1943, forty years after negotiations began, that definite reciprocal arrangements were made. In that year the New Zealand Parliament passed the Age-benefits and Invalids' Benefits (Reciprocity with Australia) Act, 1943, which came into force by Proclamation on 1st September, 1943, at the same time as a similar Act in Australia.

Under this reciprocal agreement, when determining New Zealand age and invalids' benefits, residence in Australia immediately before coming to New Zealand was treated as residence in New Zealand, and when determining Australian old-age and invalids' pensions residence in New Zealand immediately before arrival in Australia counted as residence in Australia. The more restrictive qualifications of each country applied to reciprocal benefits, and the rate of benefit could not exceed the maximum in the country with the lower rate.

* Age-benefits for the year ended 31st March, 1949, cost £13,790,971.

With the introduction of this reciprocal arrangement numbers of people in New Zealand and Australia who had not been eligible for age and invalids' benefits or old-age and invalids' pensions immediately qualified for reciprocal benefit. In New Zealand some of these people had been assisted by way of emergency benefit, but, as there was no corresponding provision in Australia, New Zealanders residing there had not received assistance.

When the Hon. P. Fraser, Prime Minister of New Zealand, was in Australia in 1946 he invited the Australian Government to send a representative to New Zealand to discuss the question of fuller reciprocity. This invitation was accepted, and in April of that year the Director-General of Social Services in Australia arrived in New Zealand for discussions. Each Government agreed in principle to extended reciprocity and was prepared to promote the necessary legislation. On 5th June, 1946, the Prime Minister of Australia, Right Hon. J. B. Chifley, announced that the Federal Cabinet had approved of an extension of the reciprocal agreement to include widows, child endowment, unemployment, and sickness benefits. However, before the necessary legislation in each country had been submitted to Parliament it was decided to hold the matter over until after the British Commonwealth Conference on National Insurance to be held in London during May, 1947.

Following this Conference further negotiations were carried on between Australia and New Zealand, and on 2nd December, 1948, the New Zealand Parliament passed the Social Security (Reciprocity with Australia) Act, 1948, which authorized the execution of a new reciprocal agreement with the Government of Australia. On 15th April, 1949, this new agreement was signed at Sydney by the Prime Ministers of Australia and New Zealand.

This new agreement, which came into operation on 1st July, 1949, superseded the 1943 agreement applicable only to age and invalids' benefits, and covered age, invalids', widows', family, unemployment, and sickness benefits with the corresponding Australian pensions. Reciprocal grants are available to permanent residents of one country who at any time have lived in the other country. Normally residence over six months is regarded as permanent. The condition that benefits were subject to the more restrictive conditions of either country has not been incorporated in the new agreement so that generally the qualifications for benefits under the reciprocal arrangements are the same as for the corresponding benefits in that country. However, this is modified in respect of the residential qualifications for male applicants for age-benefit. Residence or birth in one country is treated as residence or birth in the other, and applicants for age, invalids', or widows' benefits must satisfy the residential qualifications of both countries. In addition, male applicants for reciprocal age-benefit must be sixty-five years of age or over. The age qualification of sixty years for women is the same in both countries. Apart from the above, benefits and pensions are assessed and paid in the same way as for other applicants in the country in which the applicant is residing.

The effect of the new agreement operative from 1st July, 1949, is shown in the following very brief summary of particulars relating to reciprocal benefits.

Particulars.	Reciprocal Benefit in New Zealand.	Reciprocal Benefit in Australia.
Age—		
Annual rate	£130	£110 10s.
Qualifying age	∫ 65 (men)	65 (men)
	∖ 60 (women)	60 (women)
Residence	20 years	20 years.
Invalids—		
Annual rate	£130	£110 10s.
Residence	10 years	10 years.
Widows—		
Annual rate for widows with children ..	£208	£123 10s.
Annual rate for widows without children ..	£130	£96 4s.
Residence	5 years	5 years.
Family—		
Weekly rate	10s. each child	10s. each child after first.
Unemployment and Sickness—		
Weekly rate	£2 10s.	£1 5s.
Weekly rate for wife	£2 10s.	£1
Weekly rate for child	Family benefit	5s. for first child. Family benefit other children.

TABLE 36—RECIPROCAL BENEFITS WITH AUSTRALIA : NUMBERS IN FORCE AT
31ST MARCH, 1944–49

31st March,	Number in Force.		
	Age.	Invalids.	Total.
1944	51	20	71
1945	70	32	102
1946	117	40	157
1947	158	53	211
1948	216	55	271
1949	219	51	270

RECIPROCITY WITH GREAT BRITAIN AND NORTHERN IRELAND

Long before reciprocity was established between British countries the matter was considered at various Imperial Conferences, particularly in 1926 and 1930, but at the time it was decided that the varying nature of the benefits and qualifying conditions in different countries prevented the framing of a standard scheme acceptable to all countries. It was then left to the Governments of the different countries to negotiate separately with one another if they wished.

When reciprocal age and invalids' benefits were established between New Zealand and Australia, agreement was facilitated by the similarity of the benefits and qualifications in the two countries. Although the desirability of reciprocal arrangements with Great Britain was realized, especially in view of the probable large numbers of immigrants from the Old Country after the 1939–45 war, the different nature of the schemes in each country made the matter more difficult than was the case with Australia. In the United Kingdom benefits were paid as an insurance plan without a means test according to the number of contributions paid, but in New Zealand benefits were paid to those who qualified irrespective of the actual contributions paid. Most benefits were subject to a means and residence test. Negotiations were carried on by correspondence, but by 1945 had reached the stage where little more could be achieved by correspondence alone.

Initial discussions with the Secretary of State for the Dominions took place during the Prime Minister's visit to the United Kingdom early in 1946, and while in England that year the New Zealand Minister of Finance suggested that a conference of the British Commonwealth be held in 1947 to work out principles and administrative details for reciprocal arrangements. The conference was to be an exploratory one to enable subsequent consideration by the Governments of the countries concerned. In December, 1946, the Government of Great Britain advised that it fully recognized the value of reciprocal arrangements in social services and welcomed the proposal for official discussions at a conference early in 1947.

At this Commonwealth Conference on National Insurance held in London in May, 1947, it was felt that a standard agreement within the Empire was not practicable, and the Conference concerned itself mainly with the possibilities of bi-lateral agreements covering people who transferred permanently from one country to another.

Negotiations were carried on between New Zealand, Great Britain, and Northern Ireland after the Conference, and as child immigrants were arriving in New Zealand it was decided to concentrate first on finalizing a reciprocal agreement in respect of family benefits. The similarity of the provisions for family benefits in the three countries made this comparatively easy, and as a result of these negotiations agreements providing for reciprocity in the matter of family benefits in New Zealand and family allowances in Great Britain and Northern Ireland were concluded with the respective Governments during August, 1948. These two agreements were signed by the Hon. the Minister of Social Security for the New Zealand Government on 23rd September, 1948, and the New Zealand legislation giving effect to these agreements came into force on 1st December, 1948. Under these agreements, which apply only to children who are British subjects, residence or birth in New Zealand is treated as residence or birth in Great Britain or Northern Ireland when determining applications for family allowance in Great Britain or Northern Ireland. Similarly residence or birth in Great Britain or Northern Ireland is treated as residence or birth in New Zealand when determining applications for family benefit in New Zealand. There are no financial adjustments between the countries except where payment is made in one country in respect of children who return to the other country within six months of arrival.

Family allowances in Great Britain and Northern Ireland are paid at the rate of 5s. a week for each child after the first. In New Zealand family benefits are paid at the rate of 10s. a week for each child. There is no means test in any of the countries.

While the negotiations for reciprocal family benefits were being finalized the general question of reciprocity for age and widows' benefits was discussed, and negotiations are still proceeding.

CHAPTER X — THE INTER-RELATIONSHIP BETWEEN SOCIAL SECURITY BENEFITS AND WAR PENSIONS AND OTHER ALLOWANCES

WAR PENSIONS

IT is not strictly within the scope of this publication to deal with war pensions in detail, but, as an essential feature of social security legislation is its co-ordination with war pensions, a brief survey of war pensions will serve to illustrate the inter-relationship of the two classes of payments.

New Zealand has tended to integrate war pensions with the social security system both from an administrative and legislative point of view. As far back as 1915 war pensions and civil pensions were under one administration, and with the advent of the social security scheme the procedure was continued.

The power to grant war pensions and allowances is vested in a War Pensions Board of four members appointed by the Government, one being a registered medical practitioner and another a respresentative of members of the Forces. The Secretary for War Pensions, who is responsible for the administration of the war-pensions legislation, is also an officer of the Social Security Department. The Social Security Department and the War Pensions Department are one and the same organization, staff and accommodation are common to both fields of legislation, and this single administration provides a unified national records and index system.

At the outset it should be pointed out that war-pensions legislation makes no mention of social security benefits and is not geared to the provisions of the Social Security Act. The Social Security Act itself, however, specifies to what extent war pensioners are eligible to participate in benefits under the social security scheme. The social security system is designed to insure against want, and normally a person is not considered to be in want if she or he is in receipt of a war pension or allowance sufficient for maintenance. War pensions, being compensatory payments for war injury, are non-contributory and are paid not from the Social Security Fund, but out of the Consolidated Fund from general taxation.

Disablement pensions are free from means test, being assessed on the degree of disablement suffered while pensions to widows of servicemen are also free from a means test. Extra allowances, however, are payable in the case of need.

War pensions fall under the following headings :—

(a) *Disablement pensions* provided for disabled ex-members of the Forces. The basic rate for complete disability is £3 10s. a week ; for anything less than complete disability the rate is proportionately reduced.

(b) *Economic pensions* to ex-members of the Forces payable where the pensioner is precluded by reason of his disablement from obtaining and retaining suitable employment. The maximum rate is £2 5s. a week, which may be paid in addition to the disablement pension.

97

(c) *Pensions to dependents of deceased members of the Forces.* This applies mainly to widows, and the basic rate is £2 10s. a week, with a supplementary mother's allowance of 35s. a week if there are dependent children. Pensions are paid to other dependents at varying rates having regard to the degree of dependency.

(d) *Economic pensions for dependents.* The maximum rate is 25s. a week, which may be paid in addition to the basic pension.

(e) *Pensions to dependents of disabled members of the Forces.* The maximum rate for a wife is 25s. a week or, if there are dependent children, 35s. a week.

(f) *War veterans' allowances.* An allowance comparable with an age-benefit is payable to those ex-servicemen who, because of infirmities due to any cause whatsoever, are unfit for permanent employment. The allowance is governed by a means test less restrictive than that applied to an age-benefit. The persons to whom the allowance is paid are commonly called " burnt out " veterans, and to date most grants are payable to servicemen of the 1914–18 war. A male veteran to qualify must have had actual engagement with the enemy, but a female need only to have served overseas. The maximum rate of allowance payable is £2 10s. a week to the veteran, plus £2 10s. a week for a wife.

Under the Social Security Act the recipient of a war pension or allowance may receive a superannuation or family benefit. Provision is also made in the Social Security Act for persons who are in receipt of a war pension in respect of their own disablement. These pensioners may be granted an age, sickness, unemployment, or emergency benefit from the Social Security Fund. The amount of war pension is regarded as " other income " under the Social Security Act. A person receiving a dependent's war pension is not eligible for social security benefits other than a superannuation or family benefit. If it is desired that any other social security benefit be granted, the dependent's war pension requires to be surrendered.

Close co-ordination is maintained between war pensions and social security benefits. For instance, a war pensioner receiving a war disability pension may be granted a sickness benefit for temporary incapacity, the war pension being regarded as " other income " for social security purposes and charged accordingly. Where circumstances indicate that it is the war disability which has caused the cessation of employment and the period off work is more than a few days the war disablement pension is reviewed, and if it is to the pensioners' advantage he is advised to apply for economic pension and, if married, for dependent's pension as well. Furthermore, if indications are that he may be unfit for permanent employment, he may be advised to apply for a war veterans' allowance.

If in any particular case hardship may be occasioned through the pensioner being without adequate means of subsistence while a war pension or war veterans' allowance is being investigated an interim grant is made from the Social Security Fund. When the additional war pension is granted the Department recovers the sickness benefit advanced by " offset " from the war pension arrears due. By this means an endeavour is made to ensure that as far as possible immediate assistance is granted from the Social Security Fund to war pensioners when hardship would result from an unavoidable lapse of time in the granting of a war pension or allowance.

TABLE 37—COMPARISON OF WEEKLY RATES OF WAR PENSIONS, WAR VETERANS ALLOWANCES, AND SOCIAL SECURITY BENEFITS AS AT 1ST JUNE, 1949

—	War Pensions.			War Veterans' Allowances.		Social Security.	
	Disablement.	Disablement if Blind or Two or More Serious Disabilities.	Widows of Servicemen.	War Veterans.	Widows of Veterans.	Age, Invalids, Miners, Unemployment, Sickness.	Widows of Civilians.
	£ s.	£ s.	£ s.	£ s.	£ s.	£ s.	£ s.
Pensioner or beneficiary	3 10	5 10	2 10	2 10	5 0*	2 10	2 10
Economic pension	2 5	2 5	1 5	..	..	..	..
Wife	1 5	1 5	..	2 10	..	2 10	..
Total (if no dependent children)	7 0	9 0	3 15	5 0	5 0	5 0	2 10
Mothers' allowance	0 10	0 10	1 15	..	..	..	1 10
Total (if there are dependent children)	7 10	9 10	5 10	5 0	5 0	5 0	4 0

* For two years only from husband's death.

In addition to the above, 10s. a week is paid for each child by way of either family benefit or war pension.

REHABILITATION ALLOWANCES

In order to facilitate the reabsorption into civilian occupations of demobilized ex-servicemen and ex-servicewomen of the 1939–45 war, rehabilitation allowances were granted to discharged personnel who were fit for normal employment. These allowances were paid to bridge the gap between the cessation of service pay and gainful employment.

Although the provision of financial assistance to ex-servicemen was properly the responsibility of the Rehabilitation Department, the Social Security Department had the necessary machinery for administering cash payments, and by the co-operation of the two Departments assistance was speedily made available to demobilized men and women until they were placed in industrial employment.

The cost of these allowances was borne by War Expenses Account. A primary condition of the allowance was that applicants should enrol for employment and accept suitable work when offered.

The allowance was for a maximum period of thirteen weeks and was paid at the rate of £3 10s. a week plus £1 for a wife and 6s. for each child up to five, with a maximum of £6 a week. Allowances of ex-servicemen with less than six children were reduced by the amount of personal earnings of the servicemen, but men with six, seven, or eight children could receive 6s., 12s., and 18s. respectively in addition to the maximum allowance. Sick pay, lodge benefit, and income other than the earnings of the ex-servicemen were ignored, as were the earnings of the wife. If any social security benefit or war pension was being paid the rehabilitation allowance was reduced accordingly.

The majority of ex-service personnel were quickly reabsorbed into industry, and the need for the allowance has now passed, as is disclosed from the following figures.

Year Ended 31st March,			Allowances granted for Year.	Allowances Current at 31st March.	Expenditure.
					£
1943	..	..	849	763	7,861
1944	..	..	7,196	909	235,522
1945	..	..	4,029	338	131,733
1946	..	..	1,516	49	65,129
1947	..	..	368	1	8,244
1948	..	..	7	Nil	95
1949	..	..	3	Nil	75

DEMOBILIZATION ALLOWANCES

Until 1945 branches of the armed forces retained on service pay and allowances personnel unfit for further service but still requiring approved medical treatment. As treatment was sometimes prolonged there was unnecessary overlapping between Service Departments, the Rehabilitation Department, and the War Pensions Branch of the Social Security Department.

From the 1st August, 1945, it was decided to limit the period service personnel could be retained on pay to twelve months from the date of return to New Zealand in the case of overseas servicemen undergoing treatment, and six months from the date of commencement of treatment in the case of home servicemen. At the end of the respective periods if an incapacitated serviceman required further treatment he was discharged from the forces and placed under the control of the War Pensions Branch of the Social Security Department for the continuation of treatment and the determination of his war pension and other rights by the approved authorities.

To provide for the maintenance of unfit personnel so discharged who required continuation of treatment or medical after care and who were unable to resume civilian employment by reason of their incapacity, an allowance, known as a " demobilization allowance," was authorized. It was administered and paid by the Social Security Department through its War Pensions Branch. The payments involved were charged to War Expenses Account and not to the Social Security Fund.

The allowance, which was paid at the rate of £3 10s. a week for the ex-serviceman plus £1 for a wife and 10s. for each child, was reduced by the amount of any war pension or social security benefit. It could not be paid at the same time as a rehabilitation allowance, which was intended for those fit for work, and was not limited to any set period, but paid as long as the recipient was unable to work. Allowances were paid in 129 cases, the total expenditure to 31st March, 1949, being £11,320. There were six allowances current at 31st March, 1949.

100

CHAPTER XI—ADMINISTRATION OF CASH BENEFITS

THE Social Security Act falls into three main groups dealing with cash benefits, health benefits, and finance respectively.

The responsibility for administering the various parts of this legislation falls to the Social Security Department for cash benefits and the control of the Social Security Fund, the Health Department for the health benefits, and the Land and Income Tax Department for the collection of the social security contribution.

ADMINISTRATIVE ORGANIZATION

SOCIAL SECURITY DEPARTMENT

On the coming into force of the Social Security Act on 1st April, 1939, the newly-formed Social Security Department absorbed the Pensions Department and the greater part of the Employment Division of the Labour Department.

The Department is under the control of a Commission of three, comprising a Chairman, who is administrative head of the Department, and two other members.

As has been mentioned above, the primary function of the Department is to administer that portion of the Social Security Act which deals with the payment of cash benefits. It is also responsible for the administration of war pensions and war veterans' allowances, and acts as agent for several overseas pension authorities paying pensions in New Zealand on behalf of the Governments of the United Kingdom, Australia, Canada, India, Pakistan, South Africa, Burma, and Crown Colonies.

In addition to a Head Office in Wellington, the Department has forty-eight district offices situated throughout the length and breadth of New Zealand from Kaitaia in the north to Invercargill in the south. Of these, nineteen are principal district offices controlled by Registrars, who in turn have under their control twenty-nine sub-offices called " District Agencies." The object of this Dominion coverage is to give the greatest possible service to the public. The total staff at 31st March, 1949, was 1,329, of whom 415 were located in Head Office. In the district offices the numbers range from 180 in Auckland to one in the smallest office at Ruatoria. From the situation of the district offices it is possible, except in the very remote parts of the country, for all members of the public to have direct contact with the Department's officers, and in this way many little difficulties which may seem insurmountable to the applicant are quickly straightened out and adjusted. If an applicant lives in a particularly remote part of the country and is unable to contact the nearest office of the Department it is possible for applications for benefit to be lodged with the nearest post-office, which in turn forwards them to the Department's district offices.

District Officers make regular visits to adjoining small towns to interview and discuss social security problems with beneficiaries or intending applicants.

In order to expedite necessary inquiries District Officers are provided with or have the use of a car, and Field or Inquiry Officers provide a personal link between the beneficiaries and the Department. Apart from visiting individual beneficiaries in their homes, Inquiry Officers visit public hospitals and there take applications from patients and discuss with them, where necessary, any problems relating to social security benefits.

CHART 10—ADMINISTRATIVE ORGANIZATION

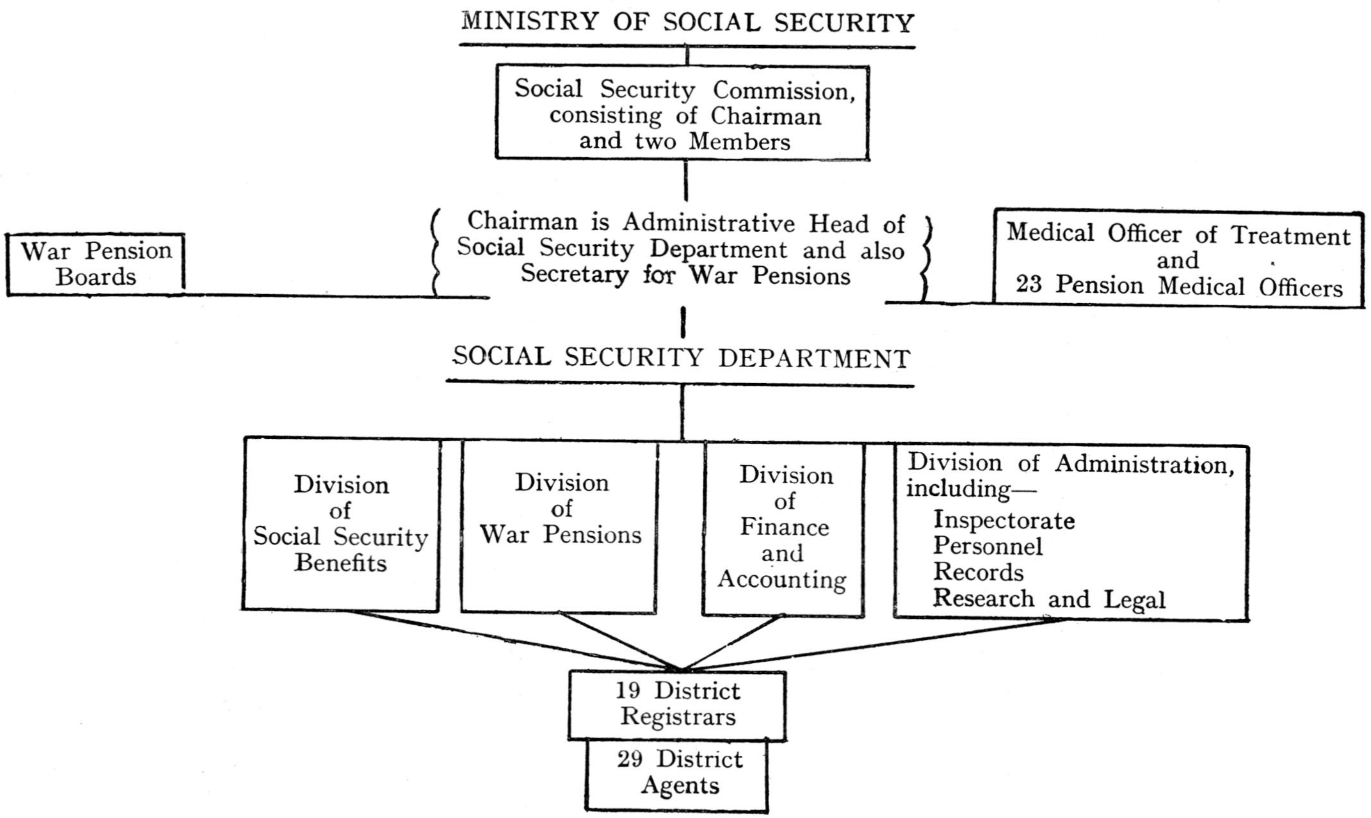

MINISTRY OF SOCIAL SECURITY

Social Security Commission, consisting of Chairman and two Members

Medical Officer of Treatment and 23 Pension Medical Officers

Chairman is Administrative Head of Social Security Department and also Secretary for War Pensions

SOCIAL SECURITY DEPARTMENT

War Pension Boards

Division of Social Security Benefits

Division of War Pensions

Division of Finance and Accounting

Division of Administration, including—
Inspectorate
Personnel
Records
Research and Legal

19 District Registrars

29 District Agents

ADMINISTRATIVE PROCEDURE

Applications for all classes of benefits are received and investigated at the local district offices, and Registrars are empowered under delegated authority which is provided in the Social Security Act to grant practically all classes of benefits, provided, of course, the applicant qualifies by law for the benefit for which application is made.

Cash benefits fall into two main groups—temporary benefits such as unemployment, sickness, and associated emergency benefits, which are paid weekly, and the more permanent benefits, which are paid monthly (quarterly at present in the case of superannuation benefits.)

APPLICATION FOR BENEFIT

Applications for benefit may be posted to a local office of the Department or left at an office of an Agent, but the most satisfactory method is for applicants to lodge their claims personally as it is then possible by interviewing to correct discrepancies, omissions, and mistakes and ensure that all necessary particulars are obtained, thus often speeding up consideration of the application by avoiding the need for subsequent inquiry and correspondence. Many people fill in the form at home before calling at the local office, and this has the advantage of enabling them to see what information is required and, when necessary, produce supporting evidence of their age, income, property, or other details when lodging their applications.

All applications are recorded in the local District Index, and in most cases a check is made of the National Index maintained at the Head Office in Wellington in order to ascertain if the person is in receipt of a benefit in another district or if any other district office is holding papers or a file relating to the person.

VERIFICATION OF INFORMATION

The next step is to verify as much of the information as is required to be checked. Where age is not a material factor, as, for example, with applicants for sickness benefit who are obviously not liable to be affected by the lower rate of benefit paid to people under twenty years of age (without dependants) and are similarly obviously under sixty years of age or with applicants for widows' benefits by widows with children, the date of birth is not verified. Where age is a material factor it may be verified by such supporting evidence as a birth-certificate submitted by the applicant, but if no evidence is submitted the Department attempts to obtain verification from the Registrar of Births. If an applicant was born out of New Zealand and has no documentary proof of age the Department attempts to verify age by whatever means are available. The stated age shown on a marriage-certificate is often a help ; also passenger-lists for practically all ships arriving at and departing from New Zealand since 1868 are held by the Department, and as these lists often show the ages of passengers they have proved of great value, particularly in verifying the ages of people who arrived in their youth. School records have been used on many occasions. If necessary, particulars of marriages or deaths are verified by sighting certificates produced by applicants or by inquiry from the Registrar of Births, Deaths, and Marriages.

Unless it is obvious that applicants are well within the residential qualifications for the type of benefit concerned the dates of arrival and period of subsequent absences from New Zealand are verified by reference to the passenger-lists of ships and aircraft.

Where income or property are material factors information declared by the applicants is verified from the appropriate source.

GRANT OF BENEFIT

Once the information has been assembled and verified the future action depends on the type of benefit applied for.

Before the Social Security Act became law applications for old-age and widows' pensions were decided by Magistrates in Chambers—all other pensions were decided by the Commissioner of Pensions. Under the Social Security Act the decision regarding all benefits is the responsibility of the Social Security Commission. The Commission, in its turn, has delegated to Registrars the power to grant all types of benefits except superannuation and miners' benefits. The restriction as far as these two latter benefits is concerned has been imposed for administrative reasons only.

District agencies have power to decide temporary benefits only—*i.e.*, unemployment or sickness benefits.

Most of the applications to be considered under the emergency provisions of the Act are referred to the Commission for decision.

Where a Registrar or District Agent is in doubt regarding an application he may forward it to the Commission for direction or decision.

RECORDS AND INDEX

District office files for age, widows', orphans', invalids', and family benefits are kept by Registrars, and files for unemployment, sickness, and emergency benefits are retained by the local office concerned, whether a District Agency or a Registrar's office. Skeleton files for all monthly benefits are kept at Head Office, as well as full files for superannuation and miners' benefits. All original applications are recorded in the District Index and also in the National Index maintained in Head Office. As far as war pensions and allowances are concerned the main files are retained at Head Office, with skeleton files in the district offices.

APPEALS

Any applicant or beneficiary aggrieved by any decision made by an officer on behalf of the Commission may, within three months, appeal to the Commission. If an applicant objects to the decision of the Registrar or District Agent, he can make further representation, and if he is still dissatisfied he can ask the local representative to submit his case to the Commission or he can communicate with the Commission himself.

As has already been mentioned, there is a special right of appeal to a Board of three medical practitioners nominated by the Commission against a decision refusing or terminating an invalid's or miner's benefit on medical grounds. These appeals must be lodged within three months. Where an invalid's benefit appeal is made against the decision of a Registrar on medical grounds the papers are forwarded to the Commission and the case is referred to the Appeal Board only if the Commission upholds the Registrar's decision.

Time Taken to Grant Benefits

The time taken from the date an application is received until payment is authorized varies according to the nature of the benefit and the circumstances of the case. Sometimes applicants and other people whom it is necessary to contact in the course of inquiries live in isolated areas, while sometimes they can be readily contacted. Information is verified easily in some cases, while in others some difficulty or delay is experienced.

Sickness benefits which are granted and paid locally usually take about ten days to dispose of. Many are finalized within a week, particularly if satisfactory medical evidence is submitted at the time of application and if the inquiry to the employer regarding earnings and cessation of work is returned promptly.

For all other benefits the average time for disposal of an application until payment of the first monthly instalment ranges from two to four weeks.

Date of Commencement of Benefits

The Social Security Act fixed the commencing date for all cash benefits except emergency benefits, as the first of the month in which the application was received or the date an applicant qualified for benefit, whichever was later. Emergency benefits commence from the date fixed by the Commission in respect of each case.

Since 1945 the law has been amended to give discretion in the hands of the Commission to pay sickness and unemployment benefits from a date either before or after the date of application, subject, however, to non-payment for the first seven days of incapacity or unemployment, except in special circumstances.

Renewal of Benefit

Under the Social Security Act, 1938, all benefits originally continued for a period not exceeding twelve months, the Commission being authorized to renew benefits from time to time for a period not exceeding one year, each application for renewal being investigated as if it was an original application for benefit. The restriction to one year of the period for which benefit could be continued without renewal was removed from 1st October, 1947, for superannuation, family, and miners' benefits, which are paid without a means test.

In practice, sickness, unemployment, and emergency benefits of a temporary nature are kept under constant review, and benefits other than those paid without a means test are renewed each year by Registrars.

In renewing benefits, breaks in the continuity of payments are avoided as far as possible, although sometimes, because of delay in the completion of the application for renewal or difficulty in verifying information and ascertaining the correct position regarding income or property, a benefit may not be renewed in time to avoid a break in payment. Registrars, however, have authority to issue payment advices if necessary to preserve continuity of payment, thus avoiding hardship to the individual.

Reviews of Benefit

Although most benefits are subject to review at the time of renewal the law provides that in the event of a change in circumstances a benefit may be reviewed at any time. Pending completion of a review which may involve investigation, payment of a benefit may be suspended, but this is done only where there are reasonable grounds for believing that a beneficiary is not entitled to further payments.

INCOME AND PROPERTY

Definition of Income

" Income " for cash benefits may include items which are ordinarily regarded as capital, and includes all moneys and the value of all benefits derived and received from any source except certain items which are specifically excluded. The items not charged as income are—

(a) Any social security benefit.

(b) Funeral benefits from any friendly society.

(c) Capital moneys received in respect of the sale or exchange of any property.

(d) Moneys received under an insurance policy in respect of the destruction of or damage to any building or other property by fire, earthquake, or other cause.

(e) Capital moneys up to £500 received by an applicant under any life-insurance policy effected on his own life.

(f) All capital moneys received from the estate of a deceased husband or wife.

(g) Capital moneys up to £500 received by way of legacy (other than from a deceased husband or wife, which is all excluded), or life insurance (other than a policy on life of applicant), or as compensation or damages for injury or death or as a compassionate grant by the Government or any employer on account of the death of the husband of an applicant.

(h) Moneys paid in respect of any military decoration and received by the recipient of the decoration.

It will be noted that clause (e) exempts from the definition of income capital moneys up to £500 received under a policy of life insurance on the applicant's own life. Clause (g) goes further and provides for a similar exemption of £500 in respect of capital moneys received under any other life insurance policy—e.g., a policy on the life of another. In effect, therefore, the exemption of £500 applies to capital moneys received under any life-insurance policy whatever.

The exemption of £500 in both clauses (e) and (g) applies to the aggregate of the amounts received during the income year from the sources mentioned in each of the clauses and is a personal exemption applicable to every person whose income is required to be taken into account. Thus if both husband and wife receive legacies from an estate each would be entitled to the exemption of £500.

Similarly, two exemptions of £500 would be allowable if an applicant received the proceeds of an endowment policy on his own life (clause (e)) and also the proceeds of an insurance policy on the life of some other person (clause (g)). If, however, he received in the same year payments from two or more sources mentioned in clause (g)—e.g., legacies and compensation—only one exemption would be allowed in respect of the aggregate of these payments. His wife, of course, would also be entitled to the exemption of £500 if she also received payments by way of legacy, compensation, &c.

Money received in trust for some other person is not regarded as income for benefit purposes. Income refers not only to " all moneys," but also to the value of all benefits derived or received by the applicant. Benefits therefore include the value of board or lodgings (on a scale fixed by the Commission), stores, property, or other payments in kind for services rendered.

Method of Ascertaining Income

Most benefits are granted for a period of one year, and the income taken into account when assessing is the estimated income for the year for which benefit is payable.

When renewing a benefit, however, the general rule is to charge income based on the actual income for the past year, but in some cases adjustments may be made in respect of anticipated income or income which has ceased. Many beneficiaries, particularly age-beneficiaries, who have been earning while receiving benefit come to the stage when, because of failing health, old age, or other reasons, future work must cease. Where it is definite that there will be no further income from such source a benefit may be renewed without taking into account past earnings which have ceased.

An amendment to the law has empowered the Commission, for the purpose of avoiding any anomaly when computing income for benefit purposes, to deduct all or part of the amount payable as social security charge on that income.

Property

When determining the value of property to be taken into account for benefit purposes the law provides that no account is to be taken of a home, furniture, personal effects, an interest in land, including a mortgage or the present value of an annuity or life insurance policy.

The property remaining after excluding the above items is called the " accumulated or chargeable " property, and it is from this " accumulated " property that the personal exemption of £500 is made in order to arrive at the net capital value of property for benefit purposes.

If it is found that property has been converted from a chargeable to one of the non-chargeable forms and the conversion was not made in good faith, but was for the purpose of securing a benefit or an increased rate of benefit, the Commission has power to disregard the transfer and include the value of property as accumulated or chargeable property. In dealing with accumulated property of husband and wife the law assumes that the couple are common owners, and for the purpose of assessing a benefit each is assumed to own half of it. For example, a married couple having £1,600 in the bank, husband £1,000, wife, £600, would each be deemed to have accumulated property of £800. After allowing the £500 personal exemption the net capital value of their property would be £300 each.

Little difficulty is experienced in verifying the stated value of most assets such as bank accounts, or company shares, or debentures which are quoted on the Stock Exchange, but the value of other assets such as shares in private companies, stock, goods, and chattels are less obvious. Where the real value of an asset is a matter of opinion a conservative value is usually adopted. Any encumbrances on an asset are deducted before arriving at its value.

Many people ceasing work on account of old age or ill health rearrange their affairs to meet the changed conditions, and there is generally no objection to people making a prudent rearrangement of their affairs to their best advantage. However, if revenue-bearing assets are deliberately disposed of the question as to whether or not it was done to secure a greater benefit is considered. It may be necessary to charge such assets in computing the benefit, notwithstanding the fact that they have been disposed of.

Many factors require to be taken into account when assessing the value of any income disposed of. Transfers of leases of farms and businesses to sons or near relatives often present difficulties, as frequently the arrangements are informal or loose and the applicant continues to live on a portion of the land or premises. The nominal consideration often bears little relation to current value, as, for example, when a son who takes over the farm or business has worked for the parent without reasonable wages in the past and that fact is reflected in the consideration for the transfer or lease. Naturally these cases require careful investigation, but it is appreciated that in dealings with near relatives genuine feelings of natural affection may have an influence and that the valuation may be reasonable under the circumstances even although it is not the highest that could be obtained under favourable market conditions. A parent would not seek to drive such a hard bargain with his children as he would with a stranger. Comparatively large sums are sometimes withdrawn from a bank account and cannot be accounted for satisfactorily after making allowances for living and reasonable expenses. Unless the benefit would be affected no inquiries would be necessary, but if it seems warranted, the cash unaccounted for may be charged. Equitable assessments in these cases are in the hands of the Social Security Commission.

PAYMENT OF BENEFITS

Under the social security scheme temporary benefits—*i.e.*, unemployment, sickness, and some emergency benefits—are paid weekly by local offices. All other benefits, except superannuation (which at present is paid quarterly), are paid monthly from the Head Office.

To get money into beneficiaries' hands regularly is the Department's most important function, for the majority of them depend on the benefit in some measure for their subsistence. To this end special arrangements operate whereby the Registrars issue the first payment advice as soon as the application has been granted. All the other payment advices are prepared and produced on Powers-Samas machines in a central pool at Head Office.

Every month approximately 394,000 social security payment advices are despatched to various paying offices. Every third month when superannuation payments are made the advices total 459,000.

The installation of these machines naturally called for skilled operators, and twenty-four female operators, with four others in training, are continuously employed on this side of the pay work. A staff of skilled mechanics is also employed to ensure that the machines are kept in first-class running-order.

From the information contained in new benefits granted by Registrars a master card is code-punched with the district number, name of beneficiary, amount of benefit, paying office, and such other details as may be required. After being interpreted and carefully checked these cards are filed away in numerical order by districts and form the basis of all future payments, a separate series being kept for each class of benefit. When any alteration has to be made, such as a change in the paying office, amount, &c., a new card must be punched and the existing one destroyed.

Every month the payment advices referred to previously must be prepared and despatched. All master cards are run through the reproducer, which produces an exact replica of the master card on a payment card called a " pay advice." At this stage the pay advices are just blanks perforated by a series of holes representing in code a figure or a letter and quite unintelligible to any person not experienced in decoding them. They are run through the interpreters which translate the holes into figures and letters and prints along the top edge of the card, the number of the benefit, paying-office number, name of beneficiary, and the amount of the benefit. Although at this stage the production of the month's advices has proceeded quite a long way, there still remains the sorting and despatching to be carried out.

Each class of benefit is machine sorted into numerical order in districts and then into paying offices. It should be explained that in each district there are quite a number of paying offices, and a beneficiary may uplift his benefit at a money-order post-office nominated by him. When it is mentioned that, in addition to payment at most of the Department's own offices, payments are made at over one thousand money-order offices throughout New Zealand, some appreciation will be gained of the amount of sorting to be done. This sorting is accomplished quickly and accurately by the sorting machines. Over seven hundred parcels of pay advices are despatched monthly to paying offices throughout New Zealand, in addition to numerous smaller lots which are forwarded in ordinary envelopes.

The production and despatch of the pay advices is a highly mechanized operation and is so arranged that advices for paying offices farthest from Wellington are produced and posted first, while those closer to Wellington are naturally the last to be completed. Production— i.e., reproducing, interpreting, and sorting—takes not less than a fortnight, and definite dates are set by which individual operations must be completed. These dates must be adhered to if the paying organization is to operate smoothly.

When benefits have been paid, the receipted advices are returned to Head Office from all paying offices throughout the country, counted and checked for irregularities such as missing signatures, &c., and then mechanically sorted back into district and numerical order. The paid advices are then marked off against the beneficiary's account in the Department's ledgers, and the total expenditure for the period assembled and charged against the Social Security Fund.

PAYMENT OUTSIDE NEW ZEALAND

The Social Security Act originally provided that payment of benefit outside New Zealand could be made up to two years for blind people receiving vocational training or medical treatment for their eyes, invalid beneficiaries if they were absent to obtain special medical or surgical treatment, and beneficiaries on miners' benefits, while age and superannuation beneficiaries could be paid in respect of six months' absence. Since 1st June, 1948, the law has been amended to enable the Commission in its discretion to pay any cash benefit in respect of any period of temporary absence from New Zealand.

Keeping the Records

Part of the National Index

Paying the People. The Old Method—Writing Payment Warrants by Hand

The New Mechanized Method—Punching Powers-Samas Cards

Producing the Monthly Pay Warrants

Sorting the Warrants to Go to Over a Thousand Paying Offices

Despatching the Warrants Each Month

An Administrative Division in Head Office

113

CHAPTER XII — GENERAL STATISTICS

NUMBER OF CASH BENEFITS IN FORCE, 1939–1949

ON the 31st March, 1939, there were 91,067 civil pensions in force, representing 561 per 10,000 of population. These were absorbed into the social security scheme the following day, and a year later, with the wider coverage provided by the Social Security Act, there were 135,291 benefits in force, or 825 per 10,000 of population. Each year thereafter the number increased, until by the 31st March, 1949, after ten years of social security, there were 463,785 benefits in force, representing 2,476 per 10,000 of population.

(It should be noted that the 463,785 benefits in force at 31st March, 1949, includes 248,726 family benefits which are paid in respect of 548,330 children, and that where a benefit includes payment for a dependent wife it is shown as one benefit only.)

CHART II—CASH BENEFITS: NUMBER IN FORCE, BY TYPE, 1940–49

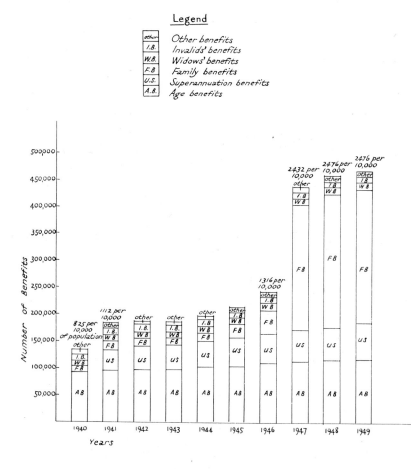

114

TABLE 39—CASH BENEFITS : NUMBER IN FORCE, BY TYPE OF BENEFIT, 31ST MARCH, 1940, TO 31ST MARCH, 1949

Number in Force

31st March,	Superannuation.	Age.	Widows.	Orphans.	Family.	Invalids.	Miners.	Maori War.	Unemployment.	Sickness.	Emergency.	Total.
1940	..	93,262	10,174	330	11,053	11,811	988	12	4,053	2,565	1,043	135,291
1941	36,602	97,606	10,569	350	16,626	11,936	931	7	1,906	3,452	2,034	182,019
1942	41,021	99,152	10,765	372	18,316	12,107	888	4	841	3,672	2,170	189,308
1943	44,448	99,671	10,589	395	14,190	11,938	841	2	373	3,699	1,821	187,967
1944	49,289	102,530	10,836	412	15,950	12,126	795	1	292	4,446	1,915	198,592
1945	53,679	104,653	10,965	421	24,251	12,205	783	1	198	4,233	2,083	213,472
1946	56,181	110,060	11,507	400	42,637	12,164	736	1	205	5,416	2,094	241,401
1947	57,992	115,287	13,133	397	230,021*	12,466	718	1	35	4,273	1,845	436,168
1948	61,612	117,161	14,145	370	243,137	10,682	685		16	4,248	2,141	454,198
1949	65,839	116,254	14,883	371	248,726	10,051	660	..	30	4,945	2,026	463,785

Percentage Distribution

31st March,	Superannuation.	Age.	Widows.	Orphans.	Family.	Invalids.	Miners.	Maori War.	Unemployment.	Sickness.	Emergency.	Total.
1940	..	68·9	7·5	0·2	8·2	8·7	0·7	†	3·0	1·9	0·8	100
1941	20·1	53·6	5·8	0·2	9·1	6·6	0·5	†	1·0	1·9	1·1	100
1942	21·7	52·4	5·7	0·2	9·7	6·4	0·5	†	0·4	1·9	1·1	100
1943	23·6	53·0	5·6	0·2	7·5	6·4	0·4	†	0·2	2·0	1·0	100
1944	24·8	51·6	5·5	0·2	8·0	6·1	0·4	†	0·1	2·2	1·0	100
1945	25·1	49·0	5·1	0·2	11·4	5·7	0·4	†	0·1	2·0	1·0	100
1946	23·3	45·6	4·8	0·2	17·7	5·0	0·3	†	0·1	2·2	0·9	100
1947	13·3	26·4	3·0	0·1	52·7*	2·9	0·2	†	†	1·0	0·4	100
1948	13·6	25·8	3·1	0·1	53·5	2·4	0·1	†	†	0·9	0·5	100
1949	14·2	25·1	3·2	0·1	53·6	2·2	0·1	†	†	1·1	0·4	100

* Family benefits paid without means test from 1st April, 1946. † Less than 0·05 per cent.

N.B.—(a) The number of family benefits in force each year denotes the number of families on benefit and not the number of chidren in respect of whom benefit is paid.

(b) In respect of other benefits where a dependent wife is included in her husband's benefit it is recorded as one benefit only.

The expenditure on cash benefits for the first year of social security—*i.e.*, for the year ended 31st March, 1940—was £(m.)9·3, or £5 14s. 4d. per head of population, almost double the amount spent on pensions for the previous year. Each succeeding year saw further increases in this expenditure, which for the year ended 31st March, 1946, amounted to over £(m.)16·6, or £9 14s. 11d. per head of population. Following the removal of the means test for family benefits, social security expenditure on cash benefits increased suddenly, and for the year ended 31st March, 1949, the tenth year of social security, was almost £(m.)34·5, or £18 12s. 3d. per head, and over three and a half times greater than the amount spent during the first year of the scheme. The total amount spent on cash benefits for the ten years to March, 1949, was £181,899,868, almost four times greater than the total amount spent on pensions in the forty years to 1939.

Expenditure on health benefits for the first year of social security was just over £(m.)1, and this has increased steadily each year to £(m.)7·9 for the year ended March, 1949. Of the total expenditure on cash and health benefits during the year ended 31st March, 1949, 81·4 per cent. was devoted to cash benefits and 18·6 per cent. to health benefits.

TABLE 40—CASH AND HEALTH BENEFITS : EXPENDITURE PER HEAD OF POPULATION, 1ST APRIL, 1939, TO 31ST MARCH, 1949

Year Ended 31st March,	Mean Population, Including Maoris.	Cash Benefits.		Health Benefits.		Cash and Health Benefits.	
		Total.	Per Head.	Total.	Per Head.	Total.	Per Head.
		£	£ s. d.	£	£ s. d.	£	£ s. d
1940	1,633,447	9,337,243	5 14 4	1,056,699	0 12 11	10,393,942	6 7 3
1941	1,635,715	10,405,460	6 7 2	1,776,685	1 1 9	12,182,145	7 8 11
1942	1,630,419	10,701,237	6 11 3	2,435,588	1 9 11	13,136,825	8 1 2
1943	1,640,191	11,711,465	7 2 10	3,721,179	2 5 4	15,432,644	9 8 2
1944	1,637,570	12,397,773	7 11 5	4,726,680	2 17 9	17,124,453	10 9 2
1945	1,664,585	13,553,463	8 2 7	5,234,713	3 2 11	18,768,176	11 5 6
1946	1,710,990	16,673,690	9 14 11	5,564,315	3 5 0	22,238,005	12 19 11
1947	1,772,787	29,909,454	16 17 5	6,211,580	3 10 1	36,121,034	20 7 6
1948	1,812,609	32,774,325	18 1 7	7,021,487	3 17 6	39,795,812	21 19 1
1949	1,851,291	34,455,758	18 12 3	7,875,448	4 5 1	42,331,206	22 17 4

Sources—Population : 1940–46, page 778, 1946 Year-Book.
1947, Table 1, page 6, *Monthly Abstract of Statistics*, March, 1948.
1948–49, Table 1, page 4, *Monthly Abstract of Statistics*, May, 1949.

(Population figures do not include members of the armed forces serving outside New Zealand.)

Amount

Year Ended 31st March.	Superannuation.	Age.	Widows.	Orphans.	Family.	Invalids.	Miners.	Maori War.	Unemployment.	Sickness.	Emergency.	Total.
	£	£	£	£	£	£	£	£	£	£	£	£
1940	..	6,517,899	785,952	14,880	252,562	942,196	92,653	1,103	434,497	208,790	86,711	9,337,243
1941	240,336	7,101,346	836,368	17,713	411,811	999,648	88,656	744	299,161	279,581	130,096	10,405,460
1942	445,686	7,190,694	844,928	18,275	539,183	1,011,375	83,258	440	138,528	304,154	124,716	10,701,237
1943	603,124	7,783,084	866,597	20,628	790,719	1,036,373	80,100	190	49,639	362,088	118,923	11,711,465
1944	778,758	8,101,668	949,099	22,442	876,858	1,067,409	76,652	119	32,316	376,878	115,574	12,397,773
1945	995,035	8,492,015	985,452	23,253	1,405,113	1,072,619	74,367	78	27,822	351,866	105,843	13,533,463
1946	1,185,508	9,817,615	1,043,593	24,178	2,611,759	1,183,537	88,359	101	31,661	565,420	121,959	16,673,690
1947	1,349,689	11,881,119	1,529,010	22,905	12,680,778	1,328,485	105,416	104	24,332	853,328	134,288	29,909,454
1948	1,593,757	12,976,286	1,770,622	24,187	13,798,648	1,367,300	110,106	111	8,358	897,093	227,857	32,774,325
1949	1,850,079	13,790,971	1,911,134	27,623	14,242,202	1,348,616	113,659	10	8,948	911,107	251,409	34,455,758
Total	9,041,972	93,652,697	11,522,755	216,084	47,609,633	11,357,558	913,226	3,000	1,055,262	5,110,305	1,417,376	181,899,868

Percentage Distribution

Year Ended 31st March.	Superannuation.	Age.	Widows.	Orphans.	Family.	Invalids.	Miners.	Maori War.	Unemployment.	Sickness.	Emergency.	Total.
1940	..	69·8	8·4	0·2	2·7	10·1	1·0	*	4·7	2·2	0·9	100
1941	2·3	68·2	8·0	0·2	3·9	9·6	0·9	*	2·9	2·7	1·3	100
1942	4·2	67·2	7·9	0·2	5·0	9·4	0·8	*	1·3	2·8	1·2	100
1943	5·1	66·5	7·4	0·2	6·8	8·8	0·7	*	0·4	3·1	1·0	100
1944	6·3	65·3	7·7	0·2	7·1	8·6	0·6	*	0·3	3·0	0·9	100
1945	7·4	62·7	7·3	0·2	10·4	7·9	0·5	*	0·2	2·6	0·8	100
1946	7·1	58·9	6·3	0·1	15·7	7·1	0·5	*	0·2	3·4	0·7	100
1947	4·5	39·7	5·1	0·1	42·4	4·4	0·4	*	0·1	2·9	0·4	100
1948	4·9	39·6	5·4	0·1	42·1	4·2	0·3	*	*	2·7	0·7	100
1949	5·4	40·0	5·6	0·1	41·3	3·9	0·3	*	*	2·6	0·7	100

* Less than 0·05 per cent.

TABLE 42—HEALTH BENEFITS : EXPENDITURE, BY TYPE OF BENEFIT, 1ST APRIL, 1939, TO 31ST MARCH, 1949

Year Ended 31st March,	Medical	Hospital.	Maternity.	Pharma-ceutical.	Supple-mentary.	Total.
	£	£	£	£	£	£
1940 ..	..	772,886	283,813	..	..	1,056,699
1941 ..	..	1,257,688	518,997	..	..	1,776,685
1942 ..	205,673	1,372,405	549,850	279,698	27,962	2,435,588
1943 ..	1,016,032	1,539,282	505,219	563,247	97,399	3,721,179
1944 ..	1,179,331	2,133,389	513,939	762,198	137,823	4,726,680
1945 ..	1,287,023	2,266,688	530,733	980,237	170,032	5,234,713
1946 ..	1,427,309	2,173,460	600,209	1,133,366	229,971	5,564,315
1947 ..	1,760,574	1,986,288	672,989	1,439,686	352,043	6,211,580
1948 ..	2,167,825	1,949,489	800,030	1,558,350	545,793	7,021,487
1949 ..	2,306,881	1,997,375	916,120	1,793,159	861,913	7,875,448
Total ..	11,350,648	17,448,950	5,891,899	8,509,941	2,422,936	45,624,374

The cost of social security for the year ended 31st March, 1940, including cash and health benefits, was £(m.)10·4, representing 4·9 per cent. of the national income and 17 per cent. of the Government expenditure from principal accounts for that year. During the year ended 31st March, 1949, the cost of social security benefits was £(m.)42·3, representing 24·6 per cent. of the Government expenditure from the principal accounts and 10·1 per cent. of the national income. Details of the cost of social security, war pensions, and other pensions, together with their relation to the national income and to Government expenditure, are shown in the following table.

| Year Ended 31st March, | National Income. | Government Expenditure (Principal Accounts— viz., Consolidated Fund, War Expenses, and Social Security. | Payments from Social Security Fund. | | War Pensions. | Cash and Health Benefits, War and Other Pensions.* |
			Cash Benefits.	Cash and Health Benefits.		
Amount						
	£(m.)	£(m.)	£(m.)	£(m.)	£(m.)	£(m.)
1940	211·4	61·27	9·34	10·39	1·9	12·29
1941	231·9	89·47	10·41	12·18	1·9	14·07
1942	254·4	100·98	10·70	13·14	2·0	15·16
1943	293·7	205·33	11·71	15·43	2·3	17·73
1944	326·9	224·09	12·40	17·12	3·1	20·26
1945	330·0	199·19	13·53	18·77	3·7	22·49
1946	350·0	212·90	16·67	22·24	3·9	26·20
1947	364·9	167·21	29·91	36·12	4·5	40·62
1948	411·2	155·40	32·77	39·80	4·5	44·33
1949	419·0	172·23†	34·46	42·33	4·6	46·94
Percentage of Nationa Income						
1940	100	..	4·4	4·9	0·9	5·8
1941	100	..	4·5	5·3	0·8	6·1
1942	100	..	4·2	5·2	0·8	6·0
1943	100	..	4·1	5·3	0·8	6·0
1944	100	..	3·8	5·2	0·9	6·2
1945	100	..	4·1	5·7	1·1	6·8
1946	100	..	4·8	6·4	1·1	7·5
1947	100	..	8·2	9·9	1·2	11·1
1948	100	..	8·0	9·7	1·1	10·8
1949	100	..	8·2	10·1	1·1	11·2
Percentage of Government Expenditure						
1940	..	100	15·2	17·0	3·1	20·1
1941	..	100	11·6	13·6	2·1	15·7
1942	..	100	10·6	13·0	2·0	15·0
1943	..	100	5·7	7·5	1·1	8·6
1944	..	100	5·5	7·6	1·4	9·0
1945	..	100	6·8	9·4	1·9	11·3
1946	..	100	7·8	10·4	1·8	12·3
1947	..	100	17·9	21·6	2·7	24·3
1948	..	100	21·1	25·6	2·9	28·5
1949	..	100	20·0	24·6	2·7	27·3

* Excluding pensions paid on behalf of other Governments.   † Includes £(m.)20·58 payment to Reserve Bank for liability due to alteration in rate of exchange.

Sources—National income, Table 46, page 49, *Abstract of Statistics,* June–July, 1949.
Government expenditure, Table 49, page 48, *Abstract of Statistics,* April, 1949.

Year.	Value of Production (Production Years).	Value of Exports (Previous 31st December).	Expenditure on Civil Pensions (to 1939) and Social Security Cash Benefits (From 1st April, 1939), Year Ended 31st March.	Social Security Cash and Health Benefits Combined (From 1st April, 1939), Year Ended 31st March.	Mean Population (Including Maoris), Year Ended 31st March.
	£(m.)	£(m.)	£(m.)	£(m.)	Millions.
1901 ..	33·9	13·2	0·2	..	0·81
1911 ..	53·4	22·2	0·4	..	1·05
1921 ..	99·5	46·4	1·1	..	1·25
1931 ..	97·2	44·9	1·6	..	1·50
1939 ..	136·1	58·4	5·0	..	1·61
1940 ..	144·8	58·0	9·3	10·4	1·63
1946 ..	201·0	81·5	16·7	22·2	1·71
1947 ..	230·9	101·3	29·9	36·1	1·77
1948 ..	265·0	129·4	32·8	39·8	1·81
1949 ..	*	147·8	34·5	42·3	1·85

* Not available.

Sources—Value of Production : 1901–31, page 729, 1946 Year-Book ; 1939–48,
Table 15, page 16, *Monthly Abstract of Statistics*, June-July, 1949.
Value of Exports : 1901–47, page 784, 1946 Year-Book ; 1948–49,
page 27, *Monthly Abstract of Statistics*, March, 1949.
Mean Population : 1901–46, page 778, 1946 Year-Book ; 1947–49,
Monthly Abstract of Statistics, March, 1948, and March, 1949.

The above table discloses that between 1940 and 1948 production increased from £(m.)144·8 to £(m.)265 (an increase of 83 per cent.), and that over the same period social security expenditure increased by 283 per cent. from £(m.)10·4 to £(m.)39·8. Expenditure on cash benefits only for the same period increased by 253 per cent.

The table also discloses that while exports increased almost threefold between 1940 and 1949 expenditure on social security benefits increased fourfold. This is consistent with the position disclosed in Table 43 on page 119, showing the increasing proportion of the national income and Government expenditure being devoted to social security.

120

Prior to the social security scheme the only pensions paid irrespective of income and property were miners' and Maori War pensions. Superannuation benefits without means test were introduced from 1st April, 1940, but these accounted for only a small part of the annual expenditure on social security. Health benefits have never been subject to a means test, and since the 1st April, 1946, family benefits have been paid irrespective of financial circumstances. The proportion of expenditure on cash benefits without means test to total expenditure on cash benefits increased from 1 per cent. in 1940 to 47 per cent. in 1949. The corresponding proportions for expenditure on cash plus health benefits were 11 per cent. in 1940 and 57 per cent. in 1949.

TABLE 45—SOCIAL SECURITY EXPENDITURE: PROPORTION WITH AND WITHOUT A MEANS TEST, 1940–49

Year Ended 31st March,	Cash Benefits.		Cash Plus Health Benefits.	
	Without Means Test.	Subject to Means Test.	Without Means Test.	Subject to Means Test.
Amount				
	£	£	£	£
1940 ..	93,756	9,243,487	1,150,455	9,243,487
1941 ..	329,736	10,075,724	2,106,421	10,075,724
1942 ..	529,384	10,171,853	2,964,972	10,171,853
1943 ..	683,414	11,028,051	4,404,593	11,028,051
1944 ..	855,529	11,542,244	5,582,209	11,542,244
1945 ..	1,069,480	12,463,983	6,304,193	12,463,983
1946 ..	1,273,968	15,399,722	6,838,283	15,399,722
1947 ..	14,135,987	15,773,467	20,347,567	15,773,467
1948 ..	15,502,622	17,271,703	22,524,109	17,271,703
1949 ..	16,205,950	18,249,808	24,081,398	18,249,808
Percentage Distribution				
1940 ..	1·0	99·0	11·1	88·9
1941 ..	3·2	96·8	17·3	82·7
1942 ..	4·9	95·1	22·6	77·4
1943 ..	5·8	94·2	28·5	71·5
1944 ..	6·9	93·1	32·6	67·4
1945 ..	7·9	92·1	33·6	66·4
1946 ..	7·6	92·4	30·8	69·2
1947 ..	47·3	52·7	56·3	43·7
1948 ..	47·3	52·7	56·6	43·4
1949 ..	47·0	53·0	56·9	43·1

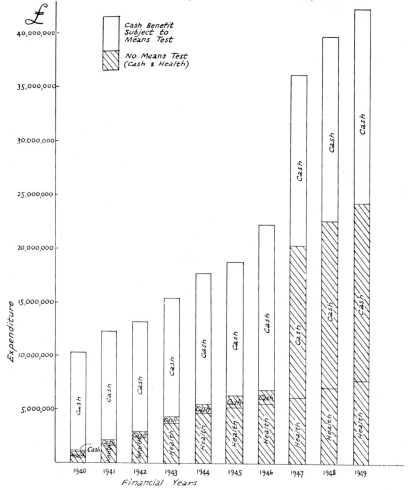

RELATION OF CASH BENEFITS TO COST OF LIVING

In recent years the rates of the various benefits have been co-ordinated, and all benefits for adults are now paid at the same basic rate of £130 a year. However, a special allowance paid to widows with children has the effect of increasing their benefits to £208.

The rates of cash benefits are fixed by statute, and there is no provision in the legislation or regulations for a review and revaluation on an actuarial basis at periodic intervals to relate the cash value of benefits to changes in the cost of living. The practical effect of any increase in the cost of living is that public opinion, often expressed through public organizations, actuates parliamentary reconsideration of what is regarded as a reasonable standard of comfort. When the scheme was framed it was not the intention of the Government that benefit rates should remain constant in relation to the varying cost of living, but, as the development and resources of the country permitted, a higher standard of living for people of smaller means should be attained and the health services extended.

The percentage increase in the rates of wages, prices, and social security cash benefits since December, 1939, are shown in the following table :—

TABLE 46—COMPARISON OF INCREASES IN SOCIAL SECURITY BENEFITS AND COST OF LIVING : DECEMBER, 1939, TO DECEMBER, 1949

Retail Price Index and Nominal Wage Rate Index—Base : 1926-30 (= 1000)

31st December.	Retail Prices, All Groups.		Nominal Wage-rate, Adult Males.		Age, Invalids', and Miners' Benefits.		Widows' Benefits: Widows With Children.		Widows' Benefits: Widows Without Children.		Unemployment and Sickness Benefits.	
	Index No.	Percentage Increase Since 1939.	Index No.*	Percentage Increase Since 1939.	Rate.	Percentage Increase Since 1939.	Rate.	Percentage Increase Since 1939.	Rate.	Percentage Increase Since 1939.	Rate.	Percentage Increase Since 1939.
					£		£		£		£	
1939	990	..	1,100	..	78	..	65	..	52	..	52	..
1940	1,035	5	1,130	3	78	..	65	..	52	..	52	..
1941	1,073	8	1,170	6	78	..	65	..	52	..	52	..
1942	1,109	12	1,222	11	81·9	5	68·25	5	54·6	5	52	..
1943	1,131†	14	1,261	15	84·5	8	78	20	65	25	52	..
1944	1,132†	14	1,274	16	84·5	8	78	20	65	25	52	..
1945	1,134†	14	1,381	26	104	33	156	140	78	50	104	100
1946	1,138†	15	1,434	30	104	33	169	160	104	100	104	100
1947	1,173†	18	1,489	35	117	50	182	180	117	125	117	125
1948	1,248	26	1,586	44	117	50	182	180	117	125	117	125
1949	..	..	..	..	130	67	208	220	130	150	130	150

* NOTE.—Wage-rates used in the compilation of index numbers (in this column) are, with certain exceptions, minimum rates specified in awards of the Court of Arbitration.
† Not strictly comparable with previous figures; obtained by linking movement in wartime price index to December, 1942, on 1926-30 base.

Sources—Retail price index and footnote relating thereto : Table 50, "Summary of Price Index Numbers," *Monthly Abstract of Statistics,* March, 1949.

Wage-rate, adult male workers, and footnote relating thereto : Table 56, "Weekly Money Wage Rates—Adult Male Workers," *Monthly Abstract of Statistics,* March, 1949.

Index numbers are indicative merely of the relative movements in each column, not of the actual relative levels in the different columns.

TABLE 47—CIVIL PENSIONS: EXPENDITURE BY TYPE OF PENSION, 1899 TO 1939

	Old Age. £	Widows. £	Maori War. £	Miners. £	Epidemic. £	Blind and Invalids. £	Family. £	Total Expenditure. £	Total Number Receiving Pension Each Year.	Mean Population (Including Maoris). Year Ended 31st March.	Expenditure Per Head. £ s. d.
1899	3,124	..	..	..	..	..	..	3,124	7,443	779,049	..
1900	157,342	..	..	..	..	..	..	157,342	11,285	792,501	0 3 11
1901	197,292	..	..	..	..	..	..	197,292	12,406	808,811	
1902	207,468	..	..	..	..	..	..	207,468	12,776	824,501	
1903	210,140	..	..	..	..	..	..	210,140	12,481	845,566	0 4 9
1904	203,164	..	..	..	..	..	..	203,164	11,926	870,047	
1905	195,475	..	..	..	..	..	..	195,475	11,770	895,108	
1906	254,367	..	..	..	..	..	..	254,367	12,582	920,615	
1907	314,184	..	..	..	..	..	..	314,184	13,257	949,650	0 6 6
1908	325,199	..	..	..	..	..	..	325,199	13,569	973,459	
1909	336,760	..	..	..	..	..	..	336,760	14,396	1,000,692	
1910	362,496	..	..	..	..	..	..	362,496	15,320	1,025,638	
1911	383,393	..	..	..	..	..	..	383,393	16,020	1,045,706	
1912	406,256	1,963	..	..	..	..	..	408,219	17,437	1,069,828	0 8 2
1913	415,761	22,114	3,681	..	..	..	..	441,556	18,390	1,096,467	
1914	416,776	27,077	29,447	..	..	..	..	473,300	20,830	1,125,628	
1915	460,814	31,619	47,616	..	..	..	..	540,049	22,528	1,145,027	
1916	479,339	36,357	48,273	1,509	..	..	..	565,478	23,137	1,150,318	
1917	480,230	38,016	45,674	8,066	..	..	..	571,986	23,191	1,149,225	0 12 9
1918	643,177	57,952	50,734	13,275	..	..	..	765,138	23,575	1,152,748	
1919	743,063	80,773	50,488	13,276	..	..	..	887,600	24,363	1,166,482	
1920	732,968	136,815	45,085	16,652	..	..	..	931,520	24,791	1,207,660	
1921	731,343	187,430	40,213	26,972	72,456	..	..	1,058,414	25,392	1,252,206	0 16 5
1922	743,620	186,457	37,737	31,212	65,486	..	..	1,064,512	25,763	1,283,546	
1923	755,324	188,021	34,004	33,447	52,371	..	..	1,063,167	26,374	1,311,382	
1924	767,805	202,818	30,350	36,084	32,702	..	..	1,069,759	26,620	1,334,029	
1925	806,953	236,378	26,848	38,506	22,881	1,036	..	1,132,602	27,265	1,359,995	

Year													£	s.	d.
1926	..	903,577	286,450	23,067	40,239	14,522	8,053	..	1,275,908	28,331	1,392,073				
1927	..	982,356	301,861	19,458	41,940	10,951	10,338	..	1,366,904	29,254	1,420,838		0	19	11
1928	..	1,010,575	304,066	16,390	45,096	8,747	12,264	37,652	1,434,790	33,476	1,443,551				
1929	..	1,060,760	313,964	13,653	48,074	7,988	13,334	54,791	1,512,564	35,694	1,460,363				
1930	..	1,107,993	323,419	11,498	51,684	7,302	14,737	61,008	1,577,641	36,609	1,478,027				
1931	..	1,158,788	325,998	9,102	58,441	6,322	15,796	63,608	1,638,055	39,692	1,498,416		1	1	10
1932	..	1,277,107	340,162	7,582	69,785	5,580	16,710	90,100	1,807,026	45,963	1,517,940		1	3	10
1933	..	1,271,157	311,317	5,831	62,563	4,197	18,065	122,810	1,795,940	51,281	1,530,119		1	3	5
1934	..	1,350,982	302,020	4,522	56,810	3,290	19,306	146,766	1,883,696	55,599	1,542,651		1	4	5
1935	..	1,519,889	296,565	3,607	58,740	1,983	21,227	152,818	2,054,829	58,323	1,554,297		1	6	5
1936	..	1,718,601	311,864	2,577	67,834	907	22,991	149,043	2,273,817	60,780	1,565,263		1	9	0
1937	..	2,413,103	412,280	1,972	83,253	253	284,760	130,730	3,326,351	76,972	1,578,757		2	2	1
1938	..	3,235,057	471,287	1,806	88,167	14	632,829	106,402	4,535,562	83,508	1,594,275		2	16	10
1939	..	3,577,129	487,216	1,338	87,094		750,748	84,436	4,987,961	91,067	1,611,362		3	1	11
						156,149*			156,149*						
Total	..	34,320,907	6,222,169	612,553	1,078,719	474,101	1,842,194	1,200,164	45,750,807	..	..				

* Expenditure on epidemic allowances by Health Department prior to 1st April, 1920.

125

Table 46 discloses that between 1940 and 1944 increases in social security benefits lagged behind prices and wages so that at that time people on benefit were worse off than in December, 1939. However, by December, 1945, the percentage increase in benefits since 1939 (33 per cent.) was greater than the corresponding increase in wages (26 per cent.) or prices (14 per cent.), so that beneficiaries were in a more favourable position than in 1939. By the end of 1948 the basic rate of cash benefits had increased by 50 per cent., the adult male wage rate only 44 per cent., and the retail price index by 26 per cent.

While, because of post-war changes, the retail price index may be unsuitable as a measuring-rod of the cost of living, the nominal wage-rate index for males affords a reasonable basis for comparing increases since 1939. However, it should be borne in mind that the wage-rate index is based on the minimum rates specified in awards of the Court of Arbitration and takes no account of wages above the minimum award rate.

PART II — HEALTH BENEFITS

CHAPTER XIII — INTRODUCTION TO PART II

PRIOR to the passing of the Social Security Act, 1938, New Zealand had no nation-wide plan for prepaid medical or hospital services. It is true that voluntary groups such as friendly societies levied on their members for this purpose, and by arrangement with doctors and with hospitals were able to offer free or partially-free medical and hospital treatment. Only a relatively small proportion of the population had taken up the friendly-society movement. For the rest each made his own arrangements and met his own costs for medical and hospital treatment as and when the need arose. Doctors engaged in individual practice and sought their fees entirely from their patients. Public hospitals provided hospital services and charged the patients at rates varying with the type of institution and with the ability of the patient to pay. Private hospitals, as at present, gave only hospital maintenance and nursing care. For the completely indigent and those in straitened circumstances private doctors afforded a measure of free treatment, and Hospital Boards, in the exercise of their charitable functions under the Hospitals and Charitable Institutions Act, gave hospital treatment and other forms of relief, either free or at a reduced charge, in keeping with the patient's financial circumstances. Such free treatment or partially-free treatment at the hands of either doctor or hospital was not obtained as of right : the patient was dependent upon the charitable disposition of doctor or hospital and upon his ability to demonstrate by means test that he was unable to meet the usual fees.

Public hospitals, with their superior equipment, diagnostic and other facilities, were regarded, and quite erroneously, as places for the treatment for the poorer classes of patient. The well-to-do preferred to receive their medical attention in the licensed private hospital.

Over twenty years ago the possibility of some form of national health insurance on a contributory basis was receiving the attention of interested organizations in New Zealand.

The General Conference of the Hospital Boards in November, 1924, resolved :—

" That the executive be urged to inquire as to the practicability and (if advisable to promote) a scheme for free hospital treatment of wage earners and dependants, the cost of same to be met by a compulsory levy on wages payable through employers direct to the Hospital Board of the district concerned."

Some preliminary work was done, and the proposal was advanced a stage further in 1933 when a sub-committee of representatives of the British Medical Association and the Hospital Boards Association was appointed to draw up a report. The Committee enlisted the assistance of the Department of Health and made a careful examination of information available on the British National Health Insurance Scheme which had been in operation since 1911. The sub-committee's report envisaged a scheme limited as to classes of persons becoming contributors in order to confer the benefits to those more generally in need of them.

A universal scheme at that stage was not contemplated.

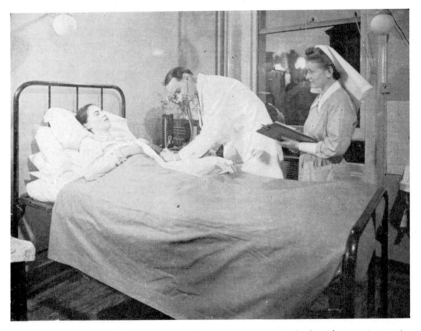

The health services ensure that there is no economic barrier to prevent every person from obtaining the best of medical care

Recognition of medical and hospital care as a social service available to all without distinction as to financial position appears in the manifesto of the Labour Party at the 1934 election. This promised a national health service which would—

Give to every citizen the right during ill-health to call in his own medical practitioner, to consult and receive the services of specialists where required, and, by the re-arrangement of our hospital system, to make available all other services that are necessary for the restoration and maintenance of health. The Labour Government will provide the necessary laboratory facilities to maintain the efficiency of the services, together with adequate payment to practitioners and others who carry out the work. The service will be available for every family.

To state this policy was one thing ; to implement it another. Its successful administration demanded careful planning, and this only after exhaustive investigation. As a first step a Committee of Labour Members of Parliament under the chairmanship of Dr. McMillan was set up, which brought down recommendations for a universal national health service, commencing with a family doctor service and maternity and hospital services, and later expanded to include specialist, nursing, and other fields.

In April, 1938, following the McMillan Committee's report, a Select Committee of the House, known as the National Health and Super-annuation Committee, was set up. Included in its membership were Mr. Savage, Mr. Nash, and Mr. Nordmeyer (as Chairman). To this Committee the Prime Minister submitted the Government's social security proposals, which read as follows :—

1. The Government proposes to provide—
(a) A universal general practitioner service free to all members of the community requiring medical attention.
(b) Free hospital or sanatorium treatment for all.
(c) Free mental hospital care and treatment for the mentally afflicted.
(d) Free medicines.
(e) Free maternity treatment, including the cost of maintenance in a maternity home.

2. The Government further proposes that these services should be supplemented when organization and finances are available, by the following additional services—
(a) Anæsthetic.
(b) Laboratory and radiology.
(c) Specialist and consultants.
(d) Massage and physiotherapy.
(e) Transport service to and from hospital.
(f) Dental benefit.
(g) Optical benefit.

3. It is also proposed to institute a free home nursing and domestic help service when the necessary staff has been trained to make such a proposal practicable.

4. Complementary to the foregoing proposals, the Government contemplates an extended educational compaign for the promotion of health and the prevention of disease.

Evidence was also taken from representatives of the British Medical Association.

The Government's proposals were adopted by the Committee, and steps were then taken to draft the relative provisions for health services which now appear in Part III of the Social Security Act, 1938.

Two essential features of the health benefits provided thereunder stand out—

(1) There is universal coverage of the total resident population regardless of economic status.
(2) The scheme is non-contributory, benefits being available to all as a matter of right regardless of the amount if any of taxes paid by the recipient of benefit.

At the 1938 elections the Labour manifesto declared—

The Social Security legislation now on the statute-book will ensure to every member of the community full and adequate hospital, santoria, medical, pharmaceutical, maternity, and other health services. Provision has been made for vigorous measures aimed at the prevention of disease.

On the Government's return to office a commencement was made with the setting-up of the necessary administrative machinery in the Health Department, and it was not until April, 1939, that the first benefit—free treatment in State mental hospitals—was brought into operation.

It is not proposed to traverse here in detail the negotiations and counter-negotiations which took place with the British Medical Association and others before the several succeeding benefits were launched. These will be treated with in the order of their introduction.

Whatever defects there may be in the Government's national health programme, and whatever gaps in its legislation to this end, the Social Security Act, 1938, has fully justified its place in the legislation of this country. Even though the aims of the legislation have not been achieved in full there can be no doubt that over the last ten years the people of New Zealand have benefited considerably. There is now no economic barrier operating against the reception of good medical care ; free radiological and laboratory services are available to assist the general practitioner in the diagnosis and treatment of his patients ; pharmaceutical services, hospital services, massage, and even a range of artificial aids are now available.

CHAPTER XIV — MATERNITY BENEFITS

THE first and perhaps the most popular benefit to be introduced was the maternity benefit, which came into operation in 1939. There are possibly few financial contingencies which bear more heavily on the young family man than the medical and hospital costs associated with an addition to the family. It is true that there is a time during which monetary provision may be made, but the doctor's bill and the hospital bill are not the only financial commitments in an event of this nature. The desirability of some form of monetary assistance in maternity cases has long been recognized. Many countries have adopted a " bonus " system, and in New Zealand prior to social security a payment of £6 on the birth of a child could be obtained from the National Provident Fund by contributors to the Fund, and by members of friendly societies. New Zealand has, however, taken the lead in an attempt to provide for the full, or substantially the full, cost of every woman's confinement.

Disregarding free treatment in State mental hospitals, operative from 1st April, 1939, the maternity benefit introduced the following month was the first new health benefit.

In April, 1939, contracts for maternity services were offered to doctors, to the licensees of private maternity hospitals, and to obstetric nurses who were in practice on their own account. However, the organized medical profession declined to enter into any contract whatever with the Government, and acceptances were received from only two medical men. Private hospitals and obstetric nurses, however, responded freely, and in a short time practically all private hospital licensees and obstetric nurses were under contract.

The attitude of medical men led to further negotiations with the British Medical Association, and in turn to the passing of the Social Security Amendment Act, 1939. This legislation replaced the proposed individual contracts between doctors and the State and introduced a statutory contract binding all doctors undertaking maternity practice. The provisions of this amendment which is still in operation are briefly :—

(1) Medical services in relation to maternity benefits were defined in an agreement between the Minister and the British Medical Association, and the appropriate fees for such services were set therein.

129

(2) Every doctor undertaking maternity work in the course of his practice is bound by this agreement and is required to collect the appropriate fees from the Social Security Fund.

(3) The fees payable from the Fund must be accepted by the doctor in full satisfaction unless he has been recognized as an obstetric specialist under the special provisions of the Act, or unless he notifies the Minister that he will not provide maternity services under the Act. Only five doctors declined service.

The effect of this arrangement has been to preserve the customary contractual relationship between the doctor and the patient. The doctor has no direct obligations to the State other than to provide proof of services signed by the patient and to collect his fees from the Social Security Fund.

The range of services offered to women under maternity benefits is—

(1) Medical services from the doctor of the patients' own choice. These services include all necessary attention during the ante-natal period, attendance at confinement, attention during the lying-in period, and one post-natal consultation following the conclusion of the lying-in period.

(2) Maternity hospital services in a public hospital or in a licensed private maternity hospital for the day of birth and for up to 14 days thereafter ; or

(3) In lieu of hospital services, attendance in the patient's own home by an obstetric nurse for the day or days of labour and up to fourteen days thereafter.

Cost of These Services

It was the intention of the Government that the services referred to above would be free or substantially free to the patient.

Medical Services

It has already been stated that doctors must accept the fees payable from the Fund in full satisfaction of their charges. The only two exceptions are the doctor who contracts out of the provisions of the Act and the obstetric specialist. The former must notify the Minister of Health, who may publish in whatever form he thinks fit the names of such doctors. Patients engaging these doctors then become responsible for the payment of the doctors' fees and have no recourse on the Fund. The second class, the obstetric specialists, are permitted to make a charge to patients over and above the fees collected from the Fund. Such specialists must obtain recognition from the Minister, and this is given only to those medical men possessing special qualifications, skill, and experience in obstetrics. In effect, then, every woman can obtain competent medical services during her pregnancy and confinement without cost to herself. The basic fee payable from the Fund was set in 1939 at £5 5s. but was increased in 1946 to £6 6s. for full services, including at least five ante-natal attendances.

Hospital Services

These are obtainable from two sources—public maternity hospitals conducted by Hospital Boards and licensed private maternity hospitals. Treatment in public hospital institutions is entirely free to the patient.

In licensed private hospitals such services are partially free. All licensees of private maternity hospitals are required to enter into contracts with the Minister of Health, and in such contract to set out the gross daily or weekly fee chargeable to the patient and to undertake to apply maternity benefit payments from the Social Security Fund in reduction of such charges.

When contracts were first made in 1939 the charges of most private hospitals ranged from £4 4s. to £6 6s. per week. The maternity benefit payable, £2 5s. for the day or days of labour, plus 12s 6d. per day for each of up to fourteen days succeeding the day of birth (maximum payment, £11), provided most private-hospital patients with substantially free hospital treatment. A great many hospitals had two or three different classes of accommodation, some of which could be obtained free and some at a slight charge over and above the social security payment. Over the last ten years, however, substantial changes have taken place. Proprietors of private hospitals have been unable to escape the impact of increased costs in both labour and goods, and their maintenance costs, together with their charges, have shown a steady advance. Private-hospital fees, in common with other charges for services, are controlled by the Control of Prices Act, and licensees to make any increase in their fees must first obtain the authority of the Price Tribunal and the concurrence of the Minister of Health. Notwithstanding the strictest scrutiny of such hospital expenses, fees have had to be increased to meet the ever mounting costs.

Many private hospitals faced with difficulties in obtaining and keeping staff, higher operating costs, and the weight of accumulated maintenance work held over during the war period have closed down, their place being largely taken by new maternity hospitals or annexes constructed or opened by Hospital Boards. In other places private hospitals are carrying on with a subsidy from the local Hospital Board.

Reference to the following maternity benefit statistics shows clearly the movement between public and private maternity hospitals.

In 1939–40, the first complete year of benefits, payments from the Fund were (to the nearest £1,000)—

1939–40

	£
Payments to public hospitals	107,000
Payments to private hospitals	216,000

This indicates that out of every three hospitalized maternity cases one was confined in a public hospital and two were confined in private hospitals—*i.e.*, the proportion in favour of the private maternity home was 2 to 1.

1947–48 presents an entirely different picture—

	£
Payments to public hospitals	301,000
Payments to private hospitals	215,000

Out of every five confinements three now take place in public hospitals and two in private maternity homes.

The cost to the patient is, or course, not the only factor involved. The birth-rate has risen from 32,000 in 1946 to 44,000 in 1948. Increased accommodation to meet these additional maternity cases has been provided in public hospitals, the number of private maternity beds over the period having shown a decline.

Under this gradual change-over the number of women obtaining entirely free maternity hospital treatment is increasing each year.

To meet the increasing costs both in public and private hospitals the benefit was raised in 1947 from a maximum of £11 to a maximum of £15—*i.e.*, £1 for the day of birth and for each of the fourteen succeeding days. This, however, has not bridged the gap between the free treatment offered by public hospitals and the additional fee over and above benefit still collected by private maternity hospitals.

OBSTETRIC NURSING SERVICES

The services of these nurses rendered in the patient's own home are entirely free to the mother. They may be given either on a full-time domiciliary basis or on a visiting basis. In the former the nurse resides with the patient for the confinement and lying-in period ; in the latter daily visits only are paid to the patient once the confinement is over. Some obstetric nurses receive patients into their own homes, and, in fact, conduct a one-bed maternity hospital, which does not require to be licensed. Under these arrangements the nurse provides her services free, but collects from the patient a sum to cover the cost of maintaining the mother and child during the lying-in period. This is, however, a matter entirely outside the nurse's contract and is subject to private arrangement between nurse and patient.

Fees payable from the Fund to obstetric nurses have recently been increased and are shown hereunder :—

	1939.	1948.
For day or days of labour—		
Midwife acting without doctor	£2	£2
Midwife or maternity nurse acting with doctor	£1	£1
For days succeeding labour, up to and including fourteenth day—		
Visiting	5s. per day	7s. 6d. per day.
Domiciliary (full-time)	13s. per day	18s. per day.

Payments for obstetric nursing services are steadily declining, and there are several factors which contribute to this, chief of which are—

(1) Public and private hospitals can now absorb all trained maternity nursing staff available at rates of salary comparable with what an obstetric nurse can earn in private practice.

(2) Doctors to-day prefer to confine their patients under proper hospital conditions, and the patients themselves usually prefer this.

(3) Economic and social conditions now operate against the home confinement. More and more families live in flats or in accommodation where there is no room for an obstetric nurse to live in.

ST. HELENS HOSPITALS

Accommodation is also available free in St. Helens hospitals conducted by the Department of Health. These are principally training schools for the training of midwives and maternity nurses, and the confinements, provided they are normal, are carried out by midwives. They operate as " closed " hospitals—that is to say, the patient who enters St. Helens for confinement cannot have the services of her own doctor during the confinement or lying-in period. Nevertheless, these institutions continue to be popular with some mothers, and some 2,500 cases per annum are now confined in St. Helens.

In the two principal St. Helens hospitals at Auckland and Wellington full-time ante-natal clinics are conducted, and mothers can attend these from the first stages of pregnancy until they enter hospital for confinement.

EFFECT OF MATERNITY BENEFITS

It is perhaps still too early to assess the social consequences of maternity benefits. Whether births have increased as the result of this form of assistance must remain a matter of speculation. The effect of the war on maternity statistics during the years 1940 to 1947 has made this period difficult to evaluate, and the introduction of universal family benefits in 1946 further clouds the issue.

It can, however, in truth be said that over the past ten years maternity benefits have made medical care available to all maternity cases regardless of the ability of parents to pay and have removed most of the financial burden of childbirth from the family to the community.

CHAPTER XV — HOSPITAL BENEFITS

HOSPITAL IN-PATIENTS

CLOSELY following the introduction of maternity benefits in May, 1939, came hospital benefits for in-patients in July, 1939. These benefits covered all in-patient treatment, other than the hospitalization of maternity cases during the maternity-benefit period, in public hospitals and in licensed private hospitals. In form these benefits consist of payments from the Social Security Fund for the period of stay in hospital. These payments were calculated in 1939 at 6s. per day, but were increased in April, 1943, to 9s. per day.

Hospital benefits do not in themselves confer any right to receive hospital treatment. Patients must still obtain admission through their own medical attendant, and priority of admission is entirely in the hands of the hospital authorities as in the past. What the benefits do provide in effect is—

(a) That treatment received in a public hospital is now free of charge to the patient.

(b) That in respect of treatment received in a licensed private hospital payment from the Fund will be accepted by the licensee in partial satisfaction of the usual hospital fees.

The rate payable from the Fund is the same for both public and private hospitals—i.e., 9s. per day. It is not to be supposed, of course, that 9s. per day meets the full cost of a patient's treatment in a public hospital; it represented in 1939 that portion of the cost which was being recovered from the patient, approximately one-third. The pattern of public hospital finance has therefore remained undisturbed. A portion of the cost of maintenance is borne by local rates, a portion by subsidy from the Consolidated Fund, and the remainder, representing that previously received from patients, is now borne by the Social Security Fund. Free treatment in public hospitals is not then given at the cost of the Social Security Fund; the balance of the cost over 9s. per day is borne by general taxation and local rates. In private hospital treatment there is no general taxation or local rating upon which the hospital can draw, and the balance of the cost of treatment over 9s. per day must be borne by the patient.

Critics of the New Zealand social security scheme have stated that hospital benefits have been a factor in filling hospitals to capacity and have necessitated their extension. It has also been said that the availability of hospital benefits has caused a large number of chronic and minor cases to fill hospital beds leaving a minimum of space available for cases in great need of hospitalization.

It is impossible, of course, entirely to refute these charges ; free service of any kind will always tend to create an artificial demand, which is exceedingly difficult to regulate. Due weight must, however, be given to other contributory factors which operate independently of hospital benefits :—

(a) Social and economic conditions tend to-day towards greater hospitalization. A large section of the city population lives in rooms or flats ; frequently husband, wife, and other members of the family are all wage-earners. There are not now the same facilities for the domiciliary treatment of the sick as existed twenty or even ten years ago.

(b) Modern treatment of disease tends more to-day towards hospitalization. Up-to-date diagnostic aids are obtainable only in well-equipped hospitals. New forms of medication call for administration under continuous skilled observation and care which cannot be provided other than in a hospital.

(c) Increased hospitalization is found also in countries where hospital benefits are not in operation.

It is probably these factors which have brought about the increased use of hospitals rather than the introduction of hospital benefits. As has already been said, these benefits give no right of admission to hospital. The patient must still satisfy the hospital authorities that admission is necessary, and, in these days of bed shortage, that the condition is urgent in relation to that of other patients seeking admission to hospital. Once admitted, too, the duration of the patient's stay is a matter for the hospital authority, and there should be no reason to keep cases in hosptial once they are fit for discharge. At the present time any serious abuse of hospital benefits is limited by the shortage of hospital beds. Over the past two or three years the number of available beds has in fact declined. This has been due largely to difficulties in obtaining staff.

The following table shows to the nearest £1,000 the trend of hospital benefits over the past decade :—

TABLE 48—HOSPITAL BENEFITS : EXPENDITURE OF IN-PATIENT TREATMENT IN PUBLIC AND PRIVATE HOSPITALS, 1939–40 TO 1948–49

Year Ended 31st March,	Expenditure.	
	Public Hospitals.	Private Hospitals.
	£	£
1940 (ten months) ..	514,000	83,000
1941	893,000	142,000
1942	954,000	147,000
1943	1,020,000	192,000
1944	1,564,000	239,000
1945	1,689,000	259,000
1946	1,768,000	265,000
1947	1,593,000	252,000
1948	1,536,000	253,000
1949	1,560,000	245,000

The first sharp increase occurs in 1943–44. This is due to the increase in the rate of benefit from 6s. to 9s. per day as from 1st April, 1943. Expenditure reaches its maximum in 1945–46, and in the following year shows an appreciable decline. This is evident both in public and in private hospitals, and is due to reduced bed states in both classes of hospitals.

The procedure governing the administration of hospital benefits is extremely simple. In the public hospital the patient or his representative completes nothing but the usual admission form. From the patient's register the hospital makes up its claim each month for benefits and renders these to the local office of the Department of Health. In the private hospital the procedure is very similar. The licensee lists the admissions, discharges, and patients remaining in for the monthly period, and submits a monthly claim to the Department. In respect of each patient on whose behalf benefits are claimed the licensee must also submit a certificate and declaration by the patient. These claims and patients' certificates are checked, and monthly payments are made by the Department to the licensee. These payments are applied in reduction of the patients' accounts.

In addition to public hospitals and licensed private hospitals benefits are available in certain approved institutions. These include principally the Karitane baby hospitals conducted by the Royal New Zealand Society for the Health of Women and Children, more commonly known as the Plunket Society. In these Karitane hospitals full benefits at the rate of 9s. per day are now payable in respect of both the baby and the mother where the latter is admitted upon the recommendation of a doctor in the interests of the baby. Benefits are also paid in a home for incurables operated under a charitable trust. All these approved institutions give treatment free of charge to the patient.

OUT-PATIENTS

Hospital Out-patients

While benefits for in-patient treatment in hospitals operated from July, 1939, it was not until 1st March, 1941, that benefits were extended to out-patient treatment at public hospitals. Much of the treatment afforded at out-patient departments is, of course, similar to that given in the surgery or in the patient's own home by a private medical practitioner. Out-patient benefits were therefore introduced coincidently with the Medical Benefits (Capitation Scheme) Regulations on 1st March, 1941.

Out-patient treatment for the purpose of benefits includes all medical, surgical, or other treatment afforded to the patient by the staff of the hospital or by any person acting by direction of the Board with the following exceptions :—

(a) Dental treatment.

(b) Supply of drugs, medicine, &c. (These are available under another benefit, the pharmaceutical benefit.)

(c) X-ray diagnostic services (already available as a separate benefit).

(d) Laboratory diagnostic services (now available as a separate benefit).

(e) Treatment afforded a patient in his own home or place of residence. This exclusion is already covered by domiciliary services under medical benefits, general medical services, and district nursing.

In addition to out-patient treatment at the hospital itself, power is given to the Minister of Health to include for the purpose of benefit treatment afforded elsewhere. These powers have already been invoked to enable Hospital Boards to make arrangements with surgeon specialists to carry out in a specially-equipped private hospital operations for cleft palate, hare-lip, and other forms of plastic surgery.

ARTIFICIAL AIDS

By an extension to the Social Security Hospital Benefits for Out-patients Regulations made in 1947 the provision of certain artificial aids has now been added to the services available as out-patient benefits.

Contact Lenses.—Persons with refractive errors which cannot be corrected by means of ordinary spectacle lenses may now obtain, through Hospital Boards, special contact lenses. The provision of this benefit has meant that patients with severe defects in vision, which in some cases would have led to complete blindness, have been able to obtain relief with the aid of these special lenses. Prior to the introduction of this benefit, contact lenses were not obtainable in New Zealand. The demand has, however, stimulated local industry, and all the lenses required can now be manufactured in this country.

Hearing-aids.—Under the regulations referred to hearing-aids are now obtainable. Persons who have a degree of deafness calling for a valve-type aid can now obtain one model free or, if they wish to purchase an imported variety, may obtain a subsidy towards its cost. Here again it is pleasing to be able to say that private enterprise in New Zealand has risen to the occasion and that the hearing-aids which are being distributed free by Hospital Boards are manufactured in the Dominion. This benefit has met a long-felt need, as aids have not in the past been freely available owing to the price in most cases being beyond the pocket of the majority of persons.

Hearing-aid clinics have been set up at the principal hospitals to administer this benefit, and the deaf and hard of hearing may obtain a thorough professional examination, an audiometric test, and skilled advice by the clinic staff as to the use of their aids.

Artificial Limbs.—Advantage has been taken of the organization set up for the manufacture and supply of artificial limbs for ex-servicemen patients to make provision for the needs of civilian amputees. Civilians, by application to the Hospital Board for the district in which they reside, can obtain the same facilities for fitting and supply as can war amputees. The supply includes artificial legs, arms, hands, and feet, and also temporary legs or pylons supplied for use before a permanent limb can be fitted. Limbs are supplied complete with the necessary " harness " or attachments, together with an initial supply of limb-socks where these are required. Eighty per cent. of the cost of limbs is borne by the Social Security Fund, but no contribution is made at present towards the cost of limb maintenance. Expensive remodelling or rebuilding of old limbs is also carried out at the cost of the Fund under these arrangements. Civilian amputees are at present entitled to only one limb by way of benefit, but it is hoped, as manufacturing resources increase, to provide two limbs for civilians as well as for war amputees.

All amputees are eligible for the benefit unless they have already received limbs as war amputees or are entitled to limbs under the provisions of the Workers' Compensation Act, 1947, which now places a liability upon the employer or his insurer in certain cases.

In procedure the operation of out-patient benefits has, as in the case of other benefits, been made as simple as possible. The patient merely applies to the hospital for the out-patient service required. Provided the requirements as regards eligibility are complied with, the patient receives the service free of charge. Hospitals claim on the Department quarterly in respect of expenditure on out patient benefits.

For general out-patient services—*i.e.*, medical, nursing, &c.—the Fund refunds 60 per cent of the ascertained costs incurred by the hospital in supplying these services. These costs include salaries and wages, materials, &c., and other direct expenditure which can be related to out-patient departments.

For both contact lenses and hearing aids the State bears the full cost of the aid supplied. Lenses cost approximately £40 per set, while the cost of a hearing-aid is about £13. For artificial limbs the Fund bears 80 per cent. of the cost of manufacture, the balance being payable by the patient or, in certain circumstances, by the Hospital Board itself.

The out-patient departments of public hospitals have developed considerably since the introduction of benefits, and a full range of general and specialist medical services is now available at most of the larger hospitals. More and more persons are taking advantage of these services.

The following table shows the expenditure from the Fund since 1941 :—

TABLE 49—HOSPITAL BENEFITS : EXPENDITURE ON OUT-PATIENT TREATMENT, 1941–42 TO 1948–49

Year Ended 31st March,			Expenditure.
			£
1942	..	.. ..	47,000
1943	..	.. ..	71,000
1944	..	.. ..	73,000
1945	..	.. ..	83,000
1946	..	.. ..	99,000
1947	..	.. ..	97,000
1948	..	.. ..	117,000
1949	..	.. ..	141,530

The sharp increase in 1947–48 marks the inclusion in these benefits of artificial aids, which were introduced on the following dates :—

Contact lenses as from 1st June, 1947.
Hearing-aids as from 1st November, 1947.
Artificial limbs as from 1st April, 1948.

These figures do not include x-ray diagnostic and laboratory diagnostic services, usually classed as out-patient services, but which are the subject of separate benefits. Expenditure on these benefits appears elsewhere.

CHAPTER XVI — MEDICAL BENEFITS

THE first endeavour to introduce benefits in respect of family doctor services was made in 1941. The Social Security Medical Benefits Regulations 1941 envisaged free medical services on the capitation system modelled on the system which has been in operation in Great Britain for many years under the National Health Insurance Scheme. The regulations offered doctors a capitation fee of 15s. per head per annum, together with a commuted payment for potential mileage calculated on the distance between the doctor's surgery or residence and the place of residence of the patient.

The medical services to be given free comprised all usual medical services except those calling for a degree of skill and experience not possessed by general medical practitioners as a class.

The system of operation of these benefits was a simple one. Application was made by the patient to the doctor. The doctor, if willing to accept the patient, signed the agreement card, which was then transmitted to the Department. Upon the current cards in hand for each doctor at each accounting period the Department calculated the half-monthly amount payable to the doctor and forwarded a cheque for this amount.

The response by doctors to these arrangements was disappointing. At no time did more than about 50 doctors agree to work the capitation system, and the largest number of patients on the combined capitation lists did not exceed 80,000. This was not altogether unexpected, as the profession had steadfastly condemned the capitation system as unsuitable except for lower-income groups as provided in the British National Health Insurance Scheme.

However, the Government was committed under the Social Security Act to provide medical services for all, and found it necessary to compromise on family doctor services on a fee-for-service basis. This was provided for in the Social Security Amendment Act of 1941, and on the 1st November, 1941, general medical services were introduced. Medical services could be provided under one or all of three systems:—

THE REFUND SYSTEM

This involved the payment of the doctor's account (usually at the rate of 10s. 6d. per visit) in full. On payment of the account and on production of the doctor's receipt giving the required details the patient could, on application to the Department of Health, obtain a refund at the statutory rate of 7s. 6d. per visit or consultation. A higher refund of 12s. 6d. was provided for night or Sunday calls where the doctor charged a correspondingly higher fee not less than 12s. 6d. Mileage is also refundable at the rate of 1s. 3d. per mile each way.

THE DIRECT CLAIM SYSTEM

Under this system the doctor made no charge on the patient. The latter merely signed the prescription form which enabled the doctor to collect the statutory amount of 7s. 6d. (or 12s. 6d. for night or Sunday calls) from the Fund upon lodging his claims with the Department of Health. Mileage is also claimed direct at 1s. 3d. per mile each way.

THE TOKEN SYSTEM

This system, though not specifically provided for, was allowable under the provisions of the Act. Instead of accepting the statutory fee of 7s. 6d. in full satisfaction of his charges he continued to charge the customary fee of 10s. 6d. Of this he collected 7s. 6d. from the Fund upon the patient's signature under the direct claim arrangements and in addition collected the balance of 3s. from the patient personally. This additional levy of 3s. became known as a " token " payment.

At the outset a substantial majority of the profession adhered to the refund system as being the one which caused the least interference with the normal conduct of medical practice. They claimed, too, that under this method the patient retained some responsibility for his own treatment and obtained a return for his social security payments without any temptation to make unnecessary calls on the doctor's time or upon the Fund. From the administrative point of view this system is cumbersome and costly. The cost of dealing with individual applications for the refund of small amounts is disproportionately high, and a large staff is required for the checking and payment of claims by postal warrants through the various post-offices.

Since the close of the war, however, there has been a gradual but steady swing towards the direct-claim system, or to the direct-claim plus token payment. Young medical men returning from war service, new graduates, and medical men from abroad setting up in New Zealand found that under the " free doctor " or direct-claim system it was comparatively easy to build up a substantial practice in a comparatively short time. Other medical men under pressure of work have apparently concluded that the sending out and collection of patients' accounts, with its attendant book-keeping and writing of receipts, is not worth while and have adopted either the direct-claim or the token system. At the present time the methods are fairly evenly divided, 34 per cent. favouring the refund and 66 per cent. the direct-claim or token system.

As may be supposed, the capitation system is not attractive side by side with the fee-for-service system, and the number of capitation patients have steadily declined as the original fifty capitation doctors (now eighteen only) have changed over either wholly or partly to general medical services. Payments under capitation have declined from £115,000 in 1941–42 to £23,000 in 1947–48.

The costs of general medical services have mounted steadily over the years. The following table, omitting payments for mileage, shows the costs to the nearest £1,000 :—

TABLE 50—MEDICAL BENEFITS : EXPENDITURE ON GENERAL MEDICAL SERVICES, 1941–42 TO 1948–49

Year Ended 31st March,	Expenditure.
	£
1942 (five months only) ..	70,000
1943	831,000
1944	1,026,000
1945	1,161,000
1946	1,291,000
1947	1,601,000
1948	1,994,000
1949	2,112,000

The charges for general practitioner services have remained practically the same over the period, nor has there been any substantial increase in the Dominion population. The increase in payments from approximately £1,000,000 in 1943–44, at which stage general medical services had been in complete operation for over two years, to approximately £2,000,000, or double the amount in 1947–48, gives food for very serious thought. It is true that medical personnel has increased, the numbers in practice in 1943–44 and 1947–48 being 1,182 and 1,750 respectively. It is equally true, however, that at the present time the public are demanding or willingly accepting an alarming amount of medical service.

There can be no doubt, of course, that the people of New Zealand have benefited considerably as the result of the introduction of general medical services ; there is now no economic barrier operating against the reception of good medical care. These advantages have, however, been purchased only at a price, and it is becoming increasingly evident that such forms of pre-paid medical care are open to abuse by both doctor and patient. A note of warning is sounded in the annual report of the Director-General of Health for 1948 :—

> It seems to be forgotten by too many of our people that health services as organized in New Zealand are a form of insurance against sickness and ill health, and that, whatever form or measure of service is demanded, it must inevitably be paid for, however indirect the payment may be. All too frequently one hears the statement that so much tax is being paid and that it behoves every one to get as much in return as possible. This attitude undoubtedly accounts for many trivial and unnecessary calls on medical men and for much unnecessary prescribing and wastage of medicines. No social measures can succeed where there is a lack of social conscience.

This statement, while applicable, of course, to all benefits, is directed particularly at general medical services.

CHAPTER XVII — PHARMACEUTICAL BENEFITS

THE Social Security Act makes provision for pharmaceutical benefits as an ancillary to medical benefits. The failure of the capitation scheme early in 1941, however, made it impossible to introduce pharmaceutical benefits under the appropriate provisions of the Act. To do so would have meant that the 80,000-odd people on the patients' lists of the handful of doctors operating on a capitation basis would also receive medicines ordered by these doctors in the course of providing medical benefits, while all other members of the community would be required to pay for their own.

Advantage was taken of the powers given under section 101 of the Act to introduce supplementary benefits, and pharmaceutical benefits were introduced under this section in May, 1941. Under the regulations covering these benefits all could now receive free pharmaceutical services irrespective of whether they were receiving medical benefits (capitation) or not. Free medicines were made available on the widest possible basis. No restrictive formulary was introduced, but the range of pharmaceutical requirements available as benefits was set out in a Drug Tariff issued under the hand of the Minister of Health.

This document sets out, by reference to official pharmacopæia and by direct inclusions or exclusions, those drugs and preparations which are a charge on the Social Security Fund. It imposes certain limits on the quantities which may be supplied, and also, by reference to a pricing schedule, which is amended from time to time, limits the prices which may be paid from the Fund for such medicines and pharmaceutical preparations. The Drug Tariff includes all official drugs and preparations—that is, those which appear in the British Pharmacopæia, the British Pharmaceutical Codex, and the official New Zealand Formulary. In addition, there are added from time to time by specific reference such new drugs of proven therapeutic value as have come into general use but have not yet appeared in the official pharmacopæia.

In general, proprietary medicines are not available at the cost of the Fund, although some are provided for, but only at the cost of the corresponding official preparation.

The State has not entered into the pharmaceutical field as a supplier, but contracts have been entered into between the Minister of Health and practically all chemists in business in New Zealand. Chemists under these contracts undertake to supply pharmaceutical requirements at the prices fixed from time to time in the official price schedule. These prices are fixed by the Pharmacy Plan Industrial Committee, in conjunction with the Price Control Division of the Department of Industries and Commerce and with the Department of Health. All price schedules require the approval of the Department of Health.

The general procedure to obtain pharmaceutical benefits is exceedingly simple so far as the patient is concerned. The doctor's prescription is taken to the nearest chemist, who dispenses the medicine, and in lieu of making a charge merely obtains the patient's signature and address. These filled prescriptions are then sent in fortnightly batches to the nearest Pricing Office of the Department of Health. A special staff at these Pricing Offices costs the ingredients, adds the appropriate dispensing fee, any special fees, together with the cost of the container, and arrives at a total price in respect of each prescription which is a charge on the Fund. The prices for all prescriptions are then machine-totalled and a payment made to the contracting chemist. Prices bear a discount of $2\frac{1}{2}$ per cent. Chemists may if they wish price their own prescriptions, subject to check by the Pricing Office, but few elect to do so and prefer to leave the pricing to the trained staff of the Department's Pricing Offices.

In addition to prescriptions, contracting chemists receive payment from the Fund for " midwifery requirements " supplied on a midwifery order issued to the patient or upon a bulk order submitted by the maternity hospital with the approval of the Department. The practice of issuing midwifery orders is now confined to patients who expect to be confined in their own homes.

Both the volume and cost of prescriptions has risen greatly since the introduction of pharmaceutical benefits. A survey conducted prior to 1938 indicated that the average number of prescriptions dispensed upon doctors' orders was not more than two and a half million a year. During the year ended March, 1949, the total was six and a half million. The following table shows the increase trend and gives the cost to the Social Security Fund of the prescriptions dispensed annually, together with the average cost per prescription :—

TABLE 51—PHARMACEUTICAL BENEFITS : NUMBER OF PRESCRIPTIONS, EXPENDITURE, AND COST PER PRESCRIPTION, 1941–42 TO 1948–49

Year Ended 31st March,				Number of Prescriptions During Year.	Expenditure for Year.	Cost Per Prescription.
					£	s. d.
1942 (eleven months)	..		..	2,170,000	279,968	2 7
1943	..	..	..	3,500,000	563,247	3 3
1944	..	..	..	4,250,000	762,198	3 7
1945	..	..	..	4,900,000	980,237	4 0
1946	..	..	..	5,400,000	1,133,366	4 3
1947	..	..	..	5,882,000	1,439,686	4 11
1948	..	..	..	6,300,000	1,558,350	4 11½
1949	..	..	..	6,500,000	1,793,159	5 6

In surveying these trends two factors are, of course, important— viz., the annual turnover in prescriptions, and the average cost per prescription.

TURNOVER

The increase in turnover is due to a variety of causes. The first of these is a lessening in the amount of " self medication." Medical services are now more freely available, and the tendency of persons to resort to " over the counter " prescriptions by chemists themselves and well-known proprietaries and patents has undoubtedly decreased. A greater number of visits are now being paid to doctors ; this is evidenced by the rising cost of general medical services themselves. Assuming the visit : prescription ratio to remain approximately the same, these additional visits bring a corresponding increase in the pharmaceutical turnover. Both these may well be legitimate increases to which no exception can be taken.

There is, unfortunately, ample evidence of inflated turnover due to the prescribing by doctors of unnecessary medicine, or where necessary in quantities greatly in excess of the patient's immediate needs. A point is made in the report of the Medical Services Committee, 1948 :—

The general medical services benefits have encouraged the public to resort to doctors for trivial complaints, with the result that there has arisen a " patient pressure " on the doctor which can only too easily be satisfied by prescribing medicines towards the cost of which neither the patient nor the doctor contributes.

It is difficult to see how a conscientious doctor can prescribe on these grounds medicines which a patient does not really need ; nevertheless, this evil does exist and lies at the door of both doctor and patient.

COST OF PRESCRIPTIONS

A number of factors, some of them complex, contribute towards the increase in " cost per prescription." The more important of these are—

(1) A substantial increase, particularly over the war years, of the wholesale cost of drugs. This increased cost also bears additional duty and increased sales tax, all of which go to swell the retail price of the drug at the point where it is paid for from the Social Security Fund.

(2) Increased labour costs. The pharmaceutical industry has not escaped the sharp rise in labour-costs which have taken place over the past ten years. Wages for pharmaceutical assistants have been increased under the appropriate awards, and it has been necessary to take this into account in fixing the prescription prices paid from the Fund. During 1947 the question of increased prices was thoroughly reviewed by a special committee, and an increase in the " dispensing fee " (as apart from ingredient costs) of approximately 40 per cent. was finally sanctioned by the Minister.

(3) The introduction over the period of review of many new and expensive drugs and preparations has also contributed largely to rising costs. During the past ten years, possibly owing to an impetus received under the needs of total warfare, many new preparations have been brought into common use. Barbiturates, though not new, are now used in increasing quantities. The sulpha drugs are in everyday use ; complex and expensive vitamin preparations are used freely. Costly glandular and hormone preparations play an increasingly large part in modern medications, and the more recent introduction of antibiotics such as penicillin and its preparations has added in no inconsiderable measure to the nation's drug bill.

(4) The unnecessary selection by doctors of the more expensive forms of medication has also been a factor. The Medical Services Committee had no difficulty whatever in including this. Not all of this unnecessary selection, however, is deliberate. Since the advent of social security, doctors generally have lost touch with the cost of the drugs they commonly use. The price is no longer a factor which has to be lined up with the financial position of the patient. Many manufacturers and wholesalers of drugs, not unnaturally, now make little attempt to inform the medical profession of the prices of their wares. More often their advertising matter is inclined to stress that the particular preparation is " free under social security." The Department, in co-operation with the British Medical Association, recently listed the more expensive drugs in common use, together with the prices, and circulated these lists to all practising medical men. There was no doubt whatever that many doctors had until then no real appreciation of the costs of their prescriptions.

In so far as the increased costs of pharmaceutical benefits can be justified, they now give no cause for alarm. It is manifestly impossible to bring within reach of all and free or substantially free of cost, the ever-increasing armament of pharmaceutical preparations called for under modern methods of the treatment of disease. To the extent to which unnecessary costs can be eliminated and the utmost economy in prescribing encouraged, everything must be done. The Department has in hand the revision of the present New Zealand Formulary with a view to its adoption as a pattern for economy in prescribing. The free use of this formulary by the profession would greatly lessen the present administrative costs in pricing prescriptions and would be an educative factor in diminishing costly prescribing.

CHAPTER XVIII — SUPPLEMENTARY BENEFITS

UNDER section 101 of the Social Security Act, 1938, the Minister of Health is empowered to introduce such supplementary benefits as are in his opinion necessary to give full effect to the principal health benefits specifically mentioned in the Act itself. These supplementary benefits may be either ancillary or additional to the principal benefits. Some are specially mentioned in section 101, but the Minister's discretion is not limited to these.

Such supplementary benefits must be general in their application— that is to say, they must be available to all who require them under the same conditions as to eligibility. It is not the intention that the Minister shall invoke section 101 to provide supplementary services for the benefit of particular individuals or to suit the particular circumstances of such individuals.

X-RAY DIAGNOSTIC SERVICES

The first of these supplementary benefits to be introduced were x-ray diagnostic services in August, 1941. These are clearly supplementary to and to provide for the more effective operation of medical benefits and general medical services. The doctor affording medical services is assisted in his diagnosis by specialist x-ray services carried out either in public hospitals or by private radiologists who have been recognized under the provisions of the regulations.

In respect of x-ray services afforded by Hospital Boards other than for in-patients of their own institutions, payments are made from the Fund according to a schedule of fees set out in the regulations, and such payments must be accepted by the Board in full satisfaction of their charges. X-ray services for " in-patients " of Hospital Board institutions are provided free of charge under the hospital benefits provisions.

In the case of a private radiologist it is necessary for the purposes of the benefits that he apply for and obtain official recognition by the Minister as a radiologist. An applicant for recognition may be granted " absolute " or " limited " recognition. " Absolute " recognition is in respect of all classes of x-ray diagnostic services, and it is usually afforded to medical practitioners wholly specializing in radiological work. " Limited " recognition may exclude certain classes of examination or may be in respect of specified classes to the exclusion of all other classes.

The arrangements for benefits in respect of x-ray examinations carried out by private radiologists were completed early in 1942, and benefits in respect of these services were made available on and from the 25th February, 1942.

The schedule of fees payable from the Fund provides two scales— namely, (a) fees payable to Hospital Boards and to radiologists afforded " limited " recognition, and (b) fees payable to radiologists whose recognition under the regulations is " absolute."

Provisions governing the recognition of radiologists enable the Minister to impose certain conditions, and one condition that has been invariably imposed is to limit to specified amounts the fees that may be charged by the radiologists over and above those payable from the Social Security Fund. The additional fees so fixed are set out in a printed list, which the radiologist is required to display in his consulting-rooms.

The range of services covered by the fees comprise—

(a) The making of x-ray examinations with the aid of a fluorescent screen :
(b) The taking of x-ray photographs :
(c) The supply and administration of any drugs or other substances for the purposes of any such examination or photograph :
(d) The provision of medical services incidental to any such examination or photograph, except medical services of a kind that are not ordinarily performed by radiologists as such (whether in any particular case such services are performed by the radiologists or by any other medical practitioner) :
(e) The provision of any other incidental services for the purposes of any such examinations or photographs.

Benefits are not, however, applicable with respect to x-ray examinations or x-ray photographs made or taken for dental purposes or for the purposes of life insurance.

Procedure affecting payment.—Claims are made directly by the radiologists on the Department for the amount of the fee payable from the Fund. The form of claim includes a certificate by the patient that he had attended, on the date or dates specified, for the purpose of x-ray examination, and includes also a statement from the radiologist as to the fee charged or proposed to be charged exclusive of that payable from the Fund. In addition, the claim must be accompanied by a signed recommendation of the medical practitioner on whose recommendation the services have been rendered, or if the x-ray services have been afforded by the radiologist to his own patient must be accompanied by a brief statement of the reasons for rendering the service.

Increasing use of these services is being made by general practitioners, and this is reflected in the expenditure figures since 1941.

Expenditure for years during which the benefit has been in full operation is given below :—

			£
1942–43	..	..	89,000
1943–44	..	..	109,000
1944–45	..	..	129,000
1945–46	..	..	133,000
1946–47	..	..	175,000
1947–48	..	..	209,000
1948–49	..	..	249,000

MASSAGE SERVICES

Next among the supplementary benefits came massage benefits, which commenced on 1st September, 1942. The object of these is to enable the medical practitioner affording medical services to give the patient the benefit of special massage and allied treatment for a definite period as part of general medical treatment.

Massage is defined as the use by external application to the human body of manipulation, remedial exercises, electricity, heat, light, or water for the purpose of curing or alleviating any abnormal condition of the body.

The general arrangement for these benefits consists of individual contracts with registered masseurs under which they are paid from the Social Security Fund a fee of 3s. 6d. for each massage treatment and undertake not to charge the patient any additional fees in excess of 3s. 6d. for each treatment afforded in the masseur's rooms, or 7s. for each treatment afforded elsewhere than in the masseur's rooms.

No massage treatment is recognized for the purpose of the benefits unless it is given on the recommendation of a medical practitioner, and no more than four weeks' treatment may be given on a single recommendation. Any treatment recognized for the purpose of benefits must, moreover, be afforded not later than six weeks after the date on which it is recommended by the medical practitioner.

It is of interest to note that only massage given by masseurs in private practice is the subject of this particular benefit. Massage services given in public hospitals form part of either in-patient or out-patient hospital benefits.

There again full advantage has been taken by general practitioners of massage services for the benefit of their patients.

The comparative annual expenditures on private massage services are :—

			£
1943–44	..	..	27,000
1944–45	..	..	32,000
1945–46	..	..	36,000
1946–47	..	..	43,000
1947–48	..	..	48,000
1948–49	..	..	57,000

DISTRICT NURSING SERVICES

In September, 1944, a further supplementary benefit covering district nursing services was introduced. These services are carried out by district nurses employed either by Hospital Boards or by the Department of Health, and operate in many sparsely-populated districts where medical services are not readily available. Certain district nursing associations are also recognized for the purpose of benefits. Prior to the introduction of benefits charges for these services were made by the agencies providing them. All such services are now free of charge to the patient.

Services afforded by district nurses employed by the Department of Health and by the Forestry Department were brought within the scope of the regulations as from 1st August, 1944, from which date the services of their nurses became free of charge to patients.

Hospital Boards employing district nurses are required by the regulations to apply for the approval of the Minister of Health, giving full particulars of the nurses employed, conditions of employment, area of service, &c., before the services of these nurses becomes the subject of benefits.

Where such services are approved, the Minister of Health appoints a date upon which these shall be the subject of benefits. The Board is then reimbursed from the Social Security Fund all expenses directly incurred in providing the services approved by the Minister. In most cases the services afforded by Hospital Boards have been approved as from 1st September, 1944, from which date charges to patients have been abolished.

Provision is also made for the recognition of voluntary associations who have in the past provided district nursing services and have been subsidized by Hospital Boards with the approval of the Minister of Health in respect of this work.

Where the services so provided by a subsidized association are approved by the Minister of Health the Hospital Board is reimbursed from the Social Security Fund the amount of the subsidy, granted with the Minister's approval, to the association. No charge is made for the treatment of patients by district nurses employed by a voluntary association whose activities have been brought within the scope of the regulations.

Though the growth of this service is somewhat limited by the nursing personnel available it has made rapid strides during the few years the benefit has been in operation.

The comparative expenditures are :—

			£
1945–46	..	..	59,000
1946–47	..	..	69,000
1947–48	..	..	83,000
1948–49	..	..	111,000

DOMESTIC ASSISTANCE

The Social Security (Domestic Assistance) Regulations 1944 provide the first step towards the inauguration of benefits under the Social Security Act in regard to domestic assistance during the incapacity of the mother for various reasons or in cases of undue hardship.

In their present form the regulations provide merely for payments by way of subsidy from the Social Security Fund to approved organizations that have been formed for the purpose of providing domestic assistance in homes.

Application from any duly incorporated association whose objects include the provision of domestic assistance may be made to the Minister of Health, who determines the conditions under which payment shall be made from the Social Security Fund and specifies the locality within which the services may be provided by the association and the classes of cases to whom such services may be afforded.

It is the duty of approved associations to engage domestic assistants to work as employees of the association in homes to which they may be allocated by the association in accordance with whatever terms and conditions are specified by the Minister.

The terms upon which domestic assistance is provided by an approved association to a householder are fixed by agreement between the association and the householder. Payment in accordance with terms so agreed upon may, if necessary, be recovered by the association by legal process.

In determining the amount to be paid to an approved association from the Social Security Fund the Minister may have regard not only to the expenses incurred in providing domestic assistance in homes, but also to expenses incurred in any scheme of registration, enrolment, or training of women and girls willing to undertake domestic work in homes, including payment to registered or enrolled assistants for the period during which they are undergoing training.

By this means encouragement is given to young women and girls to undergo proper training as domestic assistants and later to take up this work, under satisfactory conditions, as employees of an approved association.

It will be observed that the arrangements make no attempt to provide direct assistance to householders by the State, a task impossible with the number of women available during war years and to-day for domestic service.

At the present time subsidy is paid to the Women's Division, New Zealand Federated Farmers, which provides housekeeper and domestic services in many rural areas throughout New Zealand.

LABORATORY DIAGNOSTIC SERVICES

Supplementary benefits in respect of laboratory diagnostic services were introduced on 1st April, 1946, the relevant regulations being the Social Security (Laboratory Diagnostic Services) Regulations 1946 (Serial No. 1946/24). Benefits are provided in respect of laboratory services performed by or under the direct supervision of a recognized pathologist or by an approved bacteriological assistant employed by a Hospital Board and the services comprise—

(a) The supply of all materials or substances required for the purpose of providing laboratory diagnostic services ;

(b) The provision of medical services incidental to any laboratory diagnostic service except medical services of a kind that are not ordinarily performed by pathologists as such (whether in any particular case the services are performed by the pathologist or by any other recognized medical practitioner) :

(c) The provision of any other incidental services for the purposes of laboratory diagnostic services.

Benefits are not, however, applicable to examinations of specimens for public-health purposes ; to post-mortem examinations ; and preparation of sera and vaccines ; or to laboratory services for dental purposes or for purposes of life insurance.

The schedule of fees payable from the Fund now provides one scale for both Hospital Board and private pathologist.

Where services are performed by a recognized pathologist, the prescribed fee shall be accepted by the pathologist in full satisfaction of his claims in respect of those services.

A similar provision covers fees received by Hospital Boards for services afforded by a person in the employment of the Board.

Procedure affecting payment.—Pathologists claim directly on the Department for the amount of the prescribed fee, and the form of claim shall contain a certificate by the pathologist that the service to which the claim relates was duly performed. Claims from recognized pathologists must include the recommendations of the medical practitioner as to the nature of the services recommended or a statement signed by the pathologist setting out his reasons for rendering the services to which the claim relates.

Already increasing advantage is being taken of these services. The expenditure from the Fund for the past three years was as follows:—

			£
1946–47	..	..	61,000
1947–48	..	..	90,000
1948–49	..	..	117,000

DENTAL BENEFITS

The latest supplementary benefit introduced was a dental benefit for adolescent children. Since 1921 the School Dental Service, now the National Dental Service, has provided dental attention for children attending primary schools in practically all districts in New Zealand. This service is carried out by dental nurses specially trained by the Department to provide simple surgical dental treatment for schoolchildren. The object of the dental benefit is to continue for adolescents up to the age of nineteen years the dental treatment already commenced in primary schools. The services are afforded principally by registered dentists either in the employ of the State or of a Hospital Board or by those in private practice who have contracted to carry out this work at the scale of fees set out in the regulations.

So far is has been possible to extend treatment only to children up to sixteen years of age. As further dental personnel becomes available it is hoped to extend the age-group each year and to include all children up to the age of nineteen years.

The general conditions of eligibility for treatment under this benefit are as under :—

Dental benefits are available for all persons who are enrolled as patients under the regulations, but no person shall be enrolled unless he is under the age of nineteen years and is within the appropriate age-group for the time being appointed by the Minister. Any person, including any school pupil, who is above the age-group in which he would be eligible to receive treatment at a school dental clinic may be enrolled as a patient—

    (*a*) If he has received treatment at a school dental clinic within the three months immediately preceding the lodging of the application for enrolment ; or

    (*b*) If the Principal Dental Officer is satisfied that at the time of the lodging of the application for the patient's enrolment his dental and oral health is of adequate standard and no treatment except treatment of a minor character is required by him.

Provision is made for the enrolment of persons ineligible under the foregoing provisions who owing to their having resided in a locality remote from dental services or owing to other special circumstance beyond their control could not reasonably have been expected to have had their dental and oral health satisfactorily maintained.

Failure to attend for treatment or examination for any period of twelve months may render a patient ineligible to receive further benefits.

A contracting dentist or authority may stipulate the maximum number of patients, being not less than twenty, that he or it is willing to have on his or its roll.

The fees payable to contracting dentists or authorities from the Social Security Fund are—

(a) The appropriate fee specified in the Schedule ; or

(b) Where no definite fee is prescribed in the Schedule such fee as may be fixed or approved by the Principal Dental Officer. The right to claim such fee is subject to the condition that the contracting dentist or authority will not demand or accept any fee from the patient or any other person in respect of the same services.

CHAPTER XIX — THE MEDICAL SERVICES COMMITTEE REPORT

In 1947, after some six years' experience of the general medical services scheme, it became apparent both to the Department and to the leaders of the medical profession that the arrangements for the provision of general medical services were not without their defects, and were, in fact, open to a certain measure of abuse both by the public and by the more commercially-minded members of the profession. Some of the unsatisfactory features had arisen as a result of circumstance rather than from deliberate intent. The scheme had commenced during the war years with an abnormally restricted medical personnel available for civilian needs. As was to be expected, too, free or partially-free medical service itself created a greatly-increased demand. The two systems provided for under the legislation—viz., the " refund system " and the " direct claim " system—created their own special problems. Many doctors operating the direct-claim system made no additional charge to the patient and were content to collect the statutory fee of 7s. 6d. direct from the Department. Those adopting the refund system continued to follow traditional practice of charging the patient the current fee of 10s. 6d. or over and leaving the patient to collect the refund of 7s. 6d. from the State. This resulted in the diversion of a large number of patients to the " free " doctor, who became so besieged with patients that the measure of service he was able to give to each fell in value far below the statutory fee of 7s. 6d. The gross incomes of some of these doctors became the object of public criticism, and it cannot be denied that in some cases the measure of service given to patients was little more than perfunctory.

In October, 1947, the Minister of Health, Hon. Miss Howard, after some consultation with the British Medical Association, set up a special committee to inquire generally into the working of health benefits involving medical services under Part III of the Social Security Act, with special reference to the operation of the general medical services system. The Committee, which consisted of representatives of the British Medical Association and the Department of Health, sat for periods during November, 1947, and January, 1948.

The whole arrangements were closely examined, and the following extracts from the Committee's report indicate the extent of the ground covered :—

8. From the commencement of its deliberations the Committee recognized that any recommendations made by it must be governed by the wording of the order ot reference, which required it to " advise as to what alterations are necessary to give effect to the Government's policy of making available adequate and proper medical services (general and specialist) free or substantially free of cost."

9. The requirement, as a matter of Government policy, that medical services should be free or substantially free of cost to the patient relieved the Committee from the necessity of considering any suggestions that did not satisfy this requirement. In effect, this meant that the Committee was to commence its investigations with the consideration of the best means of remunerating medical practitioners from the Social Security Fund for services that should be free or substantially free to the public. This brought the Committee at an early stage to a consideration of the method of dealing with the most important aspect of medical services—the General Medical Services Scheme.

10. The information supplied to the Committee as to the payments made from the Fund under the General Medical Services Scheme disclosed cases where general practitioners were receiving annual sums much in excess of what could be regarded as reasonable and proper remuneration. The Committee was unanimous in its desire to devise a system and methods to guard against excessive payments and to eliminate abuses. To achieve this end, under such new system, the Committee recommends that steps be taken to place upon the profession itself as a body a large degree of responsibility for the ethical behaviour of its members and for the general quality of all medical services afforded in relation to benefits. This report, therefore, includes recommendations for giving responsibility of this nature to the New Zealand Branch of the British Medical Association through advisory and disciplinary committees to be set up as hereinafter suggested.

Fee-for-service System

18. Particular attention was necessarily directed to the existing General Medical Service Scheme introduced under sections 2 to 11 of the Social Security Amendment Act, 1941, which provide two alternative methods of payment from the Fund—namely, a direct payment to the doctor or a refund to the patient. Reviewing the administrative procedures involved in these two methods, the Committee came to a general agreement that there should be one method only of claiming against the Fund.

19. The Committee recommends that in lieu of the present alternative fee-for-service methods of payment from the Fund (namely, (i) direct payment, and (ii) refund), there be adopted only one method (namely, one by which the medical practitioner shall be required to claim on the Fund on behalf of the patient the appropriate amount payable from the Fund for the service and apply that amount in full or part settlement of his charge for the service).

The recommendation that the claim be made in this manner—*i.e.*, on behalf of the patient—rather than directly as is at present provided by section 4 of the Social Security Amendment Act, 1941, is made to meet the desire of the profession to preserve the doctor-patient relationship to the fullest extent. It is a matter of common knowledge that, on account of the widely held view that a direct claim by the practitioner on the Fund infringed this principle, a large number of practitioners have declined to make direct claims upon the Fund.

20. A suggested form of claim was discussed, and while the Committee recognized that the actual detail and form of the claim would be a matter for further discussion and settlement, a draft of the form considered by the Committee forms an appendix to this report as an indication of what is considered necessary.

VERIFICATION OF CLAIMS

21. It was agreed that the present invariable practice of obtaining a certificate from the patient, parent, or guardian as to the dates, &c., of attendance has only limited value. With the adoption of the system recommended in paragraph 19 it is recommended that certification by patients, &c., be discontinued.

It was recognized, however, that with the discontinuance of certification by patients some alternative method for checking the claims made by practitioners would be necessary. It is accordingly suggested that the Department devise a system of verification of service as an alternative to the patient's certification, as, for example, postal inquiry from a proportion of the patients of each practitioner. In addition, it is recommended that all practitioners be required to maintain adequate medical records of their patients in support of all claims made and that these records and daily diary sheets be subject to inspection by medical practitioners duly appointed for that purpose.

AMOUNT OF PAYMENT FROM FUND

22. The Committee recommends the following scale of payment from the Fund in respect of general practitioner services :—

(a) For an attendance at the doctor's place of residence or surgery or at a private hospital, up to 7s. 6d. :

(b) For an attendance elsewhere than at the doctor's place of residence or surgery or at a private hospital, up to 10s. :

(c) For an attendance between 9 p.m. and 7 a.m. or on a Sunday or on a public holiday in response to an urgent request at those times, 12s. 6d. :

(d) Where any attendance extends beyond a half-hour, 5s. for every additional quarter-hour :

(e) For telephone consultations in certain rural areas approved by the Medical Officer of Health, up to 5s.

It was agreed that no payment should be made either from the Fund or by a patient where the only service was to repeat a prescription.

MILEAGE

23. The Committee recommends that consideration should be given to the question of some increase in the present ordinary mileage payment from the Fund of 1s. 3d. per mile (fixed by section 5 of the Social Security Amendment Act, 1941), with the general intention that the amount paid from the Fund will be accepted in full satisfaction of the doctor's charge by way of mileage. The Committee felt that this question should be the subject of further discussions between the Association and the Department. The Committee recognized that the complete abolition of mileage charges to patients calls for some other deterrent against unnecessary and time-consuming visits to distant places.

INCREASE IN PAYMENT FOR DOMICILIARY ATTENDANCE

24. The scale of payments from the Fund recommended in paragraph 22 is substantially as at present, except that the Committee suggests an increase of 2s. 6d. for an attendance at the patient's home. Since the General Medical Services Scheme was inaugurated in 1941 a uniform fee of 7s. 6d. has been paid from the Fund for an ordinary attendance in the doctor's surgery or a visit to a patient's home or elsewhere. The Committee appreciated that the fee had been made a uniform one on the assumption that the ratio of attendances in the surgery to visits would be much the same for all general practitioners in urban areas, and that, so far as practitioners in rural areas were concerned, the mileage payments would adjust matters. It has, however, continued to be the regular custom for many practitioners to charge a higher fee for a visit than for an attendance in the surgery. The ratio of attendances to visits undoubtedly varies a good deal among practitioners. The present uniform payment encourages those individuals who are inclined to deal with unduly large numbers of patients in their surgeries. They, of course, are able to claim the same fee for every attendance, no matter how little time is involved.

The Committee feels, therefore, that a distinction should be made as regards the fee for an attendance in the surgery and an attendance in the patient's home. That this should be done by increasing the payment in respect of a domiciliary visit is conditional upon measures being taken, as recommended elsewhere in this report, to control the amounts paid to practitioners generally.

25. The Committee contemplates that the amounts payable from the Fund will in many cases be accepted in full satisfaction for the services rendered. Indeed, the Committee expects that there will be a proportion of cases, varying with the different types of practice, where less than the amounts set out in paragraph 22 will be accepted as a sufficient charge in the particular circumstances. At the same time the Committee recognizes that there will be cases where the amounts recommended in paragraph 22 will be insufficient to provide an adequate fee to the practitioner, and this aspect has caused the Committee to consider the question of the right of practitioners to recover fees from patients.

FEES PAYABLE BY PATIENTS

26. Under section 8 of the Social Security Amendment Act, 1941, a practitioner is prohibited from recovering at law a charge in respect of a general medical service above the fee payable from the Fund for that service. In fact, almost all practitioners operating under the " refund " system and a number of those operating under the " direct payment " system regularly make additional charges, which are, as a rule, readily paid by patients. Although, therefore, the provision mentioned is not very effective, it is nevertheless a source of dissatisfaction, if not resentment, on the part of a considerable number of the profession.

There was general agreement that every general medical practitioner should have the right to charge and recover a fee additional to that payable from the Fund wherever circumstances, in his opinion, warranted it.

27. The Committee accordingly recommends that section 8 of the Social Security Amendment Act, 1941, be replaced by a provision that no medical practitioner shall be entitled to recover fees (whether in respect of general medical

services or any specialist services for the time being subject to benefit from the Fund) until after the expiration of one month from the delivery of a detailed account to the patient. During the month the patient would be at liberty to refer the account to a Local Investigating Committee (referred to elsewhere in the report), which would have power, conferred by regulations, to say whether the charges were fair and reasonable having regard to the general practice of the profession and the circumstances of the case, and if excessive, to what amount they should be reduced. There should be a further provision enabling a Court to refer proceedings, pending before it for the recovery of medical charges, to the appropriate Local Investigating Committee for its views.

LIMITATION OF NUMBER OF ATTENDANCES

28. The Committee discussed the practicability of prescribing limits to the number of patients to be seen daily or, alternatively, of prescribing a limit to the amount payable from the Fund to an individual practitioner. It considered that, in view of the wide variation in local conditions, types of patients, and the capacity of practitioners, no fixed or arbitrary limits could be prescribed. Nevertheless, there are substantial grounds for believing that an average of, say, thirty attendances daily is the maximum number practicable for an efficient and conscientious practitioner, and the Committee considers that Local Investigating Committees should be vigilant to investigate cases which habitually exceed the figure mentioned. The Committee was informed that it was the intention of the Association to address its divisions throughout the country on these lines.

TRANSITIONAL PROVISIONS

29. The system of remuneration for general practitioner services now recommended is intended to be universally applied except in approved special areas where the practitioner is remunerated on a salary basis and except where the practitioner confines his practice to the capitation system. The suggestion has been made, however, that a number of medical practitioners might be reluctant to agree to operate under the system recommended in this report and that some special transitional provision be made for these cases. The Committee recommends that the Minister should have power to allow the present refund system for doctors who elect to operate thereunder if such doctors have in fact wholly operated under the present refund system since its inception in 1941. The Committee believes that there are very few practitioners who might want to take advantage of that special provision and that those few belong to the older generation of practitioners.

GENERAL ADVISORY COMMITTEE

52. The Committee recommends that there should be a General Advisory Committee constituted of members of the Association and one or more departmental medical officers, which Committee would be recognized by the Minister as the principal consultative and advisory body in all matters involving consultation with representatives of the medical profession or any branch of the profession relating to medical services. This Committee could be appointed under section 83 of the Social Security Act, 1938. The Committees already set up under this section—e.g., the Radiological Committee—would continue to function, and further committees might from time to time need to be set up under this section. The suggested General Advisory Committee would co-ordinate the activities of all committees now or hereafter set up under section 83 to deal with any particular benefits relating to medical services.

DISCIPLINARY COMMITTEE

53. Some of the existing regulations dealing with the administration of particular benefits contain provisions to enable the Minister to control and penalize practitioners who do not conform to the regulations. The Minister's powers are exercisable after reference to a committee appointed under section 83 of the Social Security Act, 1938. For example, there are provisions in the Social Security (General Medical Services) Regulations 1941 (Serial No. 1941/187) empowering the Minister, after consultation with the appropriate committee, to disallow a claim on the fund where the practitioner concerned has refused to furnish information requested of him with respect to the claim. Again, in the Social Security (Pharmaceutical Supplies) Regulations, Amendment No. 2 (Serial No. 1942/3), there is a provision which empowers the Minister to refer to the appropriate committee for investigation a complaint as to excessive prescribing, &c. If the committee so recommends, the Minister may impose certain penalties on the practitioner concerned.

The Committee considers that it will be necessary to amplify the provisions of the regulations dealing with general medical services so as to enable more effective control to be exercised in cases of over-visiting, excessive number of patients seen, and the like ; and it recommends that there be set up a Disciplinary Committee of members of the Association to which the Minister will refer for investigation and report all complaints against medical practitioners arising out of any of the regulations relating to medical benefits, and that provision be made for imposing penalties where the Disciplinary Committee so recommends.

54. The Committee suggests, however, that the Disciplinary Committee's functions should not be confined to advising the Minister in cases of alleged breaches of the various Social Security Regulations, but that it should have jurisdiction to deal with all complaints relating to the professional conduct of medical practitioners not at present falling within the jurisdiction of the Medical Council. At the present time the only provision in force enabling disciplinary powers to be exercised against practitioners are those contained in section 22 of the Medical Practitioners Act, 1914, and section 6 of the Medical Practitioners Amendment Act, 1924. These powers are, however, exercisable only in cases of " grave impropriety or infamous conduct in a professional respect." They do not apply to minor irregularities or misconduct in practice. It appeared to the Committee that there was a general opinion amongst members of the profession in favour of the constitution of a domestic body to exercise disciplinary powers in cases that were not serious or grave enough to invoke the powers conferred upon the Medical Council. If the profession is to give the assistance, which this report contemplates it will, in the control of its own members in all matters relating to medical benefits, then the case for such a domestic disciplinary body becomes much stronger. The Committee accordingly recommends that, in addition to the advisory functions referred to in paragraph 53, the suggested Disciplinary Committee should have jurisdiction to hear and determine all complaints of professional misconduct against practitioners not serious enough to give rise to the preferment of a charge of grave impropriety or infamous conduct before the Medical Council.

55. The setting-up of a Disciplinary Committee having the powers and functions recommended in this report would involve appropriate amendments to the Medical Practitioners Act, 1914. The suggestion that a committee of the Association should exercise disciplinary powers over all practitioners also gives rise to the question whether all registered practitioners should not have an automatic right to membership of the Association.

Local Investigating Committees

56. It was considered that a Central Disciplinary Committee would be unable to exercise satisfactorily the powers suggested in the preceding paragraphs of this report unless it were assisted by Local Investigating Committees in each health district. The functions of a Local Investigating Committee (consisting of members of the Association together with a medical officer of the Department) would be to make preliminary investigations into complaints against the practitioners in the district, whether such complaints were made by the Department of Health or by patients, and to obtain explanations from the practitioner concerned. It would then decide whether the complaint merited further inquiry by the Disciplinary Committee, and in particular, whether a charge should be preferred against the practitioner concerned.

In brief, the Committee's recommendations, in so far as they affect general medical services, are—

(1) The abolition, over a transitional period, of the refund system and the universal adoption of a direct-claim system.

(2) Claims by doctors on the Fund to be by means of a schedule indicating clearly the number of patients seen each day, the amounts claimed from the Fund in respect of these services and the additional amount, if any, claimed from the patient.

(3) The abolition of the present method of claim whereby the patient is required to certify as to the services received.

(4) The setting-up of advisory, investigating, and disciplinary committees by the British Medical Association to assist the Government in the administration of benefits, to investigate complaints, and to make suitable recommendations to the Minister thereon.

The Committee also considered the capitation and salaried systems as alternatives to general medical services, but were unable to find in favour of these methods under present circumstances.

Consideration was also given to the institution of benefits in respect of specialist medical services. As these are not, however, included in benefits already in operation, it is not proposed herein to traverse the Committee's recommendations in this respect.

The Committee's report was presented to both Houses of the General Assembly and following further negotiation with the British Medical Association important features of the Medical Services Committee report were given effect to in the Social Security Amendment Act of 1949.

These are—

(1) As from a date to be fixed by the Minister of Health the present refund system is to cease generally and claims are to be made by doctors direct to the Department :

Provision is made for the continuance of the refund system in the case of certain doctors where they are authorized to continue by the Council of the New Zealand Branch of the British Medical Association after consultation with the Minister :

(2) The fixed statutory fee of 7s. 6d. is replaced by "a reasonable fee not exceeding 7s. 6d."

(3) Divisional Disciplinary Committees may be appointed under the Medical Practitioners Act, 1949, to conduct investigations and to hear complaints :

(4) The restriction upon the rights of doctors to sue for fees for general medical services in excess of 7s. 6d. per visit or consultation imposed under section 8 of the 1941 amendment is removed. No doctor is, however, entitled to recover until the expiration of one month from the presentation of a detailed account to the patient. Within one month of the delivery of such account the patient may apply to the Divisional Disciplinary Committee for an examination of the account and its opinion as to the reasonableness of the fees or charges imposed. Legal action for recovery is suspended until the opinion of the Committee is made known to the Court. The Court may on its own motion refer any account to the Committee. The Court is not bound by the opinion of the Committee, but where it differs must give the Committee the opportunity of appearing by counsel before any judgment for a higher fee is entered :

(5) Provision is made for higher mileage fees in certain cases :

(6) Concurrent practice by a doctor under both the capitation scheme and the general medical services arrangement is prohibited unless the Minister otherwise determines :

(7) Provision is made for the introduction of regulations for payment for specialist medical services in accordance with a scale to be determined by agreement between the Minister and the New Zealand Branch of the British Medical Association. The regulations may include provisions for the official recognition of doctors as specialists in any branch of medicine or surgery.

The amending Act was passed only towards the end of the last session of Parliament, and to date none of its provisions has yet been brought into operation.

TABLE 52—SOCIAL SECURITY FUND MEDICAL BENEFITS : STATEMENT SHOWING EXPENDITURE SINCE COMMENCEMENT OF BENEFITS

	1939-40	1940-41	1941-42	1942-43	1943-44	1944-45	1945-46	1946-47	1947-48	1948-49
	£	£	£	£	£	£	£	£	£	£

Subdivision I—Maternity Benefits (commenced 15th May, 1939)

	1939-40	1940-41	1941-42	1942-43	1943-44	1944-45	1945-46	1946-47	1947-48	1948-49
Public-hospital fees	74,780	106,834	113,276	110,217	114,930	133,946	160,870	223,914	301,293	389,416
Private-hospital fees	139,602	216,086	227,315	207,575	209,841	210,675	222,669	202,928	214,963	221,061
Medical practitioners' fees	45,938	161,638	176,973	158,208	162,227	158,409	201,633	232,088	269,265	291,246
Medical practitioners' mileage fees	1,031	5,663	6,215	5,089	5,044	5,647	4,572	4,825	5,997	7,715
Obstetric nurses' fees	16,022	21,101	18,940	15,089	12,027	11,117	10,465	9,234	8,512	6,682
St. Helens Hospital fees	6,440	7,653	7,151	9,046	9,870	10,940	Contribution now abolished			
	283,813	518,975	549,870	505,224	513,039	530,734	600,209	672,989	800,030	916,120

Subdivision II — Medical Benefits (capitation scheme introduced 1st March, 1941 ; general medical services scheme introduced 1st November, 1941

	1939-40	1940-41	1941-42	1942-43	1943-44	1944-45	1945-46	1946-47	1947-48	1948-49
Capitation fees	..	..	114,608	71,149	55,610	42,400	38,084	31,187	22,945	16,818
Capitation and general medical services mileage	..	..	21,166	64,039	60,392	59,442	68,965	90,289	109,522	123,768
General medical services	..	..	69,898	831,397	1,026,073	1,161,326	1,291,448	1,600,601	1,993,806	2,112,304
Special arrangements under section 82	..	..	..	49,468	37,256	23,855	27,495	35,428	37,714	45,286
Purchase of sites and erection of residences for Medical Officers appointed under section 82	..	..	..	..	..	..	..	2,673	3,839	8,660
Remuneration, allowances, and expenses of medical practitioners in areas other than those covered by section 82	..	..	..	..	..	..	1,317	396	..	45
	..	..	205,672	1,016,053	1,179,331	1,287,023	1,427,309	1,760,574	2,167,826	2,306,881

Subdivision III —Hospital Benefits (commenced 1st July, 1939) ; Out-patient Benefits (commenced 1st March, 1941)

Treatment in approved institutions includes Ashburn Hall, Knox Home, Auckland, and Karitane Hospitals, payments to latter being introduced in 1940, but dated back to 1st November, 1939.

	1939-40	1940-41	1941-42	1942-43	1943-44	1944-45	1945-46	1946-47	1947-48	1948-49
Treatment in public hospitals	514,254	893,251	953,794	1,020,319	1,564,315	1,689,233	1,767,874	1,593,367	1,536,417	1,560,483
Out-patient treatment	..	..	47,162	70,720	73,187	83,412	98,972	97,287	117,385	141,530
Treatment in private hospitals	82,980	141,737	146,953	191,647	238,772	259,489	264,865	251,581	252,850	245,000
Treatment in approved institutions	1,459	37,873	28,155	38,819	43,908	56,504	41,749	44,053	42,837	50,362
Contribution to Consolidated Fund for—										
Mental hospitals	166,000	171,000	181,451	181,869	182,830	187,942	Contribution now abolished.			
Queen Mary Hospital	6,835	10,060	11,705	22,872	28,691	28,032				
Rotorua Sanatorium	2,707	4,712	4,985	4,563	5,882	6,425				
Rotorua Soldiers' Hospital	..	..	..	10,150	20,561	19,663				
	774,235	1,258,633	1,374,205	1,540,959	2,158,146	2,330,700	2,173,460	1,986,288	1,949,489	1,997,375

Subdivision IV—Pharmaceutical Benefits (commenced 5th May, 1941).

Drugs supplied by—									
Chemists		261,845	530,695	716,080	933,490	1,082,342	1,389,638	1,507,521	1,727,556
Medical practitioners		1,527	5,891	6,092	6,231	6,030	5,879	5,973	8,262
Institutions		16,326	26,661	40,026	40,516	44,994	44,169	44,856	57,341
		279,968	563,247	762,198	980,237	1,133,366	1,439,686	1,558,350	1,793,159

Subdivision V—Supplementary Benefits

Radiological services (11th August, 1941)		27,962	88,588	109,426	128,842	132,806	175,420	209,059	249,461
Laboratory services (1st April, 1946)							61,453	90,306	117,173
Massage services (1st September, 1942)			8,836	27,331	32,152	35,569	43,028	47,510	57,088
Specialist services (neuro surgery)				1,066	1,324	2,260	1,485	121	4,072
District nursing services (1st September, 1944)					7,717	58,880	68,614	82,756	111,289
Dental services								105,109	223,186
Domestic assistance (20th December, 1944)						456	2,043	2,865	3,258
Ambulance benefits*									324
Artificial-aids benefits*								8,067	96,062
		27,962	97,424	137,823	170,035	229,971	352,043	545,793	861,913
Grand totals	1,058,048	1,777,608	2,437,407	3,722,907	4,751,437	5,298,729	5,564,315	6,211,580	7,021,488	7,875,448
Recoveries†	1,350	923	1,819	1,728	24,757	64,015	27,751‡	20,384	47,630	31,814
Net totals	1,056,698	1,776,685	2,435,588	3,721,179	4,726,680	5,234,714	5,536,564	6,191,196	6,973,858	7,843,634

* £10,000 estimated for year ended 31st March, 1947, but not expended. For 1945–46 they are included in "Miscellaneous Receipts, Social Security Fund."

† These are mainly in respect of hospital benefits.

‡ Prior to 1st April, 1945, these recoveries were treated as credits in reduction of expenditure. This should be taken into account when comparing published figures relating to Social Security Fund expenditure.

PART III — FINANCE
CHAPTER XX—FINANCING OF SCHEME

SOURCE OF FUNDS

CASH and health benefits under the social security scheme are financed on a current cost basis from the Social Security Fund, which receives income from two main sources—a tax, known as the social security contribution, and annual grants from the Consolidated Fund, derived from general revenue of the Government. The fund is not built up to cover future contingencies, but expenditure each year is met from receipts into the Fund during that year.

SOCIAL SECURITY CONTRIBUTION, 1939–49

ORIGINAL RATE

The social security contribution introduced by the Social Security Act, 1938, consisted of a charge of 1s. in the pound on income of all people sixteen years of age or over ordinarily resident in New Zealand and of most companies resident in New Zealand, together with a registration fee of 5s. a quarter for men over twenty years of age, and 5s. a year for men sixteen to twenty years of age, and all women sixteen years of age or over.

CHANGES IN RATES OF CONTRIBUTION

The rate of the social security charge remained at 1s. in the pound until 1946, although during the war years, for administrative convenience only, it was collected in conjunction with the national security tax (a special war-tax), the combined rate of these charges reaching 2s. 6d. in the pound. In 1946 the registration fee was abolished, the rate of social security charge increased to 1s. 6d. in the pound, and the rate of national security tax reduced. This latter tax was repealed early in 1947.

INCOME EXEMPT FROM SOCIAL SECURITY CONTRIBUTION

There is no minimum and maximum wage limits below and above which contributions are not levied, and, apart from certain classes of income which are expressly exempted, it may be generally stated that social security charge is payable upon all income, whether derived from New Zealand or overseas.

The following classes of income are, however, expressly exempt :—
(1) Benefits from the Social Security Fund.
(2) Pensions or other benefits under any Act repealed by the Social Security Act, 1938.
(3) Sick-pay from a friendly society.
(4) Compensation received under the Workers' Compensation Act, 1922, whether as a lump sum or by weekly payments.

(5) Dividends declared on or after 1st April, 1939, by a company which is liable for social security charge on its income. (To ensure that all such dividends will have been subject to charge, provision is made whereby dividend distributions by a company in excess of income which has been chargeable to the company will, to the extent of that excess, be regarded as chargeable income in the hands of the company in the year in which the distribution is made.)

(6) Income derived by a person from any pension in respect of his services in the South African War, and income derived by any person from any pension under the War Pensions Act, 1943, or any pension granted in Great Britain, or within the British Dominions in respect of any war.

(7) All income other than salary or wages derived by any person who receives a pension granted in respect of his total disablement through service in the Great War, 1914–1918.

Under the Act as originally passed only those companies resident in New Zealand—*i.e.*, a company incorporated in New Zealand or a company with its head office in New Zealand—were liable for social security charge on income derived. These provisions were later extended to all overseas companies trading in New Zealand, which in 1941 and for subsequent years became liable to pay social security charge on income derived from New Zealand sources.

Income received from overseas sources by a New Zealand taxpayer is liable for social security charge in the hands of the taxpayer, notwithstanding that a similar levy for social services may have been paid on such income in the overseas country.

It is an interesting point that during the war years the pay of all New Zealand servicemen, whether serving in the Home Forces or overseas, was credited to them free of social security charge and national security tax, the amount involved being met out of the War Expenses Account.

METHODS OF COLLECTING CONTRIBUTION

CHARGE ON SALARIES AND WAGES

The charge on salaries and wages is deductible from the salary or wages by the employer at the time of payment and must be accounted for by him within three days of the date of deduction, or within such further time as the Commissioner of Taxes may in special circumstances determine.

Formerly the employer could account for the charge deducted by affixing special stamps for the appropriate amount in the wages records maintained by him. This method was found to be unsatisfactory in that, in the absence of a regular physical check of wages records, it was difficult to ensure that deductions were promptly accounted for or were, in fact, accounted for at all. The system at present in operation requires the employer to account in cash for all deductions where the amount of the social security charge exceeds two pounds. Where the total of the deductions is less than two pounds, appropriate stamps may be affixed and cancelled in the wages records. The procedure under the present system is as follows :—

(1) After deduction of the charge the employer prepares a declaration setting out the total of salaries or wages payable, the period for which payable, date of payment, and the amount of charge deducted.

(2) The declaration, together with the amount of the charge, is presented at any money-order post-office or at any branch of the Land and Income Tax Department, when a receipt is issued showing the relevant details as appearing on the declaration.

(3) The employer retains the receipt in his wages records as evidence of the payment of the charge.

(4) The payment is recorded in the Land and Income Tax Department, where a card is maintained for each employer, showing in respect of each payment the amount of wages paid, the amount of charge deducted, and the period to which the payment relates. Payments are examined at time of posting to the cards, and any irregularities, such as late payments, non-payment in respect of certain periods, unexplained fluctuations in amounts of payments, &c., are inquired into.

(5) Provision is made for penalties in respect of late payment, failure to deduct, and failure to account for charge deducted. In respect of late payment a penalty of 10 per cent. additional charge may be imposed, while in respect of failure to deduct or failure to account for amounts deducted there is authority to inflict a penalty equal to treble the amount of the charge not deducted or not accounted for.

CHARGE ON INCOME OTHER THAN SALARY OR WAGES

The charge on income other than salary or wages is not deductible at the source.

The recipient of the income is required to make an annual declaration of income other than salary or wages liable to the charge, and to pay the charge due thereon in two equal instalments due on the 1st July and 1st November in each year.

A 10-per-cent. penalty for late payment accrues if the instalment is not paid within one month after the due date.

The charge is calculated on the income derived during the twelve months ended 31st March (or other balance date) preceding the declaration.

Payment of the social security charge is made either at a money-order post-office or a branch of the Land and Income Tax Department, and the receipt issued for each instalment shows the total amount payable and the amount still due to complete payment.

All declarations are subsequently checked against payments made and against the return of income furnished for income-tax purposes.

Companies pay the social security charge on their income in a slightly different manner from that of individual taxpayers.

The company is not required to furnish an annual declaration for social security charge purposes.

The company's chargeable income is computed from the return furnished for income-tax purposes, and an assessment is issued to the company showing details of the social security charge payable.

Companies pay the charge in one sum in the month of February following the year ended 31st March in which the income is derived. A demand for payment of the charge is posted to each company shortly before the due date, and a 10-per-cent. penalty for late payment accrues if the charge is not paid within one month after the due date fixed.

EQUITABLE ADJUSTMENT

It will be observed that the difference in the method of payment for individuals results in the charge on salary and wages being based upon income for the *current* year, whereas in respect of income other than salary the charge is payable upon income for the year *preceding* the year of payment. This position has remained unchanged since the unemployment charge was first instituted in 1931, and there is an anomaly in that the taxpayer deriving income other than salary or wages could conceivably pay the charge for a greater period than the taxpayer on salary or wages.

To overcome this, provision is made for an equitable adjustment by way of exemption from instalments of the charge on income other than salary or wages, in those cases where a taxpayer affected by the position either dies or ceases to be ordinarily resident in New Zealand. In such a case exemption is granted in respect of instalments of social security charge which would normally have become due and payable after the date of death or the date on which the taxpayer ceases to be resident in New Zealand.

A somewhat similar equitable adjustment is made in the case of a taxpayer who ceases to derive income from a source other than salary or wages and commences to derive income from salary or wages, and who would otherwise be called upon to make a double payment of charge in the one year.

RECEIPTS OF THE SOCIAL SECURITY FUND, 1939–49

After the establishment of the Social Security Fund on 1st April, 1939, all moneys due to the Employment Promotion Fund were paid into the Social Security Fund. The balance remaining in the Employment Promotion Fund when it was abolished on 30th September, 1939, was transferred to the Social Security Fund.

Receipts of the Social Security Fund since its inception in 1939 are shown in Table 53 following, from which it will be seen that the receipts for the year ended 31st March, 1949, were four times greater than for the first year of the scheme, and that the Government contribution from the Consolidated Fund increased from 15·9 per cent. of the total receipts of the Social Security Fund in 1939–40 to 44·4 per cent. in 1946–47, falling again to 33·8 per cent. in 1948–49.

161

TABLE 53—SOCIAL SECURITY FUND : RECEIPTS, BY SOURCE, 1ST APRIL, 1939, TO 31ST MARCH, 1949

Year Ended 31st March,	Social Security Contribution.					Miscellaneous Receipts, Including Penalties and Fines.	Annual Grants From Consolidated Fund.	Total Receipts.	Percentage Government Grant to Total Receipts.
	Registration Fee.	Charge on Salaries and Wages.	Charge on Other Income of Individuals.	Charge on Company Income.	Total Social Security Contribution.				
	£	£	£	£	£	£	£	£	
1940	635,440	5,540,643	2,661,904	658,373	9,496,360	61,391	1,809,367	11,367,118	15·9
1941	604,179	6,174,092	2,828,147	1,107,338	10,713,756	54,067	3,200,000	13,967,823	22·9
1942	605,222	6,488,691	2,661,123	1,282,500	11,037,536	50,146	3,600,000	14,687,682	24·5
1943	540,921	7,548,391	2,672,180	1,403,475	12,164,967	48,673	3,800,000	16,013,640	23·7
1944	551,064	8,490,200	2,873,424	1,432,484	13,347,172	44,913	4,100,000	17,492,085	23·4
1945	574,436	8,785,454	2,873,313	2,005,091	14,238,294	38,112	4,500,000	18,776,406	24·0
1946	585,713	9,161,218	3,461,062	1,935,180	15,143,173	143,019	7,000,000	22,286,192	31·4
1947	15,287*	13,519,800	5,733,257	3,130,827	22,399,171†	120,730	18,000,000	40,519,901	44·4
1948	..	16,105,490	6,618,957	3,452,187	26,176,635	158,002	16,000,000	42,334,637	37·8
1949	..	16,744,529	7,999,000	4,635,000	29,378,384	122,080	15,000,000	44,500,464	33·8

* Registration fee abolished 1st April, 1946.   † Social security charge increased from 1s. to 1s. 6d. in pound, May, 1946.

Sources—Details for 1940–42 obtained from table on page 393 of *New Zealand Official Year-Book*, 1943.
Details for 1943–46 obtained from table on page 435 of *New Zealand Official Year-Book*, 1946.
Details of social security contribution, 1947–49, obtained from records of Land and Income Tax Department.

SUMMARY OF CASH BENEFIT RATES

	Weekly Rate.					
	31st March, 1949.			1st June, 1949.		
	£	s.	d.	£	s.	d.
BENEFITS WITHOUT MEANS TEST						
Superannuation—						
£32 10s. a year from 1st April, 1949, rising by £2 10s. a year to £130		..			12	6
Family benefits—						
Each child under sixteen years of age ..	0	10	0	0	10	0
Miners' benefit—						
Basic rate	2	5	0	2	10	0
Wife	2	5	0	2	10	0
Widow	1	15	0	2	0	0
BENEFITS SUBJECT TO MEANS TEST						
Age-benefit—						
Basic rate	2	5	0	2	10	0
Wife	2	5	0	2	10	0
Invalids' Benefit—						
Basic rate	2	5	0	2	10	0
Wife	2	5	0	2	10	0
Invalid under twenty years of age and unmarried	1	15	0	2	0	0
Widows' Benefits—						
Basic rate	2	5	0	2	10	0
Additional mother's allowance to widows with children	1	5	0	1	10	0
Orphan's Benefit—						
Each orphan	1	0	0	1	5	0
Sickness Benefit—						
Basic rate	2	5	0	2	10	0
Wife	2	5	0	2	10	0
People under twenty years of age without dependants	1	5	0	1	10	0
Unemployment Benefit—						
Basic rate	2	5	0	2	10	0
Wife	2	5	0	2	10	0
People under twenty years of age without dependants	1	5	0	1	10	0
Emergency Benefits—						
Rate determined according to circumstances		..			..	

LIST OF HEALTH BENEFITS AVAILABLE UNDER PART III OF THE SOCIAL SECURITY ACT, 1938, IN ORDER OF INTRODUCTION

Benefit.	Date From Which Operative.
Treatment in State Mental Hospitals	1st April, 1939.
Maternity Benefits	15th May, 1939.
Hospital Benefits (in respect of in-patient treatment)	1st July, 1939.
Hospital Benefits (in respect of out-patient treatment)	1st March, 1941.
Medical Benefits (under the Capitation Scheme)	1st March, 1941.
Pharmaceutical Benefits ..	5th May, 1941.
General Medical Services (as alternative to Capitation Scheme)	1st November, 1941.
X-ray Diagnostic Services	11th August, 1941.
Massage Benefits	1st September, 1942.
District Nursing Services ..	1st September, 1944.
Domestic Assistance	20th December, 1944.
Laboratory Diagnostic Services	1st April, 1946.
Dental Benefits ..	1st February, 1947.
Hospital Out-patients Benefits (General) ..	1941.
Hospital Out-patients Benefits (Artificial Aids)—	
Contact lenses..	1st June, 1947.
Hearing-aids ..	1st November, 1947.
Artificial limbs	1st April, 1948.

ACKNOWLEDGMENTS

In collecting data for publication recourse has been made to New Zealand statutes ; published reports of Government Departments ; the New Zealand Official Year-Books and publications issued by the Government Statistician ; published copies of New Zealand Parliamentary Debates and other Government publications and reports. Also reference was made to the following works :—

The Quest for Security in New Zealand, by W. B. Sutch.
Social Security in New Zealand, by A. M. Finlay.
Relief and Social Security, by Lewis Meriam.
Medical Survey in New Zealand, by Hugh MacLean, M.D., F.A.S., and Dean E. McHenry, Ph.D.

The publishers are also indebted to the departmental officers who assisted in the production of this book—in particular Mr. G. J. Brockle-hurst, B.Com., and Mr. A. R. Hutchings, who were responsible for the compilation and arrangement of the Cash and Health Benefits Sections respectively.

APPENDICES

APPENDIX I—CHRONOLOGICAL LIST OF LEGISLATIVE MEASURES RELATING TO CIVIL PENSIONS, SOCIAL SECURITY CASH BENEFITS, AND FINANCE

1894—26 June. Select Committee of House of Representatives appointed to go into question of making provision for old age.

27 Sept. Report of Committee laid before House of Representatives. Recommended establishment of old-age pensions and suggested inquiry by Royal Commission.

1896—17 Oct. *Registration of Peoples' Claims Act.* To ascertain probable cost of providing old-age pensions.

1898—24 Oct. *Old-age Pensions Act, 1898.* Came into force 1st November, 1898. Provided old-age pensions of £18 a year at sixty-five years of age, subject to a means and residence test.

1900—18 Oct. *Old-age Pensions Amendment Act, 1900.* Old-age Pensions Act, 1898, made permanent.

6 Dec. Regulations under the Old-age Pensions Act, 1898.

1901— 7 Nov. *Old-age Pensions Amendment Act, 1901.* Minor amendments. Maoris could be recommended for grant under Civil List in lieu of old-age pension.

1902— 1 Oct. *Old-age Pensions Amendment Act, 1902.* Minor amendments. Provision for transfer of home property to Public Trustee.

1903—13 Feb. *Regulations under the Old-age Pensions Act, 1898.*

1905—11 May. *Regulations Under the Old-age Pensions Act, 1898.*

22 May *Regulations Under the Old-age Pensions Act, 1898.*

29 July. *Old-age Pensions Act, 1905.* Increased rate of pension, income exemption, and allowable property.

23 Sept. *Stamp Act Amendment, 1905.* Pensions documents exempt from stamp duty.

6 Dec. *Regulations Under the Old-age Pensions Act, 1898.*

1907—29 April. *Regulations Under the Old-age Pensions Act, 1898.*

1908— 4 Aug. *Old-age Pensions Act, 1908.* Consolidation. Widened scope of former Acts.

10 Oct. *Old-age Pensions Amendment Act, 1908.* Various amendments. Uniform limit of income and pension fixed for first time.

1909—24 Dec. *Old-age Pensions Amendment Act, 1909.* Amendment to property qualification.

1910—24 Jan. *Regulations Under the Old-age Pensions Act, 1908.*

21 Nov. *Old-age Pensions Amendment Act, 1910.* Amendment to property qualification.

21 Nov. *National Provident Fund Act.* Certain money from Fund not income for old-age pensions.

1911— 5 Oct. *Regulations Under the Old-age Pensions Act, 1908.*

21 Oct. *Old-age Pensions Amendment Act, 1911.* Qualifying age for parents of two or more children under fourteen reduced to sixty years for men and fifty-five years for women. Parents of two or more children under fourteen years to receive additional allowance up to £13 a year.

28 Oct. *Widows' Pensions Act, 1911.* Came into force 1st January, 1912. Provided pension of £12 to widows with one child, increased by £6 for each additional child ; maximum, £30. Pension subject to means test.

1911—20 Nov. *Regulations Under the Widows' Pensions Act, 1911.*

1912— 7 Nov. *Widows' Pensions Amendment Act, 1912.* Extended widow's pensions to wives of mental-hospital patients who were certified incurable for twelve months.

1913— 5 Feb.   *Regulations Under the Military Pensions Act, 1912.*

     28 Aug.   *Old-age Pensions Reciprocity Act, 1913.* Agreement with Australia signed. Ratified by New Zealand but not by Australia.

     11 Oct.   *Pensions Act, 1913.* Consolidated the eight existing statutes relating to old-age, widows', and military pensions. Women qualified for old-age pension at sixty years, with reduced pension until sixty-five if less than two dependent children. Amendments *re* income and property.

1914— 5 Nov.   *Pensions Amendment Act, 1914.* Minor amendments to residence and property provisions *re* old-age pensions. Wife of mental patient entitled to widow's pension irrespective of length of time husband likely to be in mental hospital. Limitation of widow's pension to a maximum of four children.

1915—11 Oct.   *Miners' Phthisis Act, 1915.* Pensions provided for miners totally incapacitated by pneumoconiosis. Widow of miner to receive pension for two years. Funeral grant of up to £20 paid on application within one year of death.

1916— 7 Aug.   *War Legislation Amendment Act, 1916.* War pensions not to be deemed to be income for old age and widows' pensions.

1917—15 Sept.   *Finance Act, 1917.* Cost-of-living bonus added to civil pensions for duration of war and one year thereafter.

1919— 5 Nov.   *Finance Act, 1919.* Increased widows' and miners' pensions by incorporating the bonus in the statutory pension. For widows' pension the residence required by parents of children born out of New Zealand reduced if father died in New Zealand. Miners' widows' pensions payable during widowhood instead of for two years only.

1920—11 Nov.   *Finance Act, 1920.* Old-age pensions increased by incorporating bonus in statutory pension. Miners' pensions increased.

     11 Nov.   *Appropriation Act, 1920.* Cost-of-living bonus to superannuated civil servants not income for old-age or widows' pensions.

1924—29 Oct.   *Pensions Amendment Act, 1924.* Additional old-age pensions for those with no income or property and for South African war veterans. Amendments to income and property exemptions. Widows' pensions increased. Blind pensions provided for people becoming blind in New Zealand.

1925—29 Sept.   *Pensions Amendment Act, 1925.* Increased old-age and blind pensions. Amended property exemptions for old-age and widows' pensions. Blind pensions extended to people who lost sight out of New Zealand subject to residence test.

1926— 9 Sept.   *Pensions Act, 1926.* Consolidated existing law relating to old age, widows', blind, miners', and military pensions.

     9 Sept.   *Family Allowances Act, 1926.* Introduced family allowances at 2s. a week for each child in excess of two under fifteen years of age.

     9 Sept.   *National Provident Fund Act, 1926.* Sick allowance from Fund not income or property for pension purposes.

1927—11 Mar.   *Finance Act (No. 2), 1927.* Exemption from income of pensions from National Provident Fund reduced where contributions paid through local bodies.

     11 Mar.   *Regulations Under the Family Allowances Act, 1926.*

     6 June.   *Regulations Under the Pensions Act, 1926.*

1928—   Oct.   Committee set up by Government to investigate and report on unemployment problem.

1929— 8 Nov.   *Finance Act, 1929.* Miners' pension extended to miners with tuberculosis of lungs and other respiratory disease commonly associated with or following pneumoconiosis. Pensions for serious permanent incapacity as well as total incapacity.

1930—11 Oct.   *Unemployment Act, 1930.* Established Unemployment Board, provided relief, and for measures to promote employment.

     25 Oct.   *Finance Act (No. 2), 1930.* Special exemption of war pensions from income for old-age pensions purposes extended.

APPENDIX I—CHRONOLOGICAL LIST OF LEGISLATIVE MEASURES, ETC.—*continued*

1931—28 April.   *Finance Act (No. 2), 1931.* Reduced income-limit for family allowance.

22 July.   *Unemployment Amendment Act, 1931.* Re-established Unemployment Board and provided for increased funds for relief. Unemployment Relief Tax introduced.

1932—30 April.   *Unemployment Amendment Act, 1932.* Rate of unemployment charge increased.

10 May.   *National Expenditure Adjustment Act, 1932.* Reduced old-age, widows', and miners' pensions by 10 per cent. Miners' widows' pensions again restricted to two years. Income exemptions for civil pensions and family allowances reduced. Definition of income amended.

10 May.   *Finance Act, 1932.* Expenditure on pensions and family allowances to be subject to appropriation by Parliament.

19 Nov.   *Pensions Amendment Act, 1932.* Residential requirements for miners' pensions modified. Two-year limit for pensions to miners' widows current on passing of National Expenditure Adjustment Act removed. Absence from New Zealand of blind pensioner for treatment of eyes disregarded.

1933—10 Mar.   *Finance Act (No. 2), 1932–33.* Absence with armed forces not deemed to interrupt residence.

Finance Act (No. 2), 1933. Part II of National Expenditure Adjustment Act, 1932, deemed to have come into force 1st April, 1932 (validating reduction from that date).

1934—24 Sept.   Unemployment charge reduced by Order in Council.

28 Sept.   *Finance Act (No. 2), 1934.* Increased old-age pensions by 5 per cent. Income exemption for old-age and blind pensions increased.

1935—23 Sept.   Unemployment charge reduced by Order in Council.

17 Oct.   *Finance Act, 1935.* Rates of pension restored to those ruling prior to the National Expenditure Adjustment Act, 1932.

26 Oct.   *Finance Act (No. 2), 1935.* Two-year limit on miners' widows not in force on the passing of the National Expenditure Adjustment Act, 1932, removed, except where married after 26th October, 1935.

1936—15 May.   *Employment Promotion Act, 1936.* Consolidated legislation dealing with unemployment relief.

4 Sept.   *Pensions Amendment Act, 1936.* Provided pensions for invalids and deserted wives, reduced residence for old-age pensions, increased old-age, widows', and Maori War pensions, and liberalized conditions under which pensions granted.

4 Sept.   *Family Allowances Amendment Act, 1936.* Raised income limit for family allowances and permitted application by either parent instead of by father only.

13 Oct.   *Finance Act (No. 2), 1936.* Minor amendments to widows, miners', and invalidity pensions.

1937—1 Dec.   *Finance Act, 1937.* Invalidity pension paid where invalidity arose outside of New Zealand subject to residence test. Amendment to provisions regarding occasional absences from New Zealand of applicant for invalidity pension and rate of invalidity pension to person receiving overseas pension. Money received in respect of military decoration for gallantry not income for pension purposes.

1938— 9 Mar.   Select Committee on National Health and Superannuation set up to consider Government's proposals.

15 Mar.   *Finance Act (No. 2), 1937.* New Zealand seamen on intercolonial ships liable for employment tax.

15 Mar.   *Pensions Amendment Act, 1937.* Residence for old-age pensions reduced to ten years if in New Zealand on 15th March, 1938.

14 Sept.   *Social Security Act, 1938.* Into force 1st April, 1939. Replaced existing legislation relating to pensions and unemployment relief. Cash and health benefits provided. Social Security Fund established. Employment-tax replaced by Social Security charge.

APPENDIX I—CHRONOLOGICAL LIST OF LEGISLATIVE MEASURES, ETC.—*continued*

1939—21 Feb.   *Social Security Contribution Regulations (1939/13)*.

10 May.   *Social Security (Monetary Benefits) Regulations (1939/55)*.

29 Sept.   *Social Security Amendment Act, 1939.* Minor amendments affecting contributions and cash benefits.

6 Oct.   *The Finance Act (No. 2), 1939.* Temporary advances to Social Security Fund from Consolidated Fund.

7 Dec.   *Social Security Contribution Regulations 1939, Amendment No. 1 (1939/259)*.

1940—19 July.   *Social Security Amendment Act, 1940.* Family benefits paid for second child. Amendment to provisions applicable on death of an applicant before claim finalized. Overseas companies and certain public authorities liable for social security contribution.

19 July.   *Finance Act, 1940.* Income concession to widowed mothers of servicemen.

30 Aug.   *The Finance Act (No. 2), 1940.* Collection of social security charge and national security tax on issue of national savings bonds.

11 Oct.   *Finance Act (No. 3), 1940.* Adjustment in social security contribution to be made in certain cases.

6 Dec.   *Finance Act (No. 4), 1940.* Income concession for widowed mothers extended and definition of income amended.

12 Dec.   *Social Security Contribution Regulations 1939, Amendment No. 2 (1940/305.)*

1941—27 Aug.   *Finance Act, 1941.* Additional age-benefit for wife and additional age and sickness benefit for children increased. Maximum invalid's benefit increased (rate not affected). Family benefit paid for every child in family. Amendments affecting social security charge and national security tax.

17 Oct.   *Finance Act (No. 2), 1941* Income for age-benefit purposes to be reduced by all or part of the national security tax or social security charge payable.

1942—11 May.   *Finance Act, 1942.* Deduction at source of charge on income included in certain gross payments.

20 May.   *Social Security and Pensions Emergency Regulations (1942/145)* Cost-of-living bonus of 5 per cent. added to age, widows', orphans', invalids', miners', Maori War benefits, and war veterans' allowances. Bonus of 2s. a child added to family benefits and allowable income raised. Personal earnings exemption for blind beneficiaries increased.

26 Aug.   *Social Security (Employment of Age-beneficiaries) Emergency Regulations (1942/261).* Earnings while age-benefit surrended to be disregarded.

26 Oct.   *Finance Act (No. 2), 1942.* Deduction at source of charge on income included in certain payments.

25 Nov.   *Social Security and Pensions Emergency Regulations Amendment No. 1 (1942/326).* Additional £26 a year to age-beneficiary who was dependent parent of a serviceman whose death was due to service with Armed Forces.

1943—24 Feb.   *Social Security Contributions (Companies) Regulations (1943/34)*.

16 Mar.   *Finance Act, 1943.* Further provisions as to deduction at source of social security charge on income included in certain payments.

19 May.   *Social Security and Pensions Emergency Regulations Amendment No. 2 (1943/85).* Bonus incorporated in statutory family benefit.

25 Aug.   *Social Security Amendment Act, 1943.* Into force 1st July, 1943. Increased basic rates of cash benefits. Extended deserted wives' benefits to women who had taken proceedings for maintenance even if husband's whereabouts known. Liberalized definition of income. Widened and incorporated as part of the Amendment Act, the additional age-benefit for parents of deceased servicemen. A similar provision was also made in respect of parents of deceased members of the Mercantile Marine.

25 Aug.   *Age-benefits and Invalids' Benefits (Reciprocity with Australia) Act, 1943.* Established reciprocity between New Zealand and Australia for age and invalids' benefits.

1943—31 Aug. *Revocation of Social Security and Pensions Emergency Regulations (1943/144).* Bonus and war servicemen's dependant's allowance provided for by regulations in 1942 included in Social Security Amendment Act, 1943, from 1st July, 1943.

1944—15 Dec. *Finance Act (No. 3), 1944.* Qualifications for additional age-benefit for South African War veterans liberalized. Rate of family benefits and income exemption increased from 1st October, 1944.

1945—6 April. *Social Security Contribution Regulations 1939, Amendment No. 3 (1945/35).*

24 Nov. *Social Security Amendment Act, 1945.* Into force 1st October, 1945. Increased basic rate of cash benefits. Additional benefit for wife paid at same rate as basic benefit. Supplementary benefit of £52 a year provided for widows with children. Income exemption for family benefit increased until 31st March, 1946, after which family benefit paid without a means test. All benefits for children replaced by family benefit from 1st October, 1945. Qualifications for widows' and invalids' benefits and for additional age-benefit for South African War veterans liberalized. War servicemen's dependants' allowances payable in conjunction with other cash benefits, instead of merely with age-benefits as previously. Provision for diversion of benefits to Commissioner of Taxes at request of beneficiary.

7 Dec. *Finance Act (No. 2), 1945.* Payment of family benefit not to affect liability for maintenance. Rate of social security charge increased. Registration fee abolished.

1946—10 April. *Social Security Contribution Regulations 1939, Amendment No. 4 (1946/45).*

9 Oct. *Social Security Amendment Act, 1946.* Into force 1st April, 1946. Increased rates of some widows' benefits and of mother's allowance to widows. Liberalized qualifications concerning adopted children and residence for family benefit. Extended period for which benefits for children could be continued for educational purposes.

12 Oct. *Finance Act (No. 2), 1946.* Penal charge in case of evasion of social security contribution.

1947—14 Aug. *Finance Act, 1947.* Power to exempt certain allowances from social security charge.

11 Nov. *Social Security Amendment Act, 1947.* Into force 1st October, 1947. Increased basic rates of benefit. Minor amendment to qualification for widow's benefit where husband in mental hospital. Family benefit payable to children of servicemen. Amendments concerning delegation of powers of Social Security Commission, renewal of benefits and residence.

25 Nov. *Finance Act (No. 2), 1947.* Certain allowances exempt from income for social security charge. Deduction of losses from income for social security charge.

1948—19 Nov. *Family Benefits (Reciprocity With Great Britain) Act, 1948.*

19 Nov. *Family Benefits (Reciprocity With Northern Ireland) Act, 1948.*

2 Dec. *Social Security (Reciprocity With Australia) Act, 1948.* Replaced the Age-benefits and Invalids' Benefits (Reciprocity with Australia) Act, 1943, and provided for reciprocity in relation to age, invalids', widows', family, unemployment, and sickness benefits from 1st July, 1949.

3 Dec. *Finance Act (No. 2), 1948.* Amendments affecting blind beneficiaries transferred to age-benefit, date of expiry of orphan's benefit, payment of benefits during temporary absence from New Zealand. Children born during temporary absence of mother from New Zealand eligible for family benefit. Dates of payment of instalments of Social security charge altered.

1949— 9 Mar. *Social Security Contribution Regulations 1939, Amendment No. 5 (1949/27).*

21 Oct. *Social Security Amendment Act, 1949.* Increased basic rates of benefits from 1st June 1949. War Servicemen's dependants allowances extended. Other minor amendments.

APPENDIX II—LIST OF LEGISLATION AFFECTING HEALTH BENEFITS UNDER PART III OF THE SOCIAL SECURITY ACT, 1938

ACTS

Social Security Act, 1938 (Part III).
Social Security Amendment Act, 1939 (section 9–15).
Social Security Amendment Act, 1940 (section 8).
Finance Act (No. 4), 1940 (section 13–14).
Social Security Amendment Act, 1941.
Finance Act (No. 2), 1942 (section 12).
Social Security Amendment Act, 1943 (section 30).
Social Security Amendment Act, 1947 (section 20–21).
Social Security Amendment Act, 1949 (section 23–30).

REGULATIONS

Maternity Benefits—
Social Security (Maternity Benefits) Regulations (1939/43).
Social Security (Maternity Benefits) Regulations 1939, Amendment No. 1 (1939/92).
Social Security (Supplementary Maternity Benefits) Regulations (1939/93).
Social Security (Supplementary Maternity Benefits) Regulations (1940/81).
Social Security (Maternity Benefits) Regulations, Amendment No. 2 (1947/126).

Medical Benefits—
Social Security (Medical Benefits) Regulations (1941/24).
Social Security (Medical Benefits) Regulations, Amendment No. 1 (1943/156).

General Medical Services—
Social Security (General Medical Services) Regulations (1941/187).
Social Security (General Medical Services) Regulations, Amendment No. 1 (1942/13).

Pharmaceutical Supplies Benefits—
Social Security (Pharmaceutical Supplies) Regulations (1941/66).
Social Security (Pharmaceutical Supplies) Regulations, Amendment No. 1 (1941/131).
Social Security (Pharmaceutical Supplies) Regulations, Amendment No. 2 (1942/3).
Social Security (Pharmaceutical Supplies) Regulations, Amendment No. 3 (1943/155).
Social Security (Pharmaceutical Supplies) Regulations, Amendment No. 4 (1946/135).

Massage Benefits—
Social Security (Massage Benefits) Regulations (1942/255).

X-ray Diagnostic Services—
Social Security (X-ray Diagnostic Services) Regulations (1941/122).
Social Security (X-ray Diagnostic Services) Regulations, Amendment No. 1 (1942/14).

Hospital Benefits—
Social Security (Hospital Benefits) Regulations (1939/75).
Social Security (Hospital Benefits) Regulations, Amendment No. 1 (1943/98).
Social Security (Hospital Benefits for Out-patients) Regulations 1941 (1941/49).
Social Security (Hospital Benefits for Out-patients) Regulations 1941, Amendment No. 1 (1944/179).
Social Security (Hospital Benefits for Out-patients) Regulations 1947 (1947/68).

District Nursing Services—
Social Security (District Nursing Services) Regulations (1944/105).

Domestic Assistance—
Social Security (Domestic Assistance) Regulations (1944/178).

Laboratory Diagnostic Services—
Social Security (Laboratory Diagnostic Services) Regulations 1946 (1946/24).
Social Security (Laboratory Diagnostic Services) Regulations 1946, Amendment No. 1 (1949/60).

Dental Benefits—
Social Security (Dental Benefits) Regulations 1946 (1946/189).
Social Security (Dental Benefits) Regulations 1946, Amendment No. 1 (1948/191).

NOTICES (*N.Z. Gazette*)

Contact lenses : *N.Z. Gazette* No. 27, 29th May, 1947, page 654.
Hearing-aids : *N.Z. Gazette* No. 65, 6th November, 1947, page 1751.
Artificial limbs : *N.Z. Gazette* No. 17, 1st April, 1948, page 353.

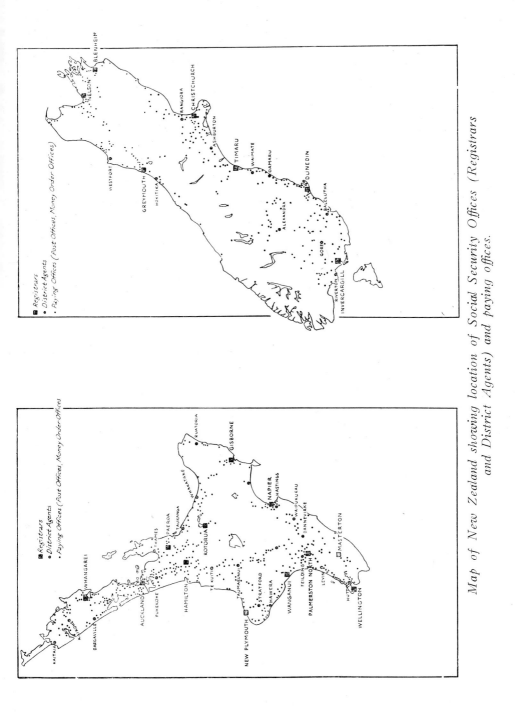

Map of New Zealand showing location of Social Security Offices (Registrars and District Agents) and paying offices.

INDEX

					PAGE
Administration of—					
Cash benefits	..	..	..	..	.. 101–113
Pensions	..	..	..	..	.. 41–43
Unemployment relief	..	..	..	.. 43–44
Administrative—					
Organization	..	..	..	..	.. 101–102
Procedure ..	..	..	..	..	.. 103–113
Advisory Committee	..	..	..	..	.. 153, 154
Age-benefits	..	..	..	..	.. 50–61
Aliens	..	..	..	..	.. 14, 23, 26, 29, 39
Appeals	..	..	..	..	.. 104
Invalids' benefits	..	..	..	..	.. 72, 104
Miners' benefits	..	..	..	..	.. 75, 104
Applications—					
Cash benefits	..	..	..	..	.. 62–63, 103
Hospital benefits	..	..	..	..	.. 137
Laboratory services	..	..	..	.. 149
Medical benefits	..	..	..	..	.. 138
Pharmaceutical benefits	..	..	..	.. 141
Widows' benefits	..	..	..	..	.. 62–63
X-ray diagnostic services	..	..	..	.. 145
Artificial—					
Aids	..	..	..	..	.. 136, 137
Limbs	..	..	..	..	.. 136, 137
Asiatics	..	..	..	..	.. 23, 26, 29, 39
Atkinson's scheme	..	..	..	..	.. 21
Attendances, medical benefits	..	..	..	.. 153
Blankets	..	..	..	..	.. 34
Blind—					
Beneficiaries	..	..	..	..	.. 71
Pensioners	..	..	..	..	.. 24, 29
Boots	..	..	..	..	.. 34
British Medical Association	..	..	..	.. 127, 128, 129, 143, 150, 151, 154, 155
Camps for single men	..	..	..	..	.. 33
Capitation system	..	..	..	..	.. 138, 139, 140, 155
Cash benefits—					
Age	..	..	..	..	.. 50–61
Disability ..	..	..	..	..	.. 46
Emergency	..	..	..	..	.. 88–92
Family	..	..	..	..	.. 47, 66–70
Invalids	..	..	..	..	.. 46, 71–74
Miners	..	..	..	..	.. 47, 75–77
Orphans	..	..	..	..	.. 26, 46, 65–66
Sickness	..	..	..	..	.. 46, 78–86
Summary of rates	..	..	..	..	.. 163
Superannuation	..	..	..	..	.. 47, 50, 53, 55, 56, 59
Sustenance	..	..	..	..	35, 46, 86
Unemployment	..	..	..	..	.. 35, 46, 86–88
Widows	..	..	..	..	.. 46, 61–65
Widowed mothers	..	..	..	..	.. 46, 61, 99
Character qualifications—					
Age-benefit	..	..	..	..	.. 50
Invalids' benefit	..	..	..	..	.. 71
Old-age pensions	..	..	..	..	.. 22, 23
Widows	..	..	..	..	.. 61
Charge—					
On company income	..	..	..	.. 161
On income other than salary or wages	..	.. 160
Salaries and wages ..	..	..	..	.. 157–160

172

	PAGE
Charitable aid ..	23, 26, 32, 78, 126
Commencement of cash benefits ..	105
Committees—	
Disciplinary Committee	153–154, 155
General Advisory Committee	153, 154
Local—	
Investigatory Committees	154
Unemployment Committees	32
Medical Services Committee	142, 143, 150–155
National Health and Superannuation Committee, 1938..	46, 47–48, 88–89, 128
Old-age Pension Committee, 1894	22
Women's—	
Employment Committees	36
Unemployment Committees	35
Compensation and sickness benefit	81
Consolidated Fund	27, 40, 133, 158, 161, 162
Contact lenses ..	136, 137
Contributions ..	40–41, 158–161, 162
Cost of living and social security	122–123, 126
Cost of prescriptions ..	143–144
Demand for pensions ..	21–24
Demobilization allowances	100
Dental—	
Benefits ..	135, 149–150
Treatment	135
Denmark : Old-age Pensions Act	22
Depression, 1930–35 ..	29
Depression measures : Unemployment relief	30–31
Deserted wives—	
Benefits ..	63–64
Pensions ..	39
Destitute Persons Act, 1877	21
Destitute Persons Act, 1910	61, 63
Diagnostic services	135, 137, 144–145, 148–149
Direct-claim system	138, 139, 150, 151, 152
Disability benefit	46, 88, 90
Disabled Soldiers' Civil Re-establishment Act, 1930	43
Disabled Soldiers' Civil Re-establishment League ..	43
Disciplinary Committee ..	153–154, 155
District nursing services	146–147, 147–148
Domestic assistance	90, 128
Domiciliary services	135, 152
Drug tariff	140–141
Education—	
Extended family benefit for	68
Extended orphans' benefit for	66
Emergency benefits	88–92
Employment of age-beneficiaries	52, 57–58
Employment promotion	35–38
Employment Promotion Act	35, 36, 41
Employment Promotion Fund ..	36, 37, 38
Epidemic allowances	28
Equitable adjustment (contributions)	161
Expenditure—	
Pensions ..	124–125
Social security ..	116–122
Unemployment relief	38
Exports and social security	120
Family allowances	24, 29, 47
Family benefits	66–70
Fee-for-service system ..	138–139, 151, 152–153, 155

		PAGE
Financing of—		
Pensions	.. ..	39–40
Social security	.. ..	47, 158–162
Unemployment relief	.. ..	40–41
Food	.. ..	35
Friendly societies	.. ..	78, 80, 126, 129
Fund—		
Employment Promotion	.. .. ..	36, 37, 38
Social Security	.. ..	49, 63, 91, 97, 98, 109 158, 161, 162
Unemployment	.. ..	30, 31, 34, 35, 40
General—		
Advisory Committee	.. .. ..	153
Medical services	.. ..	126–129, 138–140, 150–155
Statistics	.. ..	114–126
Germany : Social insurance	.. .. ..	22
Gold-miners' relief fund	.. ..	27
Gold-mining and unemployment relief	.. ..	33, 36, 37
Granting of benefits	.. ..	104
Health benefits	.. ..	49, 126–157, 164, 170
Health services	.. ..	126–129
Hearing-aids	.. ..	136, 137
Home property transferred to Public Trustee	.. ..	25
Hospital—		
Benefits	.. ..	128, 133–137
Boards	.. ..	28, 32, 126
In-patients	.. ..	133–135
Out-patients	.. ..	135–137
Services (maternity benefit)	.. .. ..	130–132
Hutchison, William	.. ..	22
Income and property	.. ..	106–108
Income exempt from contribution	.. ..	158–159
Income exemption—		
Age-benefits	.. ..	51–52
Blind pensions	.. ..	29
Emergency benefits	.. ..	89
Family allowances	.. ..	29
Family benefits	.. ..	66, 67
Invalidity pension	.. ..	38
Invalids' benefits	.. ..	71–72
Old-age pensions	.. ..	23, 25, 39
Orphans' benefits	.. ..	66
Sickness benefits	.. ..	80
Unemployment benefits	.. .. ..	87
Widow's benefit	.. ..	61, 62
Widows' pensions	.. ..	26
In-patients in hospital	.. ..	133–135
Invalid children	.. ..	29, 68
Invalidity pension	.. ..	29, 38
Invalidity and unemployment	.. .. ..	86, 88, 90
Invalids—		
Benefit	.. ..	46, 71–74
Transfer to age-benefit	.. .. ..	52
Investigation of applications	.. .. ..	41–42, 91, 103–104
Investigating Committee (local)	.. .. ..	154
Karitane baby hospitals	.. .. ..	135
Laboratory diagnostic services	.. .. ..	135, 137, 148–149
Local Investigating Committees	.. .. ..	154
Maintenance, recovery of	.. .. ..	63–64
Maoris	.. ..	23, 33, 37, 39, 52
Maori land development	.. .. ..	33
Maori War pensions	.. ..	24, 26–27
Map of New Zealand	.. ..	171
Massage services	.. ..	145–146

INDEX—*continued*

	Page
Maternity benefits	128, 129–133
McMillan report	128
Means test	121–122
Medical benefits	128, 138–140
Medical examination—	
Emergency benefits	89
Invalidity pensions	38
Invalids' benefits	72
Miners	27
Miners' benefits	75
Sickness benefit	81
Medical Services Committee report	142, 143, 150–155
Midwifery requirements	141
Mileage	152, 155
Military Pensions Act, 1911	26–27
Miner's—	
Benefit	47, 75–77
Pensions	27–28
Miners' Phthisis Act, 1915	27
Mothers' allowance—	
War pensions	98, 99
Widow's benefit	61, 99
National Endowment Act, 1907	40
National-endowment land	40
National income and social security	118–119
New Zealand Formulary	141, 144
New Zealand, location, &c.	11–16
Obstetric nursing services	132
Occupational training	89, 92
Old-age pensions	17, 19, 21–25, 30, 39, 41, 42, 43
Old-age Pensions Act, 1898	17, 19, 23–24
Organization of Social Security Department	101–102, 171
Orphans' benefits	26, 46, 65–66
Out-patients	135–137
Payment by patients	130, 132, 137, 138–139, 141, 144–145, 148, 150, 152–153, 155
Payment of benefits—	
Cash benefits	108–109, 171
Medical benefits	138–139, 151–152
Outside New Zealand	109
Sickness benefits	81
Pensions—	
Administration of	41–43
Amendment Act, 1936	35, 38–39
Blind	24–29
Demand for	21–24
Department of	41–43
Deserted wives	39
Epidemic	28
Family allowances	24, 29, 47
Financing of	39–40
Invalidity	29, 38
Maori War	24, 26–27
Miners'	27–28
Old-age	17, 19, 21–25, 30, 39, 41, 42, 43
Reductions	30
War	97–99
Widows	26, 39
Pharmaceutical benefits	128, 135, 140–143
Post Office Saving-bank accounts, payment of family benefits to	68
Powers-Samas system	108–109, 111–112

	PAGE
Pregnant single women	89
Prescriptions	141, 142, 143–144
Price Tribunal	131
Pricing Officers	141
Prisoners' dependants	90, 91
Private resources of age-beneficiaries	60–61
Production and social security	120
Promotion of employment	30–38
Property	107–108
Property exemption— ..	
Age-benefits	51–52
Blind pensions	29
Invalidity pensions	38
Invalids' benefits	72
Maori War pensions..	26
Old-age pensions	23, 25, 39
Orphans' benefits	66
Unemployment benefits	87
Widows' benefits	61, 62
Proprietary medicines	141
Public Account	27
Public Trustee—	
Re home property	25
Re Gold-miners' relief	27
Qualifications—	
Age-benefit	50, 51–52
Blind pension	29
Deserted wives' benefit	61, 63
Deserted wife's pension	39
Emergency benefit	89
Epidemic allowances	28
Family allowances	29
Family benefits	66, 67–68
Invalidity pensions	38
Invalids' benefits	71
Maori War pensions	26
Miners' benefits	75
Miners' pensions	27, 28
Old-age pensions	23, 24–25, 39
Orphans' benefits	65, 66
Sickness benefits	79
South African War allowance	25, 51
Superannuation benefit	50
Unemployment benefit	86–87
Widow's benefit	61, 62, 63
Widow's pension	26, 29
Quarantine, emergency benefits for	90
Rabbit-infested lands	32
Rates of benefit—	
Age	51
Emergency	89
Family	66
Invalids'	71, 72
Miners'	75
Orphans'	66
Sickness	79–80
Summary of	163
Superannuation benefit	50
Unemployment benefit	87
Widow's benefit	61, 62
Receipts of Social Security Fund	161–162
Reciprocity with—	
Australia	93–95
Great Britain and Northern Ireland	95–96
Reconstruction period	35–39
Records	104

	PAGE
Registration of People's Claims Act, 1896	23
Refund system	138, 139, 150, 151, 152–153, 154, 155
Rehabilitation allowances	99–100
Relatives as a resource	21, 90
Renewal of benefit	105
Reports—	
McMillan	128
Medical Services Committee	142, 143, 150–155
National Health and Superannuation Committee ..	47–48, 128
Old-age Pensions Committee, 1894	22
Residence—	
Age-benefits	50
Blind pensions	29
Emergency benefits	89
Family benefits	67–68
Invalidity pensions	38
Invalids' benefits	71
Miners' benefits	75
Miners' pensions	27
Old-age pensions	22, 23, 39
Orphans' benefits	65
Sickness benefits	79
Superannuation benefits	50
Unemployment benefits	86
Widows' benefits	61, 62
Widows' pensions	26
Review of benefit	105–106
Royal New Zealand Society for Health of Women and Children	135
Saint Helens' hospitals	132–133
Savage, Rt. Hon. M. J.	17, 18
Schemes, Unemployment relief	30–37
Scheme 1	31
Scheme 2	31
Scheme 3	31
Scheme 4A, 4B, 4F (farm and land settlement) ..	31
Scheme 5	31–32, 37
Scheme 13	34
Scheme 15 (gold-mining)	33
Scheme 16 (building)	33
Scheme 16A	34
Seasonal earnings	88
Seddon, Rt. Hon. R. J.	20, 22, 23, 24
Sickness benefits	46, 78–86
Emergency benefits in lieu of	88–89, 90
Social Security Act, 1938, scope of	48–49
Social Security Commission	101, 104
Social security contribution	41, 158–161, 162
Social Security Department	43, 44, 101–102
Social Security Fund	49, 63, 91, 97, 98, 109, 158, 161, 162
Source of funds	158, 162
South African War veterans	25, 51
Specialist medical services	137, 155
State Placement Service	30, 36, 44, 86
Subsidies—	
For Blind	29, 38, 71
Unemployment relief	30, 31, 32, 33, 34, 35, 36, 37, 40
Superannuation benefits	48, 49, 50, 53, 55, 56, 59
Summary of—	
Cash benefit rates	163
Health benefits	164

	PAGE
Supplementary health benefits	128, 144–150
Dental benefits	149–150
District nursing services	146–147
Domestic assistance	147–148
Laboratory diagnostic services	148–149
Massage services	145–146
X-ray diagnostic services	135, 137, 144–145
Sustenance	35, 46, 86
Tax adjustment	107
Taxes, payment of family benefit to Commissioner of	68
Token system	138–139, 152, 155
Training for beneficiaries	89, 92
Tuberculosis, benefits for	73, 89
Unemployment benefit	86–88, 89
Emergency benefit in lieu of	89
Unemployment relief	30–38
Alluvial-gold mining	33, 36
Administration of	43–44
Building subsidy	33, 34
Depression measures	30–37
Developments, pre-depression	30
Employment Promotion Act, 1936	35, 36, 41, 44
Employment Promotion Fund	36, 37–38
Financing of	40–41
Hospital Board relief	32
Issue of boots, blankets, food	34
Local Unemployment Committees	32
Maori land development	33
Number receiving	37
Rabbit-infested lands	32
Sickness allowances	78
Single men's camps	33
Sustenance	35
Unemployment Act, 1930	30, 40, 43
Unemployment Board	30, 31, 32, 33, 34, 35, 36, 43, 44
Unemployment Fund	30, 31, 34, 35, 40
Women	35, 36, 44
Work, full-time	34–35
Verification—	
Of claims : Medical services	139, 151, 154
Of information : Cash benefits	103–104
Of information : Pensions	41–43
Vocational training	89, 92
Voluntary unemployment	87
Waiting period	81, 87
War pensions and allowances	97–100
Administration of	101
Demobilization allowances	100
Rehabilitation allowances	99–100
War pensions	97–99
War servicemen's dependants' allowances	92
Wartime emergency benefits	91
Widowed mother's benefit	46, 61, 99
Widows' benefits	46, 61–65
Widows of miners	27, 75
Widows' pensions	26, 39
Widows—	
With children	26, 39, 46, 61
Without children	46, 61, 62
Withdrawal from employment	57–58
Wives of—	
Mental hospital patients	26, 61
Sickness beneficiaries	81
Women and unemployment relief	35, 36, 44
Women's Division, New Zealand Federated Farmers	148
Women's Unemployment Committees	35, 36, 44
Workers' compensation	27, 78, 81, 106
X-ray diagnostic services	135, 137, 144–145

R. E. OWEN, Government Printer, Wellington.

[15,000/9/49—9331